T5-ANV-421

THE PEOPLE'S PANEL

THE PEOPLE'S PANEL:

The Grand Jury in the United States, 1634–1941

RICHARD D. YOUNGER

AMERICAN HISTORY RESEARCH CENTER
BROWN UNIVERSITY PRESS
PROVIDENCE, RHODE ISLAND
1963

Library of Congress Catalog Card Number: 63-12993

Copyright

1963

BROWN UNIVERSITY

All Rights Reserved

SECOND IMPRESSION, 1965

343.1
Y 78 p

Printed in the United States of America
George Banta Company, Inc., Menasha, Wisconsin

to my mother and father

301527

Acknowledgment

I undertook this study at the suggestion of William B. Hesseltine of the University of Wisconsin. His guidance and insights were valuable at every step. My debt to him is very great. I wish also to thank the staff of the State Historical Society of Wisconsin and of the Wisconsin State Law Library. I am grateful to Leslie E. Decker of the University of Maine for his editing of the manuscript and to Forrest McDonald of the American History Research Center for his co-operation in making its publication possible.

Contents

Chapter 1

The Grand Jury

THE GRAND JURY originated in England as the accusing body in the administration of criminal justice. At the Assize of Clarendon, in 1166, Henry II provided that twelve knights or twelve "good and lawful men" of every hundred and four lawful men of every vill disclose under oath the names of those in the community believed guilty of criminal offenses. Members of this inquisitorial body were obliged to present to the judge sworn accusations against all suspected offenders. Unlike petit juries, grand juries were not to pass upon guilt or innocence but were to decide only whether an individual should be brought to trial. At first all accusations originated with the members of the inquest themselves, but gradually the juries came to consider accusations made by outsiders as well. The jurors then heard only witnesses against the accused and, if they were convinced that there were grounds for trial, indicted him. They also passed upon indictments laid before them by crown prosecutors, returning a "true bill" if they found the accusation true or a "no bill" if they found it false. However, the juries never lost their power to accuse on their own knowledge. This they did by making a presentment to the court. The presentment represented an accusation on the jury's own initiative while an indictment represented a charge that originated outside the membership. Under their power of presentment English grand juries could and did investigate any matter that appeared to them to involve a violation of the law.[1]

[1] Frederick Pollock and Frederic W. Maitland, *The History of English Law* (Cambridge, 1923), 2:642; W. S. Holdsworth, *A History of English Law* (London, 1903), 1:147–148; William Blackstone, *Commentaries on the Law of*

1

Slowly the character of the institution changed. Originally an important instrument of the Crown, it gradually became instead a strong independent power guarding the rights of the English people. The juries did not have to divulge to the court the evidence upon which they acted, and when royal officials abused their authority, they intervened to protect citizens from unfounded accusations. With the growth of royal absolutism in England the inquests became highly prized as defenders of the liberties of the people and shields against royal persecution. The refusal, in 1681, of a grand jury to indict Lord Shaftesbury on charges of treason, in spite of the insistence of Charles II, led Englishmen to look upon the grand jury system with increased respect. John Somers, Lord Chancellor of England, in his tract *The Security of Englishmen's Lives,* noted that "Grand juries are our only security, in as much as our lives cannot be drawn into jeopardy by all the malicious crafts of the devil, unless such a number of our honest countrymen shall be satisfied in the truth of the accusations." By the end of the seventeenth century the grand jury had become an important bulwark of the rights and privileges of English citizens.[2]

When English colonists went to the New World during the seventeenth and eighteenth centuries, they took with them many of their institutions—among them the grand inquest. In the succeeding three centuries the grand jury played an important role in America and became a vital force in local government, just as it had in England. Grand juries acted in the nature of local assemblies: making known the wishes of the people, proposing new laws, protesting against abuses in government, performing administrative tasks, and looking after the welfare of their communities.

England (London, 1830), 4:301; Maurice S. Glaser, "The Political and Historical Development of the Grand Jury," in *Law Society Journal,* 8:192–204 (August, 1938).

[2] Lord John Somers, *The Security of Englishmen's Lives or the Trust, Power and Duty of Grand Juries of England* (Dublin, 1766), 15, 17, 22–23; Sir John Hawles, *The Englishman's Rights* (London, 1763), 34; Henry Care, *English Liberties or Free Born Subject's Inheritance* (Providence, 1774), 222, 234; Gilbert Burnet *History of My Own Time* (Oxford, 1900), 2:301–302.

They proved their effectiveness during the Colonial and Revolutionary periods in helping the colonists resist imperial interference. They provided a similar source of strength against outside pressure in the territories of the western United States, in the subject South following the Civil War, and in Mormon Utah. They frequently proved the only effective weapon against organized crime, malfeasance in office, and corruption in high places.

But appreciation of the value of grand juries was always greater in times of crisis, and, during periods when threats to individual liberty were less obvious, legal reformers, efficiency experts, and a few who feared government by the people worked diligently to overthrow the institution. Proponents of the system, relying heavily on the democratic nature of the people's panel, on its role as a focal point for the expression of public needs and the opportunity provided the individual citizen for direct participation in the enforcement of law, fought a losing battle. Opponents of the system leveled charges of inefficiency and tyranny against the panels of citizen investigators and pictured them as outmoded and expensive relics of the past. Charges of "star chamber" and "secret inquisition" helped discredit the institution in the eyes of the American people, and the crusade to abolish the grand jury, under the guise of bringing economy and efficiency to local government, succeeded in many states.

Abolition of the grand jury left a void in local government that could be filled only by increasing the authority of judges and prosecutors. Substitution of a preliminary hearing by a committing magistrate found the judge lacking in authority to perform properly the functions of a grand jury. Magistrates possessed no power to launch investigations where specific accusations had not been made. The practice of giving the district attorneys power to bring persons to trial on an information placed too much power, power susceptible of abuse for personal and political gain, in the hands of individual officeholders. In addition, under the information system the broad inquisitorial powers of the grand jury were lost. A prosecuting attorney could inquire into wrongdoing but he lacked subpoena powers to compel the attendance of witnesses and the production of documents. Grand juries, on the other hand, could issue their own subpoenas for witnesses and records. They could cite recalcitrant witnesses for contempt and bring perjury charges against those who refused to tell the truth. They heard all testimony in secret and could indict or refuse to indict as they saw fit. Panel members in most states could not be sued for libel for statements contained in presentments or indictments. Those states that abandoned the grand jury did hold it in reserve, at the call of a judge, for instances of widespread violation of the law, but when this was done the procedure for summoning the grand jury was soon forgotten.[3]

A resurgence of grand jury activity during the second quarter of the twentieth century helped restore its prestige. Yet, new forms of investigation, particularly those practiced by legislative bodies and individual experts, constituted a further serious threat to its continued existence. At mid-century the grand inquest had perhaps as many proponents as opponents, and whether violators of the law were to be hailed before the criminal courts by modern, efficient, economical experts or by archaic, inefficient, expensive panels of the people was still an open question.

[3] Mordecai Konowitz, "The Grand Jury as an Investigating Body of Public Officials," in *St. John's Law Review*, 10:219–294 (April, 1936); William Feather, "Foreman Tells Why Criminals Fear Action by Grand Jury," in *The Panel*, 12:17 (March-April, 1934); George H. Dession and Isadore H. Cohen, "The Inquisitorial Functions of Grand Juries," in *Yale Law Journal*, 41:687–712 (March, 1932).

Chapter 2

The Colonies

THE ENGLISH COLONIES IN AMERICA patterned their legal institutions after those of the mother country, and each adopted the grand jury as a part of its judicial system. But the colonists' grand juries, like their other institutions, developed along lines of their own. In England it was common procedure to summon only the more substantial freeholders, and the colonists followed the practice by making freeholding a basic requirement, but none of the colonies except the Carolinas set a high property standard. Still, in those colonies where the sheriff or the county court named the grand jurors, the selection tended to be made from the large landowners. This was particularly true of juries attending the provincial courts held at colonial capitals. Sheriffs selected panels from the immediate vicinity of the capital and generally ignored the western areas. Absenteeism was a much greater problem in the colonies than it was in England. Poor roads, sparsely settled areas, and the tremendous size of some western counties all combined to make jury service a hardship for many. Colonial legislatures imposed fines on jurymen for failing to appear at court or upon officers for neglecting to summon grand jurors, yet many county courts went term after term without impaneling a grand inquest. Colonial juries exercised much greater independence of action than did their English counterparts. In England much of the initiative in making accusations had gradually passed to the constables, who referred bills of indictment to the grand juries. In the colonies the lack of an efficient constabulary enabled the juries to regain much of their ancient autonomy. In most

5

criminal cases tried in the colonies presentment by a grand jury preceded a bill of indictment. Colonial inquests also assumed an increasing importance in local administration as legislatures gave them numerous specific administrative tasks to perform.

The first regular grand jury to sit in the English colonies attended the Court of Assistants of the Massachusetts Bay Colony in September, 1635. Until that time, the Assistants, acting as magistrates, had exercised almost complete power in criminal matters, had made the laws and had determined who should be tried. In March, 1634, the Massachusetts General Court issued an order to town meetings to select grand jurors. Town meetings throughout the colony elected jurymen to represent them on the first grand jury. At court, the jurors took an oath to present fairly all matters that came before them and then heard the charge of Governor John Winthrop. He warned the panel to report all crimes and misdemeanors that came to its attention and, as a further guide to its deliberations, read the Ten Commandments. The jurors took their job seriously. They presented more than a hundred offenders, including several of the colony's magistrates.[1]

In general, Massachusetts patterned its grand jury system after that of England, though it did not adopt the English method of selecting jurors. Under the English system the sheriffs often abused their authority by returning men who would charge offenses against certain persons and omit charges against others. Under the Massachusetts system the clerk of the Court of Assistants or of the county court sent warrants to the constables of the various towns, requiring them to call a town meeting to elect the required number of grand jurors. A statute of 1641 required the

[1] Thomas Lechford, "Plain Dealing: or News from New England," in *Massachusetts Historical Society Collections*, third series, 3:84 (1833); John Winthrop, *A Journal of the Transactions and Occurrences in the Settlement of Massachusetts* (Hartford, 1790), 86; *Records of the Court of Assistants of Massachusetts Bay* (Boston, 1904), 2:6, 8, 57; *Records of the Governor and Company of Massachusetts Bay in New England* (Boston, 1853–1856), 1:143.

jurors to serve for a full year, and in 1649 the General Court directed that the clerks of the various courts apportion the burden of grand jury service among the towns according to their population.[2] Early Massachusetts grand juries ordinarily confined their activities to indicting and presenting persons for various violations of the law, including wife beating and "having been instigated of the divill," as well as capital crimes. Some jurors, however, turned their attention to laxity in local government, as did those of Dover County when they presented town officials for neglecting to repair the stocks.[3]

Less than a year after the meeting of the first Massachusetts grand jury, seventeen grand jurors attended the March session of the General Court of New Plymouth. As in Massachusetts, they had been elected by the town meetings. Governor William Bradford charged the jurymen that they "must enquire of all abuses within the body of the government," a charge that emphasized the investigatory powers of the grand jury.

The presentments of Plymouth grand juries revealed a great interest in community problems. In 1638, a grand jury rebuked the Town of Sandwich "for not having their swine ringed," complained of the lack of surveyors for repairing the highway, and questioned the right of the governor and assistants to sell land to certain persons. The jurymen demanded to know which lands were to be reserved for purchasers and asked why a treasurer had not been chosen for the year. A subsequent jury presented various persons who failed to serve the public: Jonathan Brewster for neglecting the ferry at North River, John Jenney for grinding corn improperly, and Stephen Hopkins for giving short measure in selling beer. Plymouth grand inquests kept a close check on the state of morality in the colony.

---

[2] *The General Laws and Liberties of Massachusetts Colony, 1600–1672*, p. 168; *Records of Massachusetts Bay*, 1:169–170; 3:174.

[3] *Massachusetts Court of Assistants*, 2:74, 78; 3:151, 187; *New Hampshire State Papers* (Concord, 1943), 40:11; *New Hampshire Court Records, 1640–1692* (Concord, 1943), 11.

They repeatedly brought in presentments for drunkenness, disgraceful speech, breach of the Sabbath, and excessive frivolity. In 1639, the General Court empowered the jurymen of each town to demand an accounting from all persons whom they suspected of idle living. If they found such persons delinquent, they were to turn them over to the constable to await trial at the next session of court.[4] In 1654, a jury condemned the condition of the highway between Plymouth and Sandwich and inquired why nothing had been done to repair the Jones River and South River bridges presented by previous grand juries. In 1655, jurors objected that the Town of Plymouth had no standards of measure and that the Town of Marshfield did not maintain stocks and a whipping post.[5]

The grand jury system of Connecticut developed on different lines than those of Massachusetts and Plymouth. From the earliest period the colony made use of the "information," a written accusation filed in the court by a prosecuting officer acting under oath; juries confined themselves almost entirely to capital cases; and the town meetings did not elect jurors. In 1643, an order of the General Court providing for the first grand jury required the clerk of the General Court to "warn" twelve men to appear at each September session.[6] In 1666, the General Court established a system of county courts and ordered each of these courts to appoint a grand jury of at least twelve men to appear at each session. The only restriction placed upon the court's power of appointment was that every plantation in the respective counties had to be represented. In 1680, the General Court ordered all grand jurors to serve for one year.

Gradually, grand jurors in Connecticut tended to become agents of the county courts. The courts appointed men who would be of service in matters concerning their respective

[4] Nathaniel Shurtleff, ed., *Records of the Colony of New Plymouth* (Boston, 1855), 1:54, 86–87, 97–98, 118; 11:11, 90.

[5] *Ibid.*, 3:69, 82.

[6] *Public Records of the Colony of Connecticut* (Hartford, 1850–1890), 1:91, 536; William T. Davis, ed., *The New England States* (Boston, 1857), 1:476.

towns. In 1690, the General Court ordered each juryman to visit families in his town whom he suspected of neglecting the order to teach all children to read. After 1712 towns in their annual elections selected two or more persons to serve as grand jurors for one year. However, the county court assembled these jurors only on special occasions. A public prosecutor for each town took over the usual inquisitorial functions of the grand inquest while the jurymen tended to act individually rather than as a body. They sometimes assisted the public prosecutor and, contrary to their powers at common law, could make presentments individually. From time to time the Connecticut legislature added duties to the office of grand juryman until he became an important official in the local government. He supervised workmen clearing the commons, presented all idle persons, assisted the county justices in levying taxes, met with the selectmen and constables to nominate tavern keepers, checked to see that Indian children were learning to read, and performed a host of other duties. Selectmen, constables, and grand jurors formed a quasi-assembly for the county in the conduct of local government. After 1731 these officials met twice each year to advise upon the suppression of vice and immorality, and after 1744 they chose the petit jurors for the county and superior courts.[7]

Although settlements in Virginia preceded those in New England, the grand jury only gradually became a part of its court system. James I did not mention the grand jury in his instructions of 1608 and none convened in Virginia during the company period. However, from the earliest years a law bound two church wardens from each parish to present all offenders against the moral law. The General Court and the courts of Oyer and Terminer summoned grand juries for serious criminal offenses as early as 1633, but they did not attend court regularly. The General Court

[7] *Connecticut Public Records,* 2:61, 98; 3:52; 4:30; 5:329; 7:338; 9:45; John T. Farrell, ed., *The Superior Court Diary of Samuel Johnson* (Washington, D.C., 1942), xv, xli–xliii; *Acts and Laws of the State of Connecticut* (New London, 1784), 92–93.

selected those freemen who happened to be at the capital
while the court was in session. Sheriffs of James and York
counties selected the grand jurymen for the courts of Oyer
and Terminer.[8] In 1645, the grand jury found its way into
the county courts. In 1658, the House of Burgesses enacted
and the Governor in Council approved a law requiring
county courts to summon a grand jury at every session, but
in the same year the House of Burgesses repealed the law.
In 1662, the system of having grand juries attend the county
court twice each year was restored.[9]

Virginia followed the English procedure in summoning
grand juries. The sheriff of each county selected a panel of
twenty-four freeholders, at least fifteen of whom had to
appear to constitute a legal jury. There were no property
qualifications for serving: any freeman could qualify. But
the selection of jurymen by the sheriffs, who were in turn
appointed by the county courts, generally led to the selection of juries that would co-operate with those in authority.
To emphasize the necessity for care in choosing grand
jurors, Governor Francis Nicholson issued a proclamation
in 1690 warning sheriffs to select grand jurymen only "from
the most substantial inhabitants of your counties."[10] At first
the law provided no penalty for the failure to summon
grand jurors, but some counties went several years without impaneling an inquest. After warning letters from the
governor proved ineffectual, a law was finally passed, in
1677, providing that any justice of the peace who neglected
to "swear a jury of inquest" before the first of April each
year be fined two thousand pounds of tobacco, and that any
grand juryman not appearing be fined two hundred pounds
of tobacco. In spite of the system of fines, Governor Thomas
Culpeper found it necessary to issue a proclamation in

[8] Arthur P. Scott, *Criminal Law in Colonial Virginia* (Chicago, 1930), 67,
71; Oliver P. Chitwood, *Justice In Colonial Virginia* (Baltimore, 1905), 464;
Virginia Magazine of History, 13:390 (April, 1906).

[9] William W. Hening, ed., *The Statutes at Large, being a Collection of all
the Laws of Virginia* (Richmond, 1810–1823), 1:304, 463, 523; 2:74.

[10] *Virginia Magazine of History*, 20:114 (April, 1912).

1682 ordering that all grand jury presentments found within the previous year be sent to the General Court. The governor complained that the laws were not being enforced
because justices failed to summon juries and jurors, in turn,
failed to make presentments.[11]

Entrance of the grand jury into the county court system
of Virginia marked an important step in extending the activities of the institution in the colony. The county courts,
presided over by the justices of the peace, were more than
mere courts. They exercised legislative and executive as
well as judicial authority. They acted as fiscal agent, levying taxes and directing disbursement of funds. They super-
intended the construction and maintenance of roads and
bridges, cared for public buildings, and appointed local
officials. Gradually, the grand jury assumed the role of an
investigatory and advisory body of the county courts. It
took on such tasks as setting the price to be paid for private
property taken for public use and reporting on the condition of roads, bridges, and public buildings. In addition, the
laws of the colony imposed upon local grand juries the tasks
of inquiring into the methods used for mulberry cultivation
and silk making, checking to see that families planted two
acres of corn for each tithable person, and examining tobacco hogsheads to make certain they were the required
size. In charging grand juries justices called their attention
to any special matters that they should consider or investigate, but the juries did not restrict themselves to items
given them in charge by either the justices or the legislature. They could and often did present other matters upon
their own initiative, as did the jurors who complained that
the local ministers were negligent "in not checking upon
those who failed to attend church on Sunday."[12]

[11] Hening, *Laws of Virginia*, 2:407–408; 3:367; Scott, *Criminal Law in Colonial Virginia*, 68; Henry R. McIlwaine, ed., *Executive Journals of the Council of Virginia* (Richmond, 1925–1945), 1:47.

[12] *Virginia Colonial Decisions, 1728–1741*, 1:197 (1909); Hening, *Laws of Virginia*, 2:120, 122–123; *Virginia Magazine of History*, 18:370 (October, 1910); *Lower Norfolk County Antiquary* (Baltimore, 1906), 5:123–124.

Maryland's first grand inquest attended the Provincial Court in February, 1637. In the next year the Assembly passed an act guaranteeing the right to an indictment in all criminal cases, but the measure failed to become law because of a dispute with the governor over the Assembly's right to initiate legislation. In the 1640's and the 1650's the Provincial Court continued to impanel grand juries for special criminal cases and occasionally they attended the county courts, but criminal cases generally came to trial on a prosecutor's information rather than on a grand jury's indictment. In 1662, the Legislative Council declared that under the common law of England, which prevailed in Maryland, every county had to impanel a grand jury quarterly. However, most county courts ignored the order until 1666, when the Assembly required regular grand jury attendance. The legislature gave sheriffs the duty of selecting jurymen but did not stipulate the number required to constitute a legal panel. In spite of the law only six of the fifty-five sessions of the Charles County Court held in the years 1666 to 1674 had a grand jury. Finally, the colony resorted to fines. In 1699, the Assembly imposed a fine of five hundred pounds of tobacco on sheriffs neglecting to impanel a jury, and ordered each county to provide two jurymen for sessions of the Provincial Court, or suffer a penalty of one thousand pounds of tobacco per year to cover the expenses of the provincial grand juries.[13]

The Maryland grand juries, like those in Virginia and the New England colonies, did not confine themselves to indictments in criminal cases. They returned a great variety of other complaints and grievances and frequently surveyed land in boundary controversies.[14]

The first use of the grand jury in Rhode Island took place after the union, in 1640, of the towns of Portsmouth and Newport. Circuit Quarter courts met alternately in the two

---

[13] *Archives of Maryland* (Baltimore, 1883), 1:49, 437–438; 2:141–142, 384; 4:21–22, 237, 240, 241, 260, 447; 13:501; 22:511–512; 60:xxiii.

[14] Carroll T. Bond, ed., *Proceedings of the Maryland Court of Appeals, 1695–1729* (Washington, D.C., 1933), xxiv, 76, 91, 112, 221.

towns and in December, 1641, and again in March, 1642, a grand jury attended sessions held at Portsmouth. After the union of Providence, Newport, Portsmouth, and Warwick in 1647, each of the four towns elected grand jurymen at their town meetings to attend the General Court of Trials. Rhode Island secured a charter in 1663, and at its first session under the new charter, the General Court ordered the four towns to provide twelve grand jurymen for each term of court. The towns paid fines of twenty shillings for each failure to elect a juryman or for each one selected who was not a freeman of the colony.[15]

In New Jersey, only ten years after the earliest settlement, the Assembly ordered that each town within the province send grand jurors to all sessions of the Provincial Court, and in the next year, 1676, it provided a penalty of thirty shillings for all constables who failed to comply with the law.[16] New Jersey grand juries, like those in the older colonies, gradually enlarged their sphere of activity beyond merely presenting or indicting those who had violated the law. In 1694, the Assembly empowered the county courts, with the assistance and concurrence of the grand juries, to levy county taxes and to audit all expenditures of county funds, and thereafter inquests in each of the New Jersey counties examined the accounts of the county treasurer every year. In 1700, the grand jury of Burlington County proposed a head tax on livestock and slaves as a means of paying the county debt. The court accepted the proposal although two jurors dissented vigorously. New Jersey jurymen also inspected county roads, and the jurors

[15] Howard M. Chapin, ed., *Documentary History of Rhode Island* (Providence, 1916–1919), 2:132–134; *Early Records of the Town of Warwick, Rhode Island* (Providence, 1926), 1:124, 128; *Early Records of the Town of Providence* (Providence, 1892–1915), 2:142; 3:12, 27; *Records of the Colony of Rhode Island* (Providence, 1856–1865), 1:502–503; 2:27–28, 83; Davis, *New England States*, 4:2366.

[16] Aaron Leaming and Jacob Spicer, *The Grants, Concessions and Original Constitutions of the Province of New Jersey* (Philadelphia, 1881), 101, 121; Edward Q. Keasby, *Courts and Lawyers of New Jersey* (New York, 1912), 1:102.

frequently complained of the condition in which they found the highways and bridges.[17]

Since the grand jury had developed in England and was not a part of continental legal systems, the Dutch in New York did not make use of it. In the New Netherlands an official known as the *schout* combined the functions of sheriff and public prosecutor. When English rule began in 1664, the English proprietor, the Duke of York, made provision neither for the grand jury nor for a representative assembly. The first grand inquest to convene in New York attended the Provincial Court of Assize in 1681 in the treason case of William Dyer. The jury indicted Dyer for treason and charged that as customs collector he had imposed unlawful customs duties and had used troops to enforce his unlawful practices. The grand jurors also took this occasion to present "the great, manifold and insupportable grievances under which the province still doth groan." They petitioned the proprietor to remedy the situation by giving the colony an elected assembly. The Court of Assize sent their petition to the Duke and he granted New York a representative assembly.[18] In 1683, at its first session, the new assembly enacted the "Charter of Liberties and Privileges," which included a guarantee of the right to indictment in all capital or criminal cases. Upon his accession to the throne the Duke disallowed the Charter and abolished the assembly, but these actions had little effect upon the grand jury in the colony. It was already in operation and it remained as a regular part of the judicial machinery without any suggestion that it be abolished.[19] Furthermore, in the absence of a

[17] Henry C. Reed and George J. Miller, eds., *The Burlington County Court Book, 1680–1709* (Washington, D.C., 1944), 234–235, 317; Leaming and Spicer, *Grants of New Jersey*, 528.

[18] "Proceedings of the General Court of Assizes," in *Collections of the New York Historical Society*, 45:11, 14–15 (1912); Julius Goebel and T. Raymond Naughton, *Law Enforcement in Colonial New York* (New York, 1944), 328–329, 334–335.

[19] *Documents Relating to the Colonial History of the State of New York* (Albany, 1853), 3:357; Charles Z. Lincoln, *The Constitutional History of New York* (Rochester, 1906), 1:102; Goebel and Naughton, *Law Enforcement in Colonial New York*, 336.

representative assembly the powers of grand juries were gradually expanded. Partly because of the lack of an efficient police system, but partly also because of a desire on the part of the colonists to extend their control over the government, the practice of indicting upon the information of a prosecuting officer eventually disappeared. Several grand juries attempted to extend their powers into the field of legislation. In 1688, for example, an Albany jury ordered that persons selling spirits must keep lodging for both horses and men. Another New York jury prohibited riding over corn fields. In this way the jurors tried to assume the ordinance-making powers that were actually in the jurisdiction of the justices of the peace.[20]

Pennsylvania, in contrast to New York, summoned grand juries from the earliest period. Its first grand inquest convened in 1683 and indicted three men for counterfeiting Spanish coins. In his Frame of Government for Pennsylvania and Delaware, written in 1682, William Penn had guaranteed the right to indictment by a grand jury in all capital cases, and the Frame of Government adopted in 1696 made special provision for those grand jurymen who "for conscience sake" could not take an oath under any circumstances. Such persons could merely attest that they would diligently inquire into and make true presentment of all matters that came before them.[21] In practice, Pennsylvania grand juries did not confine themselves to capital or even criminal cases. As early as 1683 they assisted justices in estimating county expenses and assessing taxes to meet them. Under a law of 1696 the grand jury, in co-operation with six special assessors and the county justices, supervised all county expenditures and tax levies. After 1700 grand jurors let contracts for bridge building in their respective counties. They also inspected bridges, public build-

---

[20] *Ibid.*, 355–356, 361.
[21] Benjamin P. Poore, *The Federal and State Constitutions and Colonial Charters and Other Organic Laws of the United States* (Washington, D.C., 1877), 2: 1524; Howard M. Jenkins, *Pennsylvania, Colonial and Federal* (Philadelphia, 1903), 1:296.

ings, and jails and presented to the court any evidence of the neglect of them.[22]

The constitution of the Carolinas, like that of Pennsylvania, made specific provision for grand juries. However, the elaborate and artificial Fundamental Constitutions written by John Locke also included a property qualification. In keeping with his attempt to establish a feudal aristocracy, Locke restricted grand jury service in the precinct courts to persons holding fifty acres of land and in the county and provincial courts to persons owning at least three hundred acres. Early presentments in the Carolinas followed the same pattern as those in the other colonies. In addition to indictments for various crimes and misdemeanors, the juries took an active part in local government. They presented contractors for not repairing roads and bridges properly, inspected jails and public buildings, and suggested ways of improving the moral life of the community. In 1682, the proprietors gave grand juries the unique power of initiating legislation under certain circumstances. If a majority of the county inquests suggested certain laws and the Council did not propose them within a suitable time, the Assembly could consider them without further delay.[23]

The last of the English settlements in America, James Oglethorpe's buffer colony of Georgia, summoned grand juries very early in its history. As was true in most frontier areas, they did not meet regularly. The recorders were often careless in summoning grand jurymen and jurors frequently failed to appear at court. As the older colonies had discovered, fines proved necessary to imbue prospective

[22] E. R. L. Gould, "Local Government in Pennsylvania," in *John's Hopkins Studies in Historical and Political Science*, 1:no. 3, p. 27 (1886); *Statutes of Pennsylvania*, 2:35, 39, 73 (1700–1712), 3:320 (1712–1724); 4:235 (1724–1744); Ignatius C. Grubb, "The Colonial and State Judiciary of Delaware," in *Papers of the Historical Society of Delaware*, 18:3 (1897); Charles H. B. Turner, *Some Records of Sussex County Delaware* (Philadelphia, 1909), 68–69, 128–129; Samuel Hazard, ed., *The Register of Pennsylvania* (Philadelphia, 1830), 6:329.

[23] W. L. Saunders, ed., *The Colonial Records of North Carolina* (Raleigh, 1886–1890), 1:198–199; 2:398–403; *Records in the British Public Record Office Relating to South Carolina* (Atlanta, 1928), 1:194–195.

jurors with the necessary civic spirit. However, the grand jury soon assumed an important place in the government of the colony because of Oglethorpe's paternalistic rule. Georgia, like New York, had no representative assembly. Except for a town court and the grand jury, all governmental authority rested with the proprietor. Occasionally he called meetings of the colonists but generally issued orders without consulting anyone. The strict rules of the trustees of Georgia concerning land tenures, quitrents, rum traffic, and slave owning led to grievances that had no other outlet except the grand jury. As a result, Georgia colonists early began to use the grand inquest as a means of voicing their complaints.[24]

As colonial towns grew and were incorporated, the grand jury became an instrument for popular participation in municipal as well as in county and provincial government. Grand juries operated in conjunction with the local borough courts of incorporated towns. The powers of these courts varied, but they often exercised criminal jurisdiction equal to that of the county courts. Such municipal courts constituted one of the most valuable privileges associated with incorporation, but when no municipal corporation existed, the county or provincial grand juries often turned their attention to city problems and furnished a means of agitating for municipal reforms. Through their presentments grand juries served to arouse public opinion to the need for reforms, and occasionally they managed to stir public officials to action. In some areas towns could be prosecuted upon the presentment of a grand jury. Just such a threat inspired the Boston town meeting to vote a thousand pounds for the repair of streets which the jurors had presented as being "in a ruinous condition."[25]

In 1736, a Philadelphia jury complained of the condition of the city streets, and subsequent juries took the lead in

[24] James R. McCain, *Georgia As a Proprietary Province* (Boston, 1917), 215–216; A. D. Candler, ed., *Colonial Records of the State of Georgia* (Atlanta, 1904–1916), 4:89, 92, 137, 258–259.

[25] *Report of the Boston Record Commissioners* (Boston, 1883), 26:235.

forcing the city to pave them. In 1744, Philadelphia grand jurors presented the low state of civic morality in the city, stating that tippling houses and other "nurseries of vice and debauchery" had combined to make parts of the city veritable "hell towns." By mid-century the Philadelphia City Council was acting as a closed corporation, completely out of touch with the needs of the community, and the local grand jury served as a means of focusing attention upon abuses and neglect in the city government. Presentments demanding a paid watch resulted in an ordinance setting up a board of wardens empowered to erect and maintain street lamps and to appoint watchmen.[26]

Grand juries in Annapolis followed the pattern set by those in Philadelphia when they complained of the condition of city streets, docks, and landings. In 1766, the grand inquest served as a medium of protest against incompetence and corruption in the city council. The jurors issued a "remonstrance" against neglected streets, the refusal of city officials to account for the proceeds of lotteries, and the failure of council members to attend meetings. As a result, the Annapolis City Council met more regularly, held elections to fill vacancies in its membership, and fined members for not attending its meetings.

In Charleston, grand juries attending the provincial court frequently turned their attention to municipal matters. In 1734 and again in 1742, they condemned the practice of putting slaves out to work by the week in competition with white labor. Numerous presentments complained that selling liquor to sailors and Negroes produced riots. On other occasions, juries called attention to laxity in the city administration: the failure of constables and magistrates to enforce the Sabbath observance laws, disorderly behavior of the town watch, and neglect of officials to regulate the town markets properly. They also suggested civic reforms,

[26] John Thomas Scharf and Thompson Westcott, *History of Philadelphia* (Philadelphia, 1884), 1:208, 211, 218; Ernest S. Griffith, *History of American City Government: The Colonial Period* (New York, 1938), 217, 347.

including an increased watch, better lighting, and the organization of a fire company.[27]

In the period after 1700, the American colonists gradually came to realize the value of the grand juries as a means of obtaining redress of grievances from proprietors and of opposing the power of royal officials. But this did not mean that groups in control in the various colonies now wanted juries to become an instrument of democratic government with jury service open to all. They did not wish to see the powers of grand juries restricted by royal courts and royal officers, but they did want to select those who would sit on them. In Boston, in 1702, Cotton Mather attempted to "rectify the gross abuse in the choice of jurymen" by the town meeting. As a result, the selectmen of the town each year presented to the town meeting a list of persons whom "they deemed proper to serve on juries." Only persons on this list could be nominated for service. In New York, the legislature renewed a temporary statute of 1699 placing a property qualification on the right to serve as a grand juror. The Assembly of New Jersey directed sheriffs to summon only those persons worth at least one hundred pounds in real estate located in the county in which they served. The Pennsylvania Assembly tried in 1700 and again in 1705 to restrict the jurisdiction of grand juries by taking away their power to present matters which a justice of the peace could determine, but the Queen in Council vetoed both measures. In the southern colonies the sheriffs and justices selected grand jurors from the "better classes" in the coastal areas. The North Carolina Assembly, in an address to the governor made in 1726, complained that "illegal" grand juries, particularly in the outlying areas, vilified and damaged the reputations of members of the Assembly. The legislators objected to the use of grand jury presentments for "merely petitioning redress of grievances." Until 1769

---

[27] Annapolis, *Maryland Gazette*, March 18, 20, May 1, June 19, 1766; Griffith, *American City Government*, 213–220; Carl Bridenbaugh, *Cities in the Wilderness* (New York, 1938), 359.

South Carolina's back country had no local courts and juries, and then they possessed very limited jurisdiction. In Virginia, where county courts existed in the western areas, the size of the counties and the difficulties of travel made back-country people turn to direct action rather than to grand juries as a means of redressing their grievances. Citizens of back-country North Carolina in 1750 did not use the grand jury directly as a means of protesting against a reapportionment act. Instead, they simply refused to serve on juries. In 1769, the "regulators" of Rowan County, North Carolina found the local grand jury packed against them when they attempted to bring local officials to trial for charging exorbitant fees. Only three men on the panel were not officers of the government. In March, 1771, Governor William Tryon adjourned the Superior Court of North Carolina because he was dissatisfied with the temper of the grand jury. He directed sheriffs to select as jurymen "only gentlemen of the first rank, property and probity." The resulting grand jury returned sixty-two indictments against the regulators for violating the riot act. Following this, the hand-picked jurors signed the "association" agreeing to support the government and accepted the governor's offer to accompany an armed force to crush the regulators.[28]

Though it was occasionally called upon to play a more spectacular role in provincial, county, or municipal government, the normal work of the grand jury in colonial America consisted of routine presentments and indictments, and

[28] *Boston Record Commissioners,* 8:24; *Massachusetts Historical Society Collections,* seventh series, 7:423 (1911); *Colonial Laws of New York from the Year 1664 to the Revolution* (Albany, 1894–1896), 1:387, 708, 1021; Samuel Allinson, *Acts of the General Assembly of the Province of New Jersey* (Burlington, 1776), 24; *Statutes of Pennsylvania,* 2:24, 188, 492, 529 (1700–1712); *Colonial Records of North Carolina,* 2:613–614; William A. Schaper, "Sectionalism and Representation in South Carolina," in *Annual Report of the American Historical Association,* 1895, vol. 1, p. 335; Edward McCrady, *The History of South Carolina Under the Royal Government* (New York, 1899), 2:636; John S. Bassett, "The Regulators of North Carolina," in *Annual Report of the American Historical Association,* 1894, pp. 182, 197; Archibald Henderson, ed., "Harmon Husband's Continuation of the Impartial Relation," in *North Carolina Historical Review,* 18:59–60 (January, 1941); Philadelphia, *Pennsylvania Gazette,* August 15, 1771.

most colonials, like most Englishmen, took the institution
for granted. However, in the 1680's the struggle in England
against Stuart absolutism served to renew interest in the
grand jury and was the occasion for English Whigs to set
forth in detail the rights and powers of grand juries. The
condemnation, for refusing to indict Lord Shaftesbury for
treason, of a grand jury by an English court led several
Englishmen to write expositions in defense of its powers.
Sir John Hawles, in his pamphlet, *The Englishman's
Rights*, published in 1680, denied the right or power of any
court to fine or imprison a grand jury. He characterized it
as an institution designed to prevent oppression. In 1682,
John Somers, Lord Chancellor of England, wrote a tract
entitled *The Security of Englishmen's Lives or the Trust,
Power and Duty of Grand Juries of England*. Lord Somers
hailed the grand jury as the only security against malicious
prosecution by the government and denied that courts could
"magisterially impose their opinions upon the jury." He
construed the powers of grand juries very broadly and emphasized that they were not restricted to those matters
given them in charge by the judge, but could extend their
inquiry to "all other matters which come to their knowledge." Henry Care's *English Liberties or Free Born Subject's Inheritance* was published in 1698. It emphasized
the importance of maintaining the independence of inquests
from judicial interference. Bishop Gilbert Burnet termed
the grand inquest "one of the greatest outworks of liberty."[29]

When the American colonists clashed with absentee trustees or with representatives of royal authority, they too began to see the grand jury in a different light. Instead of a
routine, burdensome institution it became the bulwark of
their rights and privileges. The writings of Hawles, Somers,
and Care soon found their way to the colonies and each went

[29] Sir John Hawles, *The Englishman's Rights* (London, 1763), 34; Lord John
Somers, *The Security of Englishmen's Lives or the Trust, Power and Duty of
Grand Juries of England* (Dublin, 1766), 15, 17, 22–23; Henry Care, *English
Liberties or Free Born Subject's Inheritance* (Providence, 1774), 222, 234;
Gilbert Burnet, *History of My Own Time* (Oxford, 1900), 2:301–302.

through several printings in America. They served the colonists as guides to the powers and duties of grand juries.[30]

Colonists in Georgia, lacking a representative assembly found a substitute in the grand jury and made a series of attempts to use the inquest as a means of airing their grievances against the trustees and their representatives. As early as 1737 a jury protested against the keeper of the trustee's store and complained that the lack of servants prevented proper cultivation of the land. The jurors urged the granting of larger tracts of land and the legalization of the ownership of Negro slaves. In the following year several members of the grand jury claimed the power to administer general oaths and to inquire into any matter they saw fit. The court denied this power, and Colonel William Stephens, Secretary to the Trustees, declared that such an oath was contrary to English usage. While waiting for a decision from the trustees in England on the matter, the justice adjourned the court for six weeks "in order to have as little to do as possible with grand jurors." Stephens confided to his journal the belief that "a few malcontents" had started the whole matter in order to take control of the government. The trustees decided that the grand juries of Georgia could require witnesses to take only an oath to testify about particular crimes. Stephens wrote elatedly to the trustees that their decision "would put a happy end to the matter of grand juries."[31]

Colonel Stephens' optimism was ill-founded. In the next year the grand jury again brought up the subject of a general oath, but finally agreed to abide by the ruling of the trustees. In July, 1741, however, the jurors were not as easily persuaded. Led by their foreman, Robert Williams, who had also been foreman of the 1738 grand jury, a ma-

[30] Charles Warren, *A History of the American Bar* (Boston, 1911), 34; Francis Hopkinson, *The Miscellaneous Essays and Occasional Writings of Francis Hopkinson* (Philadelphia, 1792), 1:198–213.

[31] McCain, *Georgia As a Proprietary Province*, 215–216; Albert E. McKinley, *The Suffrage Franchise in the Thirteen English Colonies* (Philadelphia, 1905), 166–168; *Colonial Records of Georgia*, 4:89, 92, 137; 22:264.

jority of the jurymen opposed the policies of the trustees.
They proceeded to administer a general oath to all persons
they called before them and did not tell the witnesses upon
what matters the grand inquest would examine them. Stephens, now president of Savannah County, suspected that
the action of the grand jury "tended to no good end" and
refused to go before it. He had no desire to allow the jury
to engage in a "fishing expedition" at his expense. The
jurors presented Stephens for ignoring their summons and
in the same return indicted Richard Kent, the justice of the
peace for the Indian Nations, for illegally forcing persons
to enter into recognizances before him. The jurymen interrogated other witnesses regarding the disposition of
sums of money the trustees had sent to the colony and demanded that officials make a full accounting for such funds.
At this point, the court instructed the jurors that they could
not compel persons to come before them to be examined under a general oath. Several members of the panel "grew
very warm and clamorous" when they heard the court's instructions and in the argument that ensued claimed loudly
that all grand juries enjoyed the right of sending for and
examining under oath whomsoever they pleased, touching
what matters they thought fit. After a heated debate between the bench and the jurors, the judge dismissed the
grand jury and adjourned the court.

Undaunted, the panel retired to a private residence and
sought the legal opinion of Sir Richard Everard. Sir Richard had just come to Georgia from North Carolina, where
his father was royal governor. In spite of this connection,
he immediately sided with those who opposed the local officials in the Georgia controversy. As the basis for his advice to the jurors he used Henry Care's *English Liberties*.
He advised the jurors not to submit to dismissal by the
court. They heeded this advice and continued to hold their
meetings and examine witnesses. When the court learned
of Sir Richard's action, the justices required him to post
bail and stand trial on a charge of "trying to create jealous-

ies and feuds and alienate the minds of the grand jury."
The court then adjourned for two weeks, hoping that the
matter would subside. Stephens was less hopeful this time.
Taking no chances, he began to consider means to "quash
with sufficient authority" any future pretentions on the part
of the grand jury.[32]

Blocked in their attempt to use the grand jury as a means
of protest, those opposed to the policies of the trustees
called a meeting of all settlers to discuss their grievances.
At the meeting they named Thomas Stephens, son of President Stephens, as agent to represent them in England.
Young Stephens carried with him instructions to seek land
grants equal in size to those in South Carolina, to ask for
permission to own Negro slaves, and to work for a representative assembly for the colony.[33]

South Carolina colonists also used the grand jury, with
much more success than their neighbors in Georgia, to defend their interests against those of the proprietors and
the Crown. In 1741, the Council passed and the Assembly
was about to approve an act to compel all land owners to
pay their quitrents or suffer forfeiture. Public opinion on
the measure ran high and found a spokesman in the grand
jury. Charleston jurors presented the proposed law as containing "divers clauses of a dangerous nature to the property of His Majesty's subjects of this Province." The jury's
action had a profound effect upon the Assembly. It referred
the presentment to a special committee and thereafter refused to approve the quitrent law.[34]

Individual royal officials, more often than general royal
and proprietary policies, found themselves in contention
with grand juries. It became common practice for grand
juries summoned to attend sessions of the general or provincial courts to express their opinions on matters in gen-

[32] *Colonial Records of Georgia,* 4:258–259; 4 supplement:170, 186–190; 5:588;
23:116–128.
[33] McKinley, *Suffrage Franchise,* 166–168.
[34] William Roy Smith, *South Carolina as a Royal Province* (New York,
1903), 59–60.

eral and often on the administration of the royal governor in particular. Royal governors saw the advantage of selecting jurors who would pass appropriate laudatory resolutions that could be sent to the Board of Trade. To obtain such jurymen, governors developed the practice of sending outside the capital for specially selected panel members. To prevent this in Virginia, the House of Burgesses, in 1705, ordered that grand juries at the General Court be impaneled "from the bystanders" in the court room. However, this statute did not end the influence of the governor on the selection of jurymen. In 1719, the House drafted a series of articles condemning the administration of Governor Alexander Spotswood. In his defense Spotswood sent the Board of Trade a copy of a presentment, specifically disavowing the action of the Burgesses, made by the grand inquest that had attended the last General Court. The Virginia Assembly replied that the sheriff, an appointee of the governor, selected the jurymen under the governor's "constant influence and direction." The Assembly observed that, under this system, "the country never had nor will have so bad a governor that a grand jury so pickt will not justify."[35]

By preventing the excessive use of informations signed by royal prosecutors, the grand juries constituted still another important curb on royal authority in the colonies. A Maryland statute of 1715 prohibited criminal proceedings except upon the presentment of a grand jury. The law provided a fine of five thousand pounds of tobacco for judges holding a trial upon an information of the attorney general. A committee of the South Carolina Assembly reported in 1727, that a royal official had introduced a new method of "prosecuting people by way of information." In the same year, the New York Assembly enacted a law prohibiting trial upon information except by order of the governor. The

[35] W. A. Whitehead, ed., *Archives of the State of New Jersey, 1631-1800* (Newark, 1880-1906), first series, 11:33, 34; Hening, *Laws of Virginia*, 3:368; *Virginia Magazine of History*, 22:410-411 (October, 1914); 23:71 (January, 1915); R. A. Brock, ed., "The Official Letters of Alexander Spotswood," in *Virginia Historical Society Collections*, new series, 2:320 (1895).

legislators aimed the restriction at an attorney general who had been particularly "vexatious" in bringing persons to trial. Lieutenant Governor Cadwallader Colden of New York reported to the Board of Trade that the Assembly had limited the courts of the colony by its action, as a part of "their design to weaken His Majesty's government here." Royal officers wanted to avoid referring all criminal matters to local grand juries, since such juries frequently refused to indict, especially if the official desiring the indictment was unpopular. In 1735, Chief Justice William Smith of North Carolina told grand jurors that they had perjured themselves by not bringing in a bill of indictment in a certain case. He then ordered the attorney general to bring the matter before him on an information.[36]

By the end of the Colonial period the grand jury had become an indispensable part of government in each of the American colonies. Grand juries served as more than panels of public accusers. They acted as local representative assemblies ready to make known the wishes of the people. They proposed new laws, protested against abuses in government, and performed many administrative tasks. They wielded tremendous authority in their power to determine who should and who should not face trial. They enforced or refused to enforce laws as they saw fit and stood guard against indiscriminate prosecution by royal officials.

[36] *Acts of the Assembly of the Province of Maryland* (Philadelphia, 1759), 56; "Journal of the Common House of Assembly of South Carolina," in *Colonial Records of South Carolina*, 1:68 (1946); *Colonial Laws of New York*, 2:406; *Colonial Records of North Carolina*, 4:21.

Chapter 3

The Revolution

IN THE GRAND JURY discontented American colonists had discovered a potent weapon with which to harass royal officials and protest against British authority.[1] The power of the juries lay in their ability to block criminal proceedings begun by royal officials. Simply by refusing to find a true bill they could effectively prevent the enforcement of criminal statutes, among them the laws regulating trade, and it was no secret that Colonial juries were prejudiced in favor of smugglers and patriotic mob leaders. This prejudice was particularly potent in Boston, where the radical dominated town meeting selected jurors who could be depended upon to set aside the weight of evidence and do what was expected of them. The colonists had long fought the practice of bringing individuals to trial on an information of a royal prosecutor, and British efforts to limit the powers of Colonial juries by establishing admiralty courts and providing that Colonial offenders be tried in England met with stiff resistance. Furthermore, the political importance of the juries made the colonists doubly jealous of their right to indictment before being brought to trial.[2] On the eve of the Revolution local grand juries were in an excellent position to take the lead in opposing the imperial government.

[1] The bulk of the material in this chapter originally appeared in the author's "Grand Juries and the American Revolution," in *Virginia Magazine of History and Biography*, 63:257–268 (July, 1955), and is used with permission.

[2] John Adams and Jonathan Sewall, *Political Essays Published in the Years 1774 and 1775* (Boston, 1819), 57–58; W. L. Saunders, ed., *The Colonial Records of North Carolina* (Raleigh, 1886–1890), 4:21; 7:129; *Acts of the Assembly of the Province of Maryland*, 1759, p. 56; *Colonial Records of South Carolina*, 1:68; *Colonial Laws of New York from the Year 1664 to the Revolution* (Albany, 1894–1896), 2:406 (1727).

It wasn't long before Massachusetts jurors were toasted as "volunteers in the cause of truth and humanity," defending the people from "tyrannic violence."[3]

Grand juries gave evidence of their temper very early in the struggle with England. In 1765, Boston jurors refused to indict the leaders of the Stamp Act riots, while in Williamsburg, Virginia, jurors assembled for the general court joined the mob that hanged the stamp master in effigy.[4]

Chief Justice Thomas Hutchinson of Massachusetts demanded, in March, 1768, that the grand jurors of Suffolk indict the editors of the *Boston Gazette* for libeling Governor Francis Bernard. In a long and forcible charge, the chief justice warned members of the panel that "they might depend upon being damned if they did not find a true bill."[5] Hutchinson was convinced that he had made an impression on the jurymen, but, after James Otis and other leaders of the popular party went into action, they refused to indict. In the face of this refusal the chief justice was helpless. He could only express his indignation in subsequent jury charges.[6] In August, an editorial in the *Boston Gazette* threatened that if Hutchinson continued to denounce the popular party before grand juries, "his private life and conversation" would be exposed. It was hardly necessary, however, to threaten the chief justice to silence him. He had already realized the futility of laying matters of this nature before a partisan grand jury. The inquest impaneled in September to investigate the riots of the previous June in-

[3] Josiah Quincy, *Reports of Cases in the Superior Court of Judicature of the Province of Massachusetts Bay, 1761–1772* (Boston, 1865), 278.

[4] James Truslow Adams, *History of New England* (Boston, 1927), 2:323, 334; John C. Miller, *Origins of the American Revolution* (Boston, 1943), 132; Edmund S. Morgan and Helen M. Morgan, *The Stamp Act Crisis* (Chapel Hill, 1953), 155, 182.

[5] Letter of Chief Justice Oliver, dated March 26, 1768, in the *Boston Gazette*, March 31, 1777.

[6] Letter of Governor Bernard, dated March 12, 1768, in *Letters to the Ministry from Governor Bernard, General Gage and Commodore Hood* (Boston, 1769), 13; Quincy, *Superior Court Cases*, 258, 270; letter of Thomas Hutchinson, dated October 4, 1768, in *The Letters of Governor Hutchinson and Lt. Governor Oliver* (London, 1774), 9.

cluded several persons who had raised and led the mob in its attack on the customs officers. Hutchinson stated that, in view of this, it would serve no useful purpose to bring the matter to their attention. When the attorney general sought to bring in evidence against the riot leaders, he found nobody willing to testify before the jury, since the members of the panel were ready to "mark those who would testify against the mob."[7]

Governor Bernard complained to Lord Hillsborough, Secretary of State for the Colonies, of the helplessness of royal officials in the face of partisan grand juries. The governor pointed out that the problem arose from the method by which jurors were selected in Massachusetts. The popular party easily dominated juries chosen by the town meetings. Hillsborough agreed that the popular election of grand jurors constituted a serious handicap, and proposed that the system be changed, so as to allow the sheriff to name the jurors as was done in England. However, he could not gain sufficient support in the House of Commons for the enactment of his measure.[8]

Chief Justice Hutchinson continued to call the attention of grand juries to libelous matter that appeared in Boston newspapers, although he no longer expected them to act. The chief justice dwelt upon the offenses of perjury and false swearing, reminding the recalcitrant jurors that these were serious transgressions "in the sight of God" as well as before the law,[9] but his attempts to instill the fear of heavenly retribution made little impression on the jurymen. They continued to ignore the offenses presented by the judge, and turned their attention to the British soldiers quartered among them. In March, 1769, the Boston inquest denounced soldiers quartered in the town for breaking and

[7] Governor Bernard to the Earl of Hillsborough, dated September 9, 1768, in *Letters to the Ministry*, 68–69.

[8] Chief Justice Oliver to the Earl of Hillsborough, dated February 13, 1769, in *Hutchinson-Oliver Letters*, 31; *Letters to the Ministry*, 68; Boston, *Essex Gazette*, March 14, 1769.

[9] Quincy, *Superior Court Cases*, 309–315.

entering dwellings, waylaying citizens, and wounding a justice of the peace during a riot. They also indicted Joseph Muzzele for perjury in the case of John Hancock, pending before the Court of Admiralty, but they refused to indict persons charged by the King's Attorney with enticing soldiers to desert. The jurors ended their deliberations by censuring the prosecuting officer "for having received so many lucrative court favors."[10]

It was now the turn of royal officials to block criminal prosecutions. The attorney general disposed of the indictments against British soldiers by refusing to prosecute them. This countermove brought the immediate and vehement protest of the town meetings. The Salem town meeting instructed the Massachusetts General Assembly to enquire why grand jury bills were being ignored. Residents of Boston complained that soldiers guilty of serious offenses went unpunished because the attorney general refused to prosecute them. They also claimed that the prosecutor was bringing colonists to trial upon his own information in cases where the grand juries refused to indict. In response to these complaints the Massachusetts Assembly adopted a resolution denouncing the actions of the attorney general as "a daring breach of trust and an insupportable grievance."[11] The Assembly and the town meetings could do little except protest, but the grand juries kept up their end of the dispute by continuing to return "ignoramus" all bills laid before them by the judge or royal prosecutor.[12]

A Philadelphia jury, in 1770, took up the fight, and it went beyond the purely negative tactics of refusing to indict colonists and proposed a positive program of protest against the British tax on tea. The jurors denounced the use of the proceeds of the tea tax to pay salaries of royal officials in the colony. They declared their support of the non-importation agreement recently reached by the importers of Phila-

[10] *Essex Gazette,* March 14, May 16, 1769.
[11] *Boston Evening Post,* February 6, 1769; *Essex Gazette,* May 23, June 27, July 4, August 1, 1769.
[12] Boston, *Massachusetts Gazette and News-Letter,* February 27, 1772.

delphia and, in addition, recommended that Pennsylvania attempt to "promote union with the other colonies" in order to seek redress of their collective grievances. As a start for such co-operative action, the jurors pledged themselves to work for a united colonial program of non-consumption of British goods.[13]

Back in Massachusetts, Chief Justice Peter Oliver had refused to take an oath renouncing his salary from the Crown, and, in 1774, the Massachusetts Assembly impeached him. Governor Thomas Hutchinson and the Council refused to approve the action,[14] but the local grand juries set about making it effective. At the next session of the Superior Court, the Charlestown jurors hesitated taking their oath while Oliver sat on the bench. They finally agreed to serve but issued a protest against Oliver's presiding at the trial of any offender indicted by them. At Worcester, members of the grand inquest met at a private home early on the morning before court convened and agreed not to serve if Oliver presided over the court. When the chief justice did not attend the court the jurors agreed to be sworn, but they issued a remonstrance against judges serving "while under the influence of a bribe."[15]

While the status of Chief Justice Oliver was in dispute, the British government took steps to end once and for all the harassing tactics of the Massachusetts grand juries. Lord North proposed that the act to alter the government of Massachusetts include provisions that no town meeting be called by the selectmen without prior approval of the governor and that sheriffs select grand and petit jurors formerly elected at the town meetings. Lord North convinced the House of Commons that the grand juries often included "the very people who have committed all these riots" and that it would be useless to expect any semblance of order as long as the juries continued to be "improperly

[13] Philadelphia, *Pennsylvania Gazette*, September 27, 1770.
[14] *Boston Gazette*, February 21, March 7, 1774; Charles F. Adams, ed., *The Works of John Adams* (Boston, 1856), 10:240–241.
[15] *Boston Gazette*, April 11, May 2, 1774.

chosen." Under the new law, the constable of each town was required to deliver to the sheriff a list of all freeholders qualified to serve on juries. If the constable failed to do so, the sheriff could summon those persons whom he believed to be qualified.[16]

Abolishing the elective grand jury and restricting the freedom and independence of town action struck at the very heart of local government in Massachusetts. Freeholders assembled in town meetings in violation of the new act and passed resolutions refusing their consent to any change in the Massachusetts constitution and denying the authority of any jurors chosen by the sheriffs. The Committee of Correspondence of the Town of Boston included in its circular letter of June 8, 1774, a protest against having sheriffs choose grand jurors.[17]

Before the new provisions for selecting jurors went into effect, the Superior Court of Massachusetts convened in Suffolk County. The grand jurors, including Paul Revere and Ebenezer Hancock, brother of John Hancock, protested the recent changes in the Massachusetts government and the presence of Chief Justice Oliver by refusing to take their oath. The jurors had previously drawn up a list of their reasons for refusing to serve, but the court refused to allow it read. The jurymen adjourned to the Exchange Tavern, where they voted to publish their reasons for refusing to take the oath.[18]

Protest meetings throughout Massachusetts condemned the new jury system as a subversion of justice. Counties agreed "to hold harmless" all sheriffs, constables, and jurors who would refuse to carry out the orders of the Superior Court.[19] Massachusetts towns refused to recognize the va-

[16] T. C. Hansard, ed., *The Parliamentary History of England* (London, 1813), 17:1193–1195; *Statutes at Large of England,* 14 *George III,* chapter 45; Philadelphia, *Pennsylvania Journal,* June 15, 1774.

[17] *Essex Gazette,* June 7, 1774; *Pennsylvania Gazette,* June 22, 1774.

[18] *Boston Gazette,* September 5, 1774; Hartford, *Connecticut Courant,* September 6, 1774; *Pennsylvania Journal,* September 14, 1774.

[19] *Pennsylvania Journal,* September 16, 21, 1774; *Essex Gazette,* September 13, 1774.

lidity of the act and continued to hold town meetings and elect grand jurors for their annual terms.[20] In spite of opposition to the new method of selecting grand jurors, some of the sheriffs and clerks of court proceeded to carry out the provisions of the new law. However, it did not take long for public pressure to convince them of the error of their ways. Ezekiel Goldthwait and Ezekiel Price, joint clerks of the court of Suffolk County, publicly acknowledged their "great mistake" in sending out warrants to the various town constables. Thaddeus Mason, clerk of the Middlesex court, pleaded as his excuse for complying with the new law that he had been confined with a dislocated shoulder and was thus unable to secure the proper advice.[21] Elisha Harrington, deputy sheriff of Middlesex County, apologized publicly before a large crowd and promised not to obey the new law in the future.[22]

Following passage of the Coercive Acts, grand juries in the other colonies gradually entered the dispute with England. In November, 1774, Chief Justice Frederick Smyth of New Jersey warned an Essex County grand jury that "imaginary tyranny three thousand miles distant" was less to be feared than "real tyranny of mob violence at our own doors." The jurors penned a courteous but spirited reply in which they politely suggested that the justice's charge was irrelevant to their duty as jurymen and was political rather than judicial in nature. But they pointed out that since the justice had raised the question, the presence of the British fleet and army at Boston was not "altogether visionary."[23] Chief Justice Smyth's next session of court followed by several days an impromptu tea party in the village of Greenwich. British ships had landed tea there without resistance

---

[20] *Topsfield, Massachusetts Town Records* (Topsfield, 1917), 2:345, 354, 367, 372, 388; *Records of the Town of Plymouth* (Plymouth, 1903), 3:311, 328.
[21] *Essex Gazette*, September 6, 1774.
[22] *Boston Gazette*, September 12, 1774.
[23] *Pennsylvania Journal*, November 23, 1774; "Provincial Courts of New Jersey," in *Collections of the New Jersey Historical Society*, 3:175, 177 (1849); Peter Force, *American Archives* (Washington, D.C., 1837–1853), fourth series, 1:967–968.

and the chests had been placed in the cellar of a house fronting on the market place. Forty of the local townsmen assembled in the dusk on the evening of November 22, 1774, removed the tea chests from the cellar, and burned them in an adjoining field. The chief justice spoke strongly to the grand jurors of Cumberland County on the subject of the "wanton waste of property" and mob violence, but the jurymen had no intention of returning bills against their neighbors for opposing the tax on tea. They refused to indict any of the participants. Smyth lectured the jurors a second time and sent them out to reconsider the matter, but still they refused to return indictments.[24]

As the dispute with the mother country became more heated, grand jury charges and presentments served as excellent mediums of propaganda. Judges used their position to declaim before grand juries on the state of the dispute with England. Generally they did not confine themselves to legal arguments but dwelt upon the depravity of the British leaders and the cruelty of their policies. Not to be outdone, the juries responded with stinging denunciations of Great Britain and stirring defenses of their rights as Englishmen. These patriotic pronouncements were not only effective in arousing the people of the immediate vicinity: newspapers copied them and gave them wide publicity.

Chief Justice William Henry Drayton of South Carolina quickly recognized the propaganda value of patriotic grand jury charges. During the winter of 1774 and 1775 he traveled from district to district in upper South Carolina urging the people to assert their rights and maintain their freedom. Drayton was not disappointed in the reaction to his efforts. The grand jurors of the Camden district responded with "a veritable little Declaration of Independence" in which they denounced the "most dangerous and alarming nature of the power exercised by Parliament" to tax and legislate for the American colonies. Other grand juries answered the chief justice's address by returning equally stirring pronouncements. They requested that their declarations be laid before the Provisional Assembly, thus strengthening the position of those who desired a complete break with England.[25]

Grand juries in other colonies followed the lead of those in South Carolina. New York City jurors issued a protest in February, 1775, against "the many oppressive acts of Parliament," citing for special condemnation the law establishing admiralty courts and the act providing for the payment of judicial salaries by the Crown.[26] Grand jurors of New Castle, Delaware, took a more practical approach to the dispute with England. They agreed to vote for and promote a tax of one shilling and six pence to the pound on all taxable property. Money thus collected would constitute a fund for the defense of Delaware "and our brethren in the other colonies."[27] In Rhode Island the legislature required grand juries to report "any person who declares their late King to be their rightful Lord and sovereign."[28]

In the spring of 1776, Chief Justice Drayton of South Carolina again utilized his grand jury charges for a patriotic end, this time to support the movement for complete independence. Addressing the jurors of Charleston in April, 1776, he declared that absolute independence for the colonies was "the necessity of manifest destiny" and that "the Almighty created America to be independent." Drayton recounted in lurid terms the details of British oppression and praised the new state constitution. As they had previously done, the grand juries of Charleston and the other districts throughout the state echoed the sentiments of the chief justice. They presented as a grievance "the unjust, cruel and diabolical acts of the British Parliament" and warned those who "through an ignorance of their true interests and just rights and from a want of proper information may be

[25] Force, *American Archives,* fourth series, 1:959–962; *New York Journal,* January 19, 1775; *Essex Gazette,* January 31, February 21, 1775; Williamsburg, *Virginia Gazette,* December 30, 1780; *Historic Camden: Colonial and Revolutionary* (Columbia, South Carolina, 1905), 1:106–107.
[26] Force, *American Archives,* fourth series, 1:1227.
[27] *Ibid.,* 2:633.
[28] *Philadelphia Gazette,* August 7, 1776.

misled by our enemies." After the Continental Congress adopted the Declaration of Independence in July, 1776, Drayton addressed grand juries at great length on the topic of British oppression. Warning the jurors that the colonists still had to win their freedom on the field of battle, the chief justice said that the cause of independence could be "powerfully aided" by an alert grand jury. The jurors congratulated the Continental Congress on its declaration.[29]

In the months following independence, many grand juries adopted patriotic resolutions denouncing Great Britain and enjoining all persons to support "the war for freedom." Some acted in response to stirring addresses of presiding judges, while others took the initiative themselves. They also took occasion to warn persons in the community who were not in sympathy with the Revolution. Frequently they endorsed the newly drafted state constitutions, expressing "unfeigned satisfaction" with the liberties guaranteed.[30]

Revolutionary grand juries did not confine themselves to agitating against English rule. They continued to deal with local problems important to the people of their districts and did not neglect the practical aspects of everyday life. Some juries recommended price controls for bacon, flour, and other essentials and complained when produce wagons were delayed in coming from the back country. Others protested against the poor conditions of roads and ferries and the laxity of local law enforcement. Grand juries did much to prevent anarchy in the interregnum between royal and state government. They made certain that basic agencies of local government continued to function while political changes took place on higher levels. They checked upon public officials and complained when they discovered neglect of duty. They gave their attention to the problem of law enforcement and recommended new laws to meet special situa-

---

[29] Hezekiah Niles, *Principles and Acts of the Revolution in America* (New York, 1876), 327–335; Force, *American Archives,* fourth series, 5:1025–1034.

[30] *Archives of New Jersey,* second series, 1:229–230; Force, *American Archives,* Fourth series, 5:1205–1206; 6:514–515; Charleston, *South Carolina Gazette,* December 10, 1772, January 31, 1774.

tions. They inspected public records, audited county or town books, and set tax rates. In short, in the tradition of their colonial forerunners, grand juries representing the people of each community continued to preserve order and watch over local affairs during the course of the Revolution.[31]

Only two of the new state constitutions drafted in 1776 and 1777 specifically guaranteed the right to indictment by a grand jury, but both Revolutionary leaders and ordinary citizens took the institution for granted. Each of the states enacted laws providing for grand juries and gave no thought to abolishing the institution. Since the early days of the struggle against England, Revolutionary leaders had effectively labeled the information of a prosecutor as an odious instrument of British tyranny, while at the same time they had hailed indictment by a grand jury as one of their rights as Englishmen.[32]

As the military aspects of the Revolution became more important, judges used grand jury addresses to encourage support of the war. Again Chief Justice Drayton used his position to support the cause, reviewing military events at each grand jury session and continually berating those who engaged in horse racing or were "anxious for private gain."[33] James Iredell of North Carolina opened each session of court with a heated discussion of the causes of the Revolution. In his charges to grand juries he urged greater effort in the war and warned the people not to flatter themselves with the dangerous idea that independence was almost won.[34] Judge Samuel Ashe traveled his circuit in North Carolina appealing for united effort against England and bewailing the fact that all citizens were not contributing to

[31] Niles, *Principles and Acts,* 334–346; Force, *American Archives,* fifth series, 2:1047–1059.
[32] Only North Carolina and Georgia Constitutions guaranteed the right to indictment by a grand jury in all criminal cases. *Colonial Records of North Carolina,* 10:1003; Francis N. Thorpe, ed., *The Federal and State Constitutions* (Washington, D.C., 1909), 2:784.
[33] Niles, *Principles and Acts,* 347–352.
[34] Stephen B. Weeks, ed., *State Records of North Carolina* (Winston, Goldsboro, Charlotte, 1895–1905), 13:431–438; Griffith J. McRee, *Life and Correspondence of James Iredell* (New York, 1857), 1:382–390.

the defense of their state. He advised jurors to be on their guard against "the fascinating spirit of avarice and extortion" rampant in the state. As a guide to their deliberations, Judge Ashe defined the crime of treason and listed the punishments for counterfeiting public bills of credit.[35]

Grand juries often commended their judges for the "pure disinterested patriotism" of their charges,[36] but they also took the initiative in investigating and indicting for offenses that grew out of the war. A South Carolina jury demanded, in October, 1777, that the legislature require all citizens who were in Europe to return to the state to assist in its defense.[37] Juries returned treason indictments against those who joined the British army or gave information to the enemy. Frequently they indicted persons for passing counterfeit Continental currency and warned all citizens to be on guard against it.[38] When Continental troops reoccupied Philadelphia in 1779, the grand jury indicted many of those who had co-operated with the British during the occupation. The June meeting of the grand inquest issued a general presentment against the wives of British soldiers who remained in the city. The jurors charged that they continued to correspond with their husbands, providing the British army with valuable intelligence. After the British retreat from before the city, Philadelphia juries continued to indict for informing to the English in New York.[39]

To meet specific problems arising from the conflict, the wartime legislatures of the new states often restricted the membership or added to the duties of the grand inquest. In Pennsylvania the legislature attempted to keep tories off grand juries by disqualifying all those who refused to renounce George III and take an oath of allegiance to the

[35] *North Carolina State Records*, 13:438-443.
[36] *Ibid.*, 444.
[37] Niles, *Principles and Acts*, 353.
[38] *Archives of New Jersey*, second series, 2:283, 355-356; *Providence Gazette*, January 8, 1780; Joseph R. Sickler, *History of Salem County, New Jersey* (Salem, New Jersey, 1937), 171.
[39] J. Thomas Scharf and Thompson Westcott, *History of Philadelphia* (Philadelphia, 1884), 1:400.

state.[40] Rhode Island experienced difficulty in some districts in assembling a sufficient number of grand jurors, because many persons had not "subscribed the Test" and were thereby disqualified. Several courts were forced to adjourn for this reason, until the Assembly authorized other towns to supply grand jurors.[41] The Rhode Island Assembly also provided that the estates of those who remained loyal to Great Britain could be confiscated and sold at public auction. Proceedings for confiscation did not have to be instituted by a grand jury, but could be carried out by the court on the basis of an information filed by the prosecutor.[42] In New York the legislature created an emergency body known as the Commissioners for Detecting and Defeating Conspiracies. This committee moved from place to place throughout the state, and with the assistance of the army sought out and arrested "enemies of the state." Although the commissioners had unlimited authority to confine persons, those arrested had to be indicted by a grand jury before they could be brought to trial. Grand juries thus served to prevent suspected individuals from being tried without sufficient evidence to warrant prosecution, and local juries frequently released persons arrested by the commissioners.[43] Virginia grand juries performed the function of assessing the value of tobacco in terms of paper money. Public officials, including the governor and members of the legislature, received their salaries in tobacco at the rate set by the grand jury of the General Court at Richmond. This rate of exchange also determined the value of tobacco in the purchase of military provisions and in loans made to the state.[44]

In a few instances during the Revolution, grand juries played a leading and sometimes spectacular role in opposing English authority. More often, and throughout the con-

---

[40] *Statutes of Pennsylvania,* 9:112.

[41] J. R. Bartlett, ed., *Records of the Colony of Rhode Island and Providence-Plantations in New England* (Providence, 1856–1865), 9:258.

[42] *Providence Gazette,* October 11, November 1, 1780.

[43] *Minutes of the Commissioners for Conspiracies, Albany County Sessions, 1778–1781* (Albany, 1909), 1:11, 13, 99, 274–276, 278, 280.

[44] *Virginia Gazette,* August 23, November 25, 1780.

test, they served as propaganda agencies, giving both judges and jurors the opportunity to denounce the enemy and rally support for the war. Grand juries played an important part in wartime law enforcement, investigating abuses which grew out of the struggle with England and indicting persons for offenses connected with the war. However, their importance during the American Revolution lay not only in their extraordinary activities, but in the fact that their purpose remained unchanged in spite of the emergency. Grand juries continued to concern themselves with the solution of problems important to the local community. Because of the multiplication of extralegal committees and organizations that were in no way responsible to the people, grand juries assumed an added importance as safeguards against promiscuous prosecution by public officials caught up in the excitement of wartime hysteria.[45] The grand inquest emerged from the American Revolution with the added prestige and public support which attached to all institutions that had assisted in the struggle for independence.

[45] Niles, *Principles and Acts*, 353.

Chapter 4

The New Nation

THE GRAND JURY entered the post-Revolutionary period high in the esteem of the American people. The institution had proved valuable indeed in opposing the imperial government and indictment by a grand jury had assumed the position of a cherished right. Francis Hopkinson, Revolutionary pamphleteer, reflected this feeling when he pictured the grand jury as "a body of truth and power inferior to none but the legislature itself."[1] However, though their dramatic role in the Revolution had served to focus public attention and admiration upon them, most grand jurors went quietly about their traditional routine work. They listened patiently while the judge instructed them in their duties and held forth on the problems of the day, often launching into a purely political discourse. Occasionally they commended the judge for the tenor of his remarks or thanked him for addressing them, but more often they merely accepted his digressions as a part of the system and busied themselves with problems of law enforcement and local government.

In the months following the close of the Revolution, judges often used their grand jury charges to review the events of the recent war and to call attention to the increased "violence and licentiousness" which followed it. In some districts they pointed to a need for reconciliation and a spirit of "forget and forgive" toward those who had worked for an English victory. Grand juries did not always respond kindly to addresses urging reconciliation, for they often resented being told to forgive those whom they regarded as traitors.

[1] *The Miscellaneous Essays and Occasional Writings of Francis Hopkinson* (Philadelphia, 1792), 1:229–235.

41

In general, the juries confined their activities to questions of local importance. They recommended such things as the suppression of "dram shops," advised against the further erection of wooden bridges because of the fire hazard, called attention to the "ruinous state" of public works due to the war, and recommended the establishment of police systems. The problems of local law enforcement, complicated by wartime laxity, led some grand juries to suggest reviving the old penalty of public whipping for all idle persons, as well as enacting strict laws governing the movement of vagrants. Occasionally, they reflected the general distrust of lawyers as a class. In 1783, a South Carolina grand jury complained that most people were at a loss to explain the fee system used by attorneys. The jurors recognized that "the employing of lawyers in our courts of justice is a grievance that at present seems necessary," but they urged passage of a law strictly regulating legal fees.[2]

Grand juries of the Confederation period also reflected the concern of propertied groups for the security of their wealth. They complained of "ignorance and idleness" as potential threats, denounced paper money schemes, and expressed their "utter abhorrence" of legislative interference with private contracts between debtors and creditors. A South Carolina grand jury warned of "the pernicious influence" of legislative interference, stating that it was far better that a few individuals should suffer rather than stigmatize a whole community "for a want of faith and a total disregard to national honor."[3]

In Massachusetts, Chief Justice William Cushing confided to the Middlesex grand jurors at Concord his fears that insurgent groups would be successful in altering the conservative state constitution drafted in 1780. The chief justice's fears were well founded. In September, 1786, mobs of farmers, in an effort to prevent the hearing of actions for debt

[2] Charleston, *South Carolina Gazette,* June 10, December 18, 1783, May 11, December 1, 1784.
[3] *American Museum,* 7:appendix no. 2, pp. 10–11 (1790).

and foreclosure of mortgages, forced the courts in western Massachusetts to adjourn. Fearing indictments against them in the State Supreme Court, insurgent leaders also moved to close that court.[4] On September twenty-ninth, the date for the convening of the Supreme Court at Springfield, between seven hundred and a thousand farmers faced eight hundred militia sent to guard the court. Captain Daniel Shays demanded of the court that the grand jury not be permitted to deal with the question of indicting insurgent leaders and that trial of all civil cases be suspended until legislative relief could be secured. The court agreed to adjourn after both insurgents and militia had disbanded, but mobs continued to prevent court sessions, threaten property, and ask the redress of their grievances. Shays' Rebellion assumed serious proportions. Instead of seeking to alleviate the situation of those in revolt, the Massachusetts legislature suspended the writ of habeas corpus, declared the existence of a state of rebellion, and sent troops under General Benjamin Lincoln to crush all opposition.[5] Although the legislature pardoned most of those who took part in the uprising, grand juries indicted the most prominent leaders of the movement for treason. Chief Justice Cushing delivered to grand juries violent tirades against the rebel leaders, calling their attempt at revolution "as foolish and rash as it was wicked and unprovoked." The chief justice declared that there could never be a reason for rising in arms against a free government such as that of Massachusetts. He went on to attribute the difficulties of the western farmers to "their own imprudence and extravagance and want of frugality and economy." At each court on his circuit, Cushing thanked the troops who had assisted in stamping out "incipient treason." The Supreme Court had sentenced the insurgent leaders to death, but in June, 1787, the legislature pardoned them. This led Cushing to lecture subsequent

[4] Oscar Handlin and Mary F. Handlin, *Commonwealth: Massachusetts, 1774–1861* (New York, 1947), 46.
[5] James Truslow Adams, *New England in the Republic, 1776–1850* (Boston, 1926), 150, 154–155, 162–163.

grand juries on "the fatal consequences" of suspending the execution of "the traitors."[6]

Shays' Rebellion acted as an imporant catalytic agent in hastening the call for a national constitutional convention. Men who had long advocated a stronger central government were now imbued with a greater sense of urgency. Following the Philadelphia Convention, Federalist judges and grand juries praised the new document and urged its adoption. A Newark, New Jersey, grand jury hailed ratification as "a great national event" which altered the basic relationship between the states and the central government. Chief Justice Cushing of Massachusetts differentiated between "liberty and licentiousness of the press" and urged grand juries to take action against anti-Federalist attackers of the Constitution. Chief Justice Nathaniel Pendleton told jurors of Georgia that he hoped the new Constitution would mark "the beginning of a general reformation" in the whole country, doing away with paper money and state laws that interfered with the right of contract. Judge John Grimke of South Carolina warned Charleston grand jurors to anticipate the intrigues and secret combinations "of our internal enemies" who would seek to destroy the Constitution. Donning the garb of a prophet, Judge Grimke predicted that "future ages will honor the Constitution as the masterpiece of political wisdom."[7]

The Constitution of the United States, as it went into force in 1789, did not mention grand juries in any way. It was not at all certain that there would be separate grand inquests for the federal government, because the Constitution did not require separate federal inferior courts. Delegates to the Constitutional Convention had discussed the details of a federal judiciary but slightly. Federalists regarded inferior courts as one of the vital agencies for main-

---

[6] Boston, *Massachusetts Centinel,* May 26, August 29, 1787.
[7] *Massachusetts Centinel,* July 30, 1788; Edenton, *State Gazette of North Carolina,* May 28, 1789; Philadelphia, *Gazette of the United States,* December 9, 1789.

taining federal supremacy and for checking the pretentions of the states. But they also knew that many opposed the establishment of lower federal courts. Vagueness and the use of general terms were used to confuse those who opposed an elaborate federal judiciary. As a result, the judicial article of the Constitution emerged as a broadly worded passage that left much to be determined by Congress. Gouverneur Morris explained Federalist tactics regarding the judiciary, saying, "On that subject it became necessary to select phrases which would not alarm others." To have defined clearly the relationship of federal to state courts might have raised an insuperable barrier to ratification.[8]

The necessity of an express guarantee of the right to indictment by a grand jury in all criminal cases became a disputed issue before several of the state ratifying conventions.[9] Reminding delegates of their experiences with British officials, Abraham Holmes warned the Massachusetts convention that an officer of the proposed new government would be able to file informations and "bring any man to jeopardy of his life" without indictment by a grand jury. Supporters of the Constitution did not deny this possibility, but reminded the objecting delegate that just because officers of the new government could abuse their authority, did not mean that they would. Refusing to rely solely upon the integrity of future federal officials, the Massachusetts convention recommended that the Constitution be amended to provide that no person could be tried for a capital offense unless previously indicted. The ratifying conventions of New York and New Hampshire followed the lead of Massachusetts and proposed similar amendments. At its first session, in 1789, the first congress under the Constitution proposed twelve amendments, among them an amendment

[8] Anne C. Morris, ed., *The Diary and Letters of Gouverneur Morris* (New York, 1888), 2:416.

[9] Jonathan Elliot, ed., *Elliot's Debates on the Federal Constitution* (Philadelphia, 1901), 1:322–323, 326, 328; *Debates and Proceedings in the Convention of the Commonwealth of Massachusetts held in 1788* (Boston, 1856), 214.

guaranteeing the right to a grand jury indictment for all
infamous or capital crimes. After ratification by the required number of states, this became a part of the fifth
amendment to the Constitution.[10]

The problem of the creation of a federal judicial system,
which the Philadelphia Convention had deliberately avoided,
came before Congress in 1789. Federalists were determined
to take full advantage of the almost unlimited authority
given Congress to establish inferior courts with jurisdiction
equal to that of the Supreme Court. Oliver Ellsworth, Federalist leader, headed the Senate committee which drafted
the judiciary bill, and he made certain that it provided for
three federal circuit courts and thirteen federal district
courts. Anti-Federalists attempted to nullify the power of
the lower courts by limiting them to admiralty and mari-
time cases, but they were unsuccessful. The Judiciary Act
of 1789 provided that grand juries were to attend each session of the circuit and district courts. Federal marshals were
responsible for choosing jurors by lot or according to the
method used by the state in which the court was sitting.
Qualifications for grand jury duty also followed the laws of
the several states.[11]

Although federal marshals selected federal grand juries
in the same manner as did the states and from among the
same group of eligible citizens, there remained vital differ-
ences between the two. State grand juries were free to investigate and present to the court any criminal matter that
violated the common law. Federal grand jurors were far
more limited in the scope of their investigations. They had
the power to investigate and present only those offenses that
violated specific federal laws. State grand juries operated at
the county level where the jurors were familiar with condi-

[10] *Elliot's Debates*, 1:338–340.

[11] *Annals of Congress*, 1st Congress, 1st session (1789), 783–806, 813–833;
Edgar S. Maclay, ed., *Journal of William Maclay* (New York, 1890), 85–117;
Charles Warren, "New Light on the History of the Federal Judiciary Act of
1789," in *Harvard Law Review*, 37:59–63 (November, 1923); *United States
Statutes at Large*, 1:88.

tions in their own communities. They regarded themselves
as the appointed investigators of the people and as such they
did not hesitate to reprimand local officials or to suggest
improvements and changes in local government. They often
went far beyond mere law enforcement and dealt with community problems that touched the everyday lives of every
one of them. Federal grand juries, however, because they
were restricted to the investigation of statutory offenses,
tended to become instruments of the central government
rather than representatives of the people. Federal grand
jurors had little opportunity to become sufficiently familiar
with the operation of the national government to check on
the performance of federal officials or to suggest federal
policies as did their counterparts in the state courts. The
grand jury functioned best in conjunction with a government that was close to the people and it lost much of its
effectiveness under a centralized administration.

From the first, the new federal judges regarded their
addresses to grand juries as excellent opportunities to deliver political orations. Though grand jury charges originated for the purpose of instructing the jurors in their
duties, judges had long used them as a means of disseminating political propaganda. English jurists had frequently
given vent to their political feelings in grand jury charges.
In Colonial America, judges had usually lectured on political matters, while during the American Revolution jury
charges denouncing England and the Loyalists had become
an accepted and patriotic practice. In this tradition, Federalist jurists delighted in comparing the strength of the
new Constitution with the weaknesses of the Articles of
Confederation. Justice James Wilson joyously declared,
"We now see the circle of government beautiful and complete." He congratulated the grand jurors of Philadelphia
upon their new Constitution under which "the power of the
people is predominant and supreme."[12] The newly appointed
Chief Justice of the United States, dour John Jay, enthusi-

[12] *Massachusetts Centinel,* May 1, 1790.

astically enumerated the advantages offered by the Constitution which the previous government had "proved too feeble and ill constructed to produce." Jay toured the eastern circuit carrying from court to court his message of salvation from discord and anarchy. Grand juries acknowledged "with pleasure" the chief justice's message and Federalist newspapers hailed the jury charges as "containing a species of information which cannot be too often published."[13] Judge David Sewall painted a dramatic scene of discord, bloodshed, and foreign intervention for the edification of grand jurors in Portland, Maine, so they might know the perils from which the Constitution had rescued them.[14] As early as April, 1791, District Judge John Sitgreaves pointed with pride to reviving agriculture and commerce and to the increased stability of public and private credit, all resulting, he said, from the new national government. He called the attention of South Carolina grand jurors to the energy and stability of the central government in contrast to its previous impotence.

Federal judges endeavored to impress upon grand jurors the necessity for the strict enforcement of federal laws. In South Carolina Judge Sitgreaves made it clear that it was one thing to evade payment of import duties when America was a part of the British Empire, but quite a different matter now that it had achieved independence. What may have been honorable and patriotic at one time was now to "be execrated."[15] Judges constantly urged upon federal grand juries the vital importance of rigidly enforcing the revenue laws. Chief Justice Jay lauded the unpopular excise on whiskey as "the people's revenue" and denounced as defrauders of the people those who evaded it. He hailed the success of Alexander Hamilton's financial program as an unprecedented instance of a nation providing for its financial needs without resorting to direct taxation.[16] The federal

---

[13] *Ibid.*, May 29, 1790; *Gazette of the United States,* June 16, 1790.
[14] Boston, *Columbian Centinel,* August 25, 1790.
[15] *Gazette of the United States,* May 4, 1791.
[16] *Ibid.*, August 11, 1792.

grand juries frequently voiced their approval of charges given them, but they returned few indictments for violations of federal laws.[17]

Following President Washington's Neutrality Proclamation of 1793, federal judges warned grand juries to present all persons guilty of violating the neutrality acts. Chief Justice Jay reminded grand jurors of Richmond, Virginia, of their duty to be strictly impartial in their deliberations and to bring to trial all persons guilty of recruiting men or outfitting privateers for the aid of France. In spite of judicial urgings, grand juries indicted only a few persons for violation of the neutrality laws and in almost every case brought to trial, the petit juries refused to convict. In some instances popular celebrations greeted refusals to indict or convict.[18]

As political divisions in the new nation became more pronounced, partisan harangues before grand juries became even more common. As a rule they did not stampede jurymen into returning indiscriminate indictments on political grounds. Instead, jurors often reacted against the heated charges and refused to indict. However, the partisan orations of Federalist jurists did serve to arouse the bitter opposition of anti-Federalists, who resented the advantage which possession of the federal judgeships gave their opponents. They replied in kind through the columns of their newspapers, accusing federal judges of "converting the holy seat of law, reason and equity into a rostrum from which they can harangue the populace under the pretense of instructing a grand jury."[19]

Justice James Iredell became particularly adept at arousing the ire of anti-Federalists through his intemperate

---

[17] *Ibid.*, June 1, 1791; *Massachusetts Centinel*, May 1, 1790; Charles Warren, *The Supreme Court in United States History* (Boston, 1923), 1:59.

[18] Henry P. Johnston, ed., *The Correspondence and Public Papers of John Jay* (New York, 1891), 3:480–482; *Gazette of the United States*, July 31, 1793; *United States vs. Henfield* in Francis Wharton, *State Trials of the United States During the Administrations of Washington and Adams* (Philadelphia, 1849), 1, 2, 49.

[19] Warren, *Supreme Court*, 1:165.

tirades before grand juries. In May, 1797, in an animated charge to a Richmond, Virginia, grand jury, Iredell denounced those who criticized federal officials merely "to gratify malignant or grovelling purposes of their own." In response to Iredell's address, the jurors presented Samuel J. Cabell, member of Congress from Virginia, for having "disseminated unfounded calumnies" against the government of the United States in a letter that he had circulated among his constituents.[20] Although the presentment could not serve as the basis for criminal proceedings in the federal court, anti-Federalist leaders sprang immediately to Cabell's defense. Cabell's district in western Virginia seethed with anger, and Thomas Jefferson, one of his constitutents, charged that Federalist judges had perverted grand juries "from a legal to a political engine" by inviting them "to become inquisitors on the freedom of speech." Seeking an effective means of protest, Jefferson, with the assistance of James Madison, drew up a petition of protest to be signed by the residents of Cabell's district. They planned to present the protest to the United States House of Representatives, but fear that a Federalist majority would pass a vote of approbation dissuaded them. As a second choice, Jefferson laid the petition before the Virginia House of Delegates in August, 1797. The petition censured the grand jury's action as a crime, "wicked in its purpose and mortal in its consequences," tending to subvert the legislative department to the caprice of the judiciary.[21]

The Sedition Act, passed by Congress in 1798, resulted from confusion over whether federal grand juries had the power to return indictments where a federal law had not been violated. Chief Justice Oliver Ellsworth told grand jurors that they could indict persons for acts which were criminal under the common law, but most Federalist leaders

[20] Griffith J. McRee, *Life and Correspondence of James Iredell* (New York, 1857), 2:506–510; Paul L. Ford, *Writings of Thomas Jefferson* (New York, 1892–1899), 8:325.

[21] Ford, *Writings of Jefferson*, 8:302, 322–331, 334, 338–339; *Letters and Other Writings of James Madison* (Philadelphia, 1865), 2:118.

had their doubts.[22] Federal judges became active prosecutors under the Sedition Act, urging juries to bring individuals to trial. In an attempt to secure indictments, Justice William Cushing portrayed the horrors of the French Revolution and warned jurors to be on their guard against French wiles.[23] Justice Iredell defended the law before grand juries as being entirely consistent with the principles of the United States Constitution and launched into violent tirades against those who dared to criticize the government. Seeking to frighten the grand jurors into indicting, Iredell announced that "dreadful confusion must ensue and anarchy will ride triumphant" if opposition to the federal government were not ended.[24] Iredell's charge prompted the grand jury to return nine indictments for treason.[25] Justice Samuel Chase succeeded in persuading a Richmond grand jury to indict Thomas Callender, publisher of *The Prospect Before Us*, because he defamed the Congress and president of the United States.[26] A federal grand jury in Vermont indicted Matthew Lyon, member of Congress, for characterizing President John Adams as a person with "an unbounded thirst for ridiculous pomp, foolish adulation and selfish avarice." Shortly thereafter, Anthony Haswell denounced the president as a "hard hearted savage" for holding Congressman Lyon in prison. This accusation secured Haswell the indictment of a federal grand jury.[27] Anti-Federalists frequently objected that grand juries that returned indictments under the Sedition Act were partisan. They charged

[22] Charles G. Haines, *The Role of the Supreme Court in American Government and Politics, 1789–1835* (Berkeley, 1944), 159–160; Frank M. Anderson, "Enforcement of the Alien and Sedition Laws," in *Annual Report of the American Historical Association*, 1912, p. 119; James M. Smith, *Freedom's Fetters* (Ithaca, 1956), 125, 188; John C. Miller, *Crisis In Freedom* (Boston, 1952), 79–80.

[23] Warren, *Supreme Court*, 1:166.

[24] Wharton, *State Trials*, 466, 481; McRee, *Iredell*, 2:551–564.

[25] Frankfort (Kentucky) *Palladium*, May 23, 1799.

[26] *Ibid.*, June 19, 1800; *United States vs. Callender*, 25 *Federal Cases* 239 (1800).

[27] Wharton, *State Trails*, 333; *United States vs. Haswell*, 26 *Federal Cases* 218 (1800).

that Federalist officials were able to pack juries with those who would listen sympathetically to requests for indictments by federal judges and adopt resolutions echoing sentiments contained in partisan jury addresses.[28]

After Jefferson's election in 1800, Judge Samuel Chase continued to harangue grand juries on political matters. Repeal by the Republicans of the Judiciary Act of 1801 drew his fire in the form of heated grand jury charges. Articles of impeachment, which the Republicans brought against Chase in 1804, included charges that he had made improper attempts to induce grand juries to indict newspaper publishers on political grounds and that he had delivered a large number of intemperate political addresses to grand juries.[29]

While the federal grand jury, intimately involved as it was in the political and constitutional battles of the 1790's, had yet to prove itself, the local grand jury remained an accepted and essential part of American democratic government. The new states of Kentucky and Tennessee, which came into the Union in 1792 and 1795, both included in their constitutions specific provisions making indictment by a grand jury mandatory in all criminal cases. Newly drafted constitutions for the states of Pennsylvania and New Hampshire also contained guarantees against criminal prosecution except upon indictment by a grand jury.[30] Juries sitting in each of the counties throughout the new nation continued to hear the complaints and protests of any and all persons, to supervise law enforcement activities of the sheriff and the constables, and to keep a watchful eye on all other public officials. Grand juries became thoroughly agitated over the condition of public highways in their particular area, appeared shocked at the alarming increase in disorderly houses in towns, recommended laws for the consideration of the state legislature, and publicly rebuked those public

[28] Anderson, "Alien and Sedition Laws," 125.
[29] *Annals of Congress*, 8th Congress, 2nd session (1804–1805), 148.
[30] *Gazette of the United States*, July 7, 1792; Francis N. Thorpe, ed., *The Federal and State Constitutions* (Washington, D.C., 1909), 3:1275; 6:3423.

officials guilty of laxity or corruption. Grand juries also
served to educate those who served upon them, giving the
jurymen valuable experience in the workings of local government as well as an opportunity to voice their own opinions. Most citizens accepted the responsibility thrust upon
them by grand jury duty and rose to the occasion. For many
this service on the grand inquest constituted the only active
part, save perhaps for voting, they would ever take in their
government.[31]

Occasionally state jurists, like their federal counterparts,
made use of grand jury addresses to make known their
political opinions. Those who were Federalists emphasized
the importance of a vigorous central government to national
prosperity. Judge John Grimke directed the attention of
Camden, South Carolina, grand jurors to the economic advantages for their state of the assumption program. He explained that, by taking over the South Carolina debt of four
million dollars, the federal government had removed the unpleasant dilemma of higher taxes or repudiation. The judge
ventured to predict that such a "wise measure" would serve
to reconcile many who at first had opposed the new government.[32] Chief Justice Thomas McKean of Pennsylvania
severely castigated those persons in his state who organized
to oppose enforcement of the tax on whiskey. He drew from
the grand jurors of Philadelphia a spirited echo denouncing
the villainy of those who combined to evade federal revenue
laws. Western grand juries viewed the excise on whiskey in
a far different light. Jurors of Abbeville County, South
Carolina, condemned the tax as a "grievance of the highest
nature" and denounced all excises as incompatible with
liberty. They expressed a fear that the whiskey tax would
give northern distillers an advantage.[33] Judge Andrew Sin-
nickson of New Jersey lectured grand jurors on the indis-
pensability of laws protecting private property and warned

[31] *Gazette of the United States,* July 6, 1791.
[32] *Ibid.,* February 19, 1791.
[33] *Ibid.,* September 3, 1791, November 17, 1792.

that without them the world would become an "uncivilized common."[34] County Judge Jedidiah Peck of Cooperstown, New York, lamented the fact that there were those who opposed the Constitution and wished to destroy the federal government.[35]

A few Federalist state judges undertook to defend the Alien and Sedition acts before grand juries. Judge Alexander Addison of Pennsylvania approved a limit on freedom of the press as necessary to curb licentiousness and dwelled upon the "horrors of revolution" that would result from a refusal to uphold those in authority. During the presidential election of 1800, Addison delivered political speeches in support of President Adams to his grand juries. Chief Justice Francis Dana of Massachusetts, speaking before a grand inquest in 1800, denounced Jefferson and the Republican candidates for Congress as "apostles of atheism and anarchy, bloodshed and plunder."[36] Judge William Patterson of New Hampshire, while acting as a Federalist presidential elector, held the Republicans up to grand juries as "disorganizers of our happy country,"[37] and compared them to the French Jacobins.

Republicans replied to Federalist judges through their newspapers, but on occasion local Jeffersonian judges retaliated by means of grand jury charges. Judge Richard Parker of Virginia rebuked federal judges when he warned jurors of the General Court to remain clear of political presentments. Parker told the jurors that such matters were entirely out of their province. At the time of the Alien and Sedition trials Judge Harry Innes advised a Frankfort, Kentucky, grand jury that its proper place was "as a strong barrier between the supreme power of the government and the citizens," rather than as an instrument of the state. Taking a slap at partisan federal judges, Innes told the grand

---

[34] *Ibid.*, October 6, 1792.

[35] *The Panel*, 17:no. 1, p. 3 (January-February, 1939).

[36] *Palladium*, January 15, 29, 1799; Warren, *Supreme Court*, 1:275–276.

[37] William H. Hackett, "The Circuit Court for the New Hampshire District One Hundred Years Ago," in *Green Bag*, 2:264 (June, 1890).

jurors that their duty was to shield the innocent from "unjust persecutions."[38]

Though local juries had no authority to indict for infringements of federal statutes, occasionally they did adopt resolutions giving voice to their opinions. In most instances, however, they listened patiently to the partisan orations of the presiding judge, then, in the tradition of their English and colonial forerunners, turned their attention to problems of local importance.

To many, the federal courts were reminiscent of the royal courts before the Revolution. Political prosecutions under the Sedition Act, militantly partisan grand jury addresses, and Republican charges that Federalist officials had packed grand juries all tended to dim the luster of federal grand juries. Their reputation suffered still more because they were often entangled in the political strife of the 1790's. Many persons came to regard them as mere appendages of the federal courts rather than as representatives of the people. As agents of the federal government they became unpopular in the eyes of groups out of power and with those opposed to centralization. State and local grand juries, on the other hand, possessing full common law powers of investigation and indictment and concerning themselves principally with problems of local government, continued to be viewed by most individuals as barriers between the citizen and the government, the role that had made them popular during the Revolution.

[38] *Palladium,* October 23, 1798; November 25, 1800.

Chapter 5

Tradition and Reform, 1800–1865

AT THE CLOSE OF THE EIGHTEENTH CENTURY the grand jury was an accepted part of the judicial system in both England and the United States, and people, most people, looked upon it as a fundamental part of their legal heritage.[1] But the traditional role and past services of the grand inquest had not served to quash opposition. Lawyers, jurists, and utilitarian philosophers now replaced representatives of royal authority as its principal attackers. The aims of the new attack—reform—were different but the ends were the same: the abolition of the grand jury.

In England, the movement received its early impetus from Jeremy Bentham, the great codifier and legal reformer. He denounced the grand jury as "an engine of corruption, systematically packed" on behalf of the upper classes, and charged that juries in Britain had become assemblies composed almost exclusively of gentlemen, "to the exclusion of the Yeomen." Bentham also opposed it on the grounds of efficiency. As a utilitarian, he had little patience with a body composed of a "miscellaneous company of men" untrained in the law. He believed a professionally trained prosecutor could perform the functions of a grand jury with far greater efficiency, and with less expense to the people and less bother to the courts.[2] Bentham's criticism attracted

[1] The bulk of the material in this chapter originally appeared in the author's "The Grand Jury Under Attack, Part One," in *Journal of Criminal Law, Criminology and Police Science*, 46:26–37 (Mary-June, 1955), and is used with permission.

[2] Jeremy Bentham, *The Elements of the Art of Packing, As Applied to Special Juries* (London, 1821), 14–28; John Bowring, ed., *The Works of Jeremy Bentham* (Edinburgh, 1843), 2:139–140, 171.

support and gradually bore fruit in the form of proposals to abolish the system entirely. Robert Peel was one of the first to suggest that a responsible public prosecutor should be appointed in its place.[3]

Suggestions that Parliament do away with the institution led both defenders and attackers to present their cases to the public. A citizen writing to the London *Times* under the name, "an admirer of grand juries," praised them as protectors of liberty and warned that it would take a bold man to bring a bill into Parliament to abolish them. An answering letter, signed "a Middlesex Magistrate," advocated a parliamentary inquiry into the exorbitant expenses of the juries, and expressed satisfaction that the proposals for abolition were gaining ground.[4] In 1834 and again in 1836 parliamentary resolutions to curtail their use aroused interest in English legal circles, but were not successful.[5]

By mid-century a strong movement to abolish the grand jury completely had developed in England. Many English judges acquired the habit of calling attention to the uselessness of the system in their jury addresses. In February, 1848, the mayor and aldermen of Southampton petitioned the House of Commons to do away with all grand juries. Later in the same year, grand jurors attending the Central Criminal Court of London recommended abolition of the institution and sent a copy of their resolution to the Secretary of State for the Home Department. In 1849, grand inquests of both the Central Criminal Court and the Middlesex sessions announced their opposition to the grand jury system.[6]

Many English barristers entered the lists, most of them on the side of reform. W. C. Humphreys, a prominent law

[3] "Grand Juries," in *Jurist*, 1:190–202 (June, 1827); Peter Laurie, *The Use and Abuse of Grand Juries* (London, 1832), 5.

[4] Letters to the Editor," in London *Times*, December 23, 30, 31, 1833, September 2, 1834.

[5] Proposed Abolition of the Grand Jury," in *Legal Observer*, 9:129 (December 13, 1834); 11:492 (April 30, 1836).

[6] *Journal of the British House of Commons*, 103:265 (1847–1848); *Accounts and Papers of the House of Commons*, 51:211 (1847–1848); *Hansard's Debates*, third series, 145:1426 (1857).

reformer, stated that grand inquests were a potential menace to the country because they assisted rather than suppressed crime, and in a pamphlet entitled "Inutility of Grand Juries," joined the crusade for their abolition.[7] The committing magistrate of Old Bailey Prison declared the grand jury the "first hope" of the criminal, because it afforded "a safe medium for buying off a prosecution and is often resorted to for that purpose." Writing to the London *Times* under the name *"Billa Vera,"* another lawyer claimed that intelligent and respectable jurors were "ashamed and disgusted" with their functions. He also revealed that a committee to investigate grand juries appointed by the Corporation of the City of London had uncovered evidence "decidedly hostile to the system."[8] On December 20, 1858, T. Chambers, a solicitor, read a paper before the Juridical Society of London on the future of the grand jury. He opposed tampering with the institution and expressed a fear that, like many other modern reforms, the effect would be to "withdraw the people from the tribunals and replace them by officials." He also warned that justice should not be made to "rush through professional and official conduits" but should be passed upon by the people themselves. In the discussion following Chambers' paper, several members took vigorous exception to his position and insisted that increased efficiency would follow if "a professional inquiry" replaced the grand jury. The debate did not end that evening. As late as April, 1859, a letter to the London *Times* answered Chambers with the complaint that inquests too often encroached upon the duties of the trial jury and performed unnecessary work.[9]

Before 1860 efforts in Parliament to curtail the powers of the grand inquest, though often supported by leading

[7] W. C. Humphreys, "Inutility of Grand Juries," reviewed in *Solicitor's Journal and Reporter,* 1:326 (April, 1857).

[8] London *Times,* January 9, 1849.

[9] T. Chambers, "On the Institution of the Grand Jury," in *Juridical Society Papers,* 1858, vol. 2: pp. 120, 122, 126–127; *Solicitor's Journal and Reporter,* 3:135 (December 25, 1858); London *Times,* April 15, 1859.

jurists, achieved only partial success. In 1849, Lord J. Jervis, Attorney General of England, introduced in Parliament a bill to nullify the power of grand juries sitting in the metropolitan police districts. Under the attorney general's proposal, a jury could not indict a person until he had had a preliminary hearing before a police court magistrate. The measure failed of passage. Attorney General Sir Frederick Thesiger introduced other such measures in 1852, in 1854, and in 1857. Each time he sought to convince his colleagues that in view of improved methods of police investigation, the grand jury was useless in large cities. He pointed out that many of the jurors themselves looked upon their job as a fruitless one. After the proper judicial urgings, juries in the metropolitan district of London had presented themselves year after year as "an impediment to the administration of justice." In spite of all his efforts, Sir Frederick also failed to work up sufficient enthusiasm among members of Parliament to persuade them to curtail use of the institution. However, opponents of the grand inquest finally attained a measure of success when, in July, 1859, Parliament enacted the Vexatious Indictments Law. Thereafter, a private citizen had to present certain cases to a police magistrate, who would then determine whether or not he could go before a grand jury.[10]

British reform proposals received wide circulation in the United States and soon led American legal scholars to debate the value of the grand jury. But, at least one American jurist, Judge Alexander Addison of Pensylvania, had anticipated the early Benthamite attacks by some years. In a charge delivered in 1792, Judge Addison went on record as favoring restrictions upon grand juries. He feared that danger lay in giving inquests too free a hand in their investigation and cautioned the jurors that they could act only when a matter came within the actual knowledge of one of them, or when the judge or district attorney submitted an indict-

[10] *Ibid.*, April 14, 1849, July 12, 1854; *Hansard's Debates,* third series, 120:806 (1852); 122:1115 (1852); 145:1425–1426 (1857); 152:1046 (1859).

ment for their consideration. They could investigate matters of public importance only if the judge charged them to do so. In this restricted view of the powers of the grand jury it could neither summon witnesses on its own initiative nor indict on the basis of testimony received from such witnesses. In effect the jury was placed entirely under the control of the court.[11] Judge Addison was ahead of his time. It would be some years before such opinions would be widely voiced. The far more popular position in these early years of the new nation was that voiced by Justice James Wilson of the United States Supreme Court, in a series of law lectures delivered in Philadelphia only two years earlier. Justice Wilson placed no limit upon a grand jury's area of inquiry. He viewed the inquest as an important instrument of democratic government. As Wilson saw it the jury served as "a great channel of communication between those who make and administer the laws and those for whom the laws are made and administered."[12]

The campaign of the anti-jury forces in the United States gathered momentum only gradually. Some early reformers, like those in Britain, came to the conclusion that public indifference and apathy had seriously impaired the usefulness of the grand jury. They blamed juries themselves as being partly responsible for criticism of the institution because they frequently neglected to conduct investigations into the conditions of prisons, roads, bridges, and nuisances within the community.[13] Edward Livingston, prominent Jeffersonian, became a disciple of Bentham and an ardent advocate of codification. In 1821, Louisiana commissioned him to study and to revise and codify its criminal laws. The procedural provisions of the completed Livingston Code con-

[11] Alexander Addison, *Reports of Cases in the County Courts of the Fifth Circuit* (Washington, D.C., 1800), part 2, pp. 37–46.
[12] Bird Wilson, ed., *The Works of James Wilson* (Philadelphia, 1804), 2:365–367; Charles Warren, *History of the American Bar* (Boston, 1911), 347; Charles P. Smith, *James Wilson, Founding Father, 1742–1798* (Chapel Hill, 1956), 308–310.
[13] "Cottu on English Law," in *North American Review*, 13:347 (October, 1821).

fined grand juries to passing upon indictments submitted
to them. They could only determine whether persons had
violated criminal laws of the state, but they had no power
to initiate presentments or express their opinions on other
matters. Livingston limited judges to a mere statement of
the law when addressing grand juries, ruling out all remarks of a political nature.[14] These restrictions met the
whole-hearted approval of Chancellor James Kent of New
York, in spite of his disapproval, in principle, of codification. The New York jurist and law professor congratulated
Livingston on the section of his code that severely limited
grand jury activity, stating, "I am exceedingly pleased with
the provision confining grand juries to the business of the
penal law and not admitting any expression of opinion on
other subjects."[15]

While a few eastern legal scholars were hoping to curb
the inquisitorial powers of grand juries, a western court
spoke out forcefully in favor of giving them very broad
powers. In 1829, a grand jury in St. Louis, Missouri, embarked upon a gambling investigation. It subpoenaed a
great many witnesses, questioned them on a wide variety
of subjects, and indicted various persons on the basis of
this testimony. Several of those indicted asked the court to
quash the indictments on the grounds that the grand jurors
had exceeded their authority by engaging in a "fishing expedition" with no particular offense in mind. The Supreme
Court of Missouri, however, upheld the jurors and declared
that to hold overwise "would strip them of their greatest
utility and convert them into a mere engine to be acted
upon by circuit attorneys or those who might choose to
use them."[16] Chief Justice Lemuel Shaw of Massachusetts
echoed the sentiments of the Missouri court. He told mem-

---

[14] *The Complete Works of Edward Livingston on Criminal Jurisprudence*
(New York, 1873), 1:372; 2:249–250.

[15] James Kent to Edward Livingston, February 17, 1826, one of "Two Letters
of Chancellor Kent," in *American Law Review*, 12:485 (April, 1878); John T.
Horton, *James Kent: A Study in Conservatism* (New York, 1939), 171.

[16] *Ward vs. State*, 2 *Missouri* 120 (1829).

bers of a Massachusetts inquest that they alone, because
of the method of their selection and the temporary nature
of their authority, were "beyond the reach of fear or favor,
or of being overawed by power or seduced by persuasion."[17]
   But the restricted view of the role of the grand inquest
gained more and more support. In an article written in 1832
for Francis Lieber's *Encyclopaedia Americana,* Justice
Joseph Story of the United States Supreme Court described
a grand jury as acting only "at the instigation of the government." He made no mention of jurors acting independently of the court or initiating investigations of their own.[18]
The supreme courts of both Vermont and Tennessee lent
support to Story's views. In Vermont, the state constitution
did not specifically guarantee the right to indictment by a
grand jury in all criminal cases. As a result, many lesser
crimes came to trial at the instance of the public prosecutor.
In 1836, the defendent in a criminal trial challenged this
procedure, claiming that the state had violated the fifth
amendment of the United States Constitution by prosecuting him on an information. The Supreme Court of Vermont
held that the restrictions imposed by the fifth amendment
applied only to the federal government and not to the states:
that the states were free to abolish grand juries entirely
insofar as the federal Constitution was concerned.[19] In 1837
the grand jury of Sullivan County, Tennessee, initiated a
sweeping investigation of illegal gambling and, in the course
of the probe, summoned a large number of individuals to
testify. A state law empowered the jurors to summon witnesses to investigate "illegal gaming." Among the indictments based upon testimony of witnesses returned by the
jury was one for betting on an election. The Supreme

[17] "Chief Justice Shaw's Charge to the Grand Jury," in *American Jurist,*
8:216 (July, 1832).
   [18] Francis Lieber, ed., *Encyclopaedia Americana* (Philadelphia, 1831), 8:284;
Frank Freidel, *Francis Lieber, Nineteenth-Century Idealist* (Baton Rouge,
1947), 69.
   [19] Francis N. Thorpe, ed., *The Federal and State Constitutions* (Washington,
D.C., 1909), 6:3740; *State vs. Keyes, 8 Vermont* 57 (1836).

Court of Tennessee quashed the indictment and warned future grand juries that they did not possess "general inquisitorial powers" and could call witnesses only if specifically authorized by law. The court also held that betting on elections could not be construed as "illegal gaming."[20] Several years later, jurors of Maury County, Tennessee, indicted a master for permitting his slave to sell liquor. The inquest had become aware of the offense from a witness it had summoned to testify on another matter. Again the Tennessee Supreme Court restricted the power of grand juries to act independently and held that indictments had to be based on the actual knowledge of one of the panel members.[21]

In Cincinnati, a newly appointed federal judge, Timothy Walker, expressed the same restricted view of grand jury powers. Walker was not a newcomer to western legal circles. He had studied under Joseph Story at Harvard and gone to Cincinnati in 1830. There he organized a law school, founded the *Western Law Journal,* and became an ardent advocate of legal reform. In 1842, he told a jury, "Your sole function is to pass upon indictments. The term presentment confers no separate authority. . . . Yet in some states advantage has been taken of a similar expression to convert a grand jury into a body of political supervisors."[22]

Two years after Timothy Walker read his restrictive charge before a Cincinnati jury, the question of grand jury powers came up in Pennsylvania. In May, 1844, the convention of the Native American Association in Philadelphia ended in a series of destructive riots when Irish groups attempted to break up the meeting. After mobs had burned several buildings the governor called up the state militia. At this point Charles J. Jack, a member of the Native American group, addressed a letter to the grand jury then in session, protesting that the call for troops was an effort

[20] *State vs. Smith,* 19 *Tennessee* 99 (1838).
[21] *State vs. Love,* 23 *Tennessee* 255 (1843).
[22] "Charge Delivered by T. Walker," in *Western Law Journal,* 1:337–338 (May, 1844); "Obituary of Timothy Walker," in *Law Reporter,* 18:708 (April, 1856).

to crush the Native Americans by military force. When he learned of the letter, Judge Anson V. Parsons of the Philadelphia Court of Quarter Sessions cited Jack for contempt of court and declared that it was an "indictable offense" for a private individual to communicate with a grand jury. Furthermore, Parsons announced that grand jurors were officers of the court under its legal direction and that only the court could convey information and instructions to them.[23] In the following year, a Philadelphia grand jury informed the court that one of its members had charged Richard L. Lloyd and Benjamin E. Carpenter, members of the City Board of Health, with stealing public funds. The jurors asked the court to call witnesses and order the Board of Health to produce its books. Judge Edward King refused the request, stating that grand jurors could not proceed to investigate a matter unless the judge gave it to them in charge or the district attorney brought it to their attention. He told the jurors that they were free to initiate presentments only where all the facts of the offense were known to one of their members.[24]

Judicial rulings restricting the independence of grand juries found ready acceptance among several American legal scholars. Francis Wharton, recognized authority in the field of criminal law, noted with approval the decisions of the Tennessee and Pennsylvania courts making grand inquests mere adjuncts of the court. Wharton stated that the value of grand juries depended upon the political tendencies of the age. While they may have been important at one time as a barrier to "frivolous prosecutions" by the state, in the United States they were more useful as restraints upon "the violence of popular excitement and the malice of private prosecutors." If they were necessary at all, Wharton thought

---

[23] *Commonwealth ex rel Jack vs. Crans,* 3 *Pennsylvania Law Journal* 443 (1844).

[24] *In the matter of the Communication of the grand jury in the case of Lloyd and Carpenter,* 5 *Pennsylvania Law Journal* 55 (1845); George H. Dession and Isadore H. Cohen, "The Inquisitorial Functions of Grand Juries," in *Yale Law Journal* 41:695 (March, 1932).

it was to serve as a means of protecting established institutions from the actions of the people.[25] Edward Ingersoll, prominent reforming member of the Pennsylvania bar, published an essay on grand juries in 1849. Condemning the institution as incompatible with the American constitutional guarantee of freedom, Ingersoll approved limitations placed upon their investigating activities because he believed that their secrecy and power to indict upon the knowledge to their own members, without additional evidence or witnesses, was "at variance with all modern English theory of judicial proceeding." He declared that inquests, if retained at all, should be limited to passing upon cases where the defendant had already had a preliminary hearing before a committing magistrate.[26] In 1849, the Code Commissioners of New York, headed by David Dudley Field, long a proponent of legal reform and codification, presented to the legislature of that state their draft of a proposed code of criminal procedure. The commissioners left no doubt about their position on the grand jury. They referred to jury service as a burdensome duty and stated flatly that they would have recommended complete abolition of the institution in New York, had it not been for guarantees contained in the state constitution. The commissioners did the next best thing, however, and recommended to the legislators that "limits must be placed to the extent of its powers and restraint must be placed upon their exercise." The New York legislature did not adopt the proposed criminal code nor did it heed the advice of the commissioners and curtail the power of grand juries.[27] In February, 1850, the *United States Monthly Law Magazine* reported the progress of the abolition movement in England

[25] Francis Wharton, *A Treatise on the Criminal Law of the United States* (Philadelphia, 1857), 227–234.

[26] Edward Ingersoll, *The History and Law of the Writ of Habeas Corpus with an Essay on the Law of Grand Juries* (Philadelphia, 1849), 47; Allen Johnson and Dumas Malone, eds., *Dictionary of American Biography* (New York, 1928–1944), 9:467.

[27] New York Constitution of 1846, article 6, section 24, in Thorpe, *Federal and State Constitutions*, 5:2666; *Fourth Report of the Commissioners on Practice and Pleading, Code of Criminal Procedure* (Albany, 1849), 37, 128.

and commented editorially that it hoped American judges
would follow the example of those in Britain and take an
active stand against the institution. The editorial also asked
American newspapers "to keep the matter before the public
until a similar bill shall be before our legislative bodies, and
passed."[28]

After 1850, opposition to the grand jury moved from the
courts and the pages of the law journals and textbooks to
the floors of state constitutional conventions and legislative
assemblies. In 1850, conventions to revise existing constitutions met in three states and in each of them abolition of the
grand jury became an important issue. In the constitutional
conventions of two of the new states admitted to the Union
between 1850 and 1865 the issue was hotly debated, and in
a third the way for legislative abolition was quitely left
open. At the same time opponents of the institution in at
least two states made concentrated efforts to obtain direct
legislative abolition or legislative support for constitutional
amendments designed to achieve the same end.

In Michigan the Committee on the Bill of Rights reported to the convention at Lansing that it had struck
out the provision guaranteeing the right to indictment by a
grand jury in all criminal cases. When delegate Samuel
Clark moved to restore the provision, the line of battle was
drawn and a sharp debate ensued. Clark admitted that
abuses might have crept into the system but he contended
that these could easily be corrected. He warned that complete reliance on public prosecutors would be "a dangerous
innovation." James Sullivan, an attorney, answered Clark.
He maintained that no district attorney could possible be
more arbitrary or dangerous than a secret *ex parte* body
which held its sessions "like the inquisition of the star
chamber." He dwelt long on the average juror's complete
ignorance of the law and pointed to the great expense of
maintaining such a useless institution. The convention voted
to strike out the grand jury guarantee, but abolitionist

[28] *United States Monthly Law Magazine*, 1:200 (February, 1850).

forces pressed for a provision specifically doing away with it. A majority of the delegates was unwilling to go that far however, and the convention left the question for the legislature to decide.[29]

The Indiana constitutional convention also became the scene of a struggle regarding the future of the grand jury. Delegates were sharply divided, as they had been in the Michigan convention. Some hailed it as an essential bulwark of liberty while others denounced it as a "remnant of the barbaric past." Anti-jury forces worked for a constitutional provision doing away with all grand juries, but the best they could get in the face of determined opposition was a clause authorizing the legislature "to continue, modify, or abolish" the system at any time. Indiana was the first state to include such a provision in its constitution.[30]

Opponents of the grand inquest were less successful in the Ohio constitutional convention than they had been in Michigan and Indiana. B. P. Smith, an attorney from Wyandot County, proposed substituting the information for the indictment, but only a handful of anti-jury men supported him. They pointed to the arbitrary nature of grand jury powers and pictured the inquests as an unnecessary tax burden, but all to no avail. A majority of the delegates favored retaining the institution, and the revised constitution made indictment by a grand jury a mandatory step in all criminal prosecutions.[31]

In 1857, delegates met at Salem, Oregon to draft a constitution for statehood. David Logan, a member of the territorial bar, tossed the question of the future of the grand jury into the lap of the convention with a resolution to replace the system with professional prosecutors. Logan reviewed in detail the origin and history of the grand inquest,

[29] *Report of the Proceedings and Debates in the Convention to Revise the Constitution of the State of Michigan* (Lansing, 1850), 27, 54, 84–85, 202–219.
[30] *Journal of the Convention of the State of Indiana to Amend the Constitution* (Indianapolis, 1851), 28, 60, 116, 946.
[31] *Report of the Debates and Proceedings of the Ohio Constitutional Convention, 1850–1851* (Columbus, 1851), 2:328–329.

and argued that conditions that had once made the institution necessary no longer existed in the United States. He urged Oregon to take the lead in getting rid of the grand jury and predicted that it would be only a matter of time before most other states followed suit. George H. Williams, Territorial Chief Justice, came to its defense, emphasizing its peculiar suitability in a frontier area such as Oregon. He admitted that, like most newly opened areas, Oregon had more than its share of lawlessness. Many "desperadoes" had come to the territory from the gold fields of California. In view of such conditions, the chief justice favored a secret method of entering complaints as a means of protecting citizens from possible reprisals. He explained to the convention that many persons refused to make complaints before justices because it might cost them their property or even their lives. Former Territorial Chief Justice Matthew P. Deady also joined the fight to save the grand jury. Opponents, however, accused the judges and lawyers who defended the grand jury of retaining outmoded legal machinery merely because they were familiar with the system. Logan placed them in the same class as those persons who stood against popular election of judges. Anti-jury forces failed to secure the outright abolition of the grand inquest, but they, like their Indiana counterparts, did get a constitutional provision empowering the legislature to nullify the system at any time.[32]

The first attempt to abolish the grand jury system by legislative action was made in Michigan in 1859. The state constitution, as revised in 1850, no longer guaranteed the right to a grand jury indictment, and the Judiciary Committee of the Michigan Assembly heartily endorsed a plan to end the use of inquests. It issued a scathing report, characterizing the grand jury as "a crumbling survivor of fallen institutions . . . more akin to the star chamber." Led by Alexander W. Buell, a Detroit attorney, the committee

[32] Charles H. Cary, ed., *The Oregon Constitution and Debates of the Constitutional Convention of 1857* (Salem, Oregon, 1926), 197, 212–215.

called upon the state to discard an institution dangerous to individual liberty. It bemoaned the lack of learning of most jurors and the inability of the courts to control the direction of their investigations. It referred to the "wholesome" curbs which Pennsylvania courts had placed upon grand juries but feared that such decisions would be difficult to enforce and would prove an unsatisfactory solution to the problem of lay interference. The committee's vigorous report proved effective in rallying legislative support for a bill abolishing the grand jury in Michigan. In February, 1859, the legislature provided that all crimes be prosecuted upon the information of a district attorney. Only a judge could call a grand jury for purposes of an investigation.[33]

Anti-jury forces in neighboring states watched with interest the success of their brethren in Michigan. In Wisconsin they drew encouragement and sought to use the example of Michigan as an opening wedge in a campaign to rid their own state of the institution. The *Milwaukee Sentinel* published with approval the Michigan legislative report and attacked grand juries editorially as cumbersome and expensive "instruments of private malice." Legislative action alone would not be sufficient to abolish the grand inquest in Wisconsin. The people would have to approve the required constitutional amendment.[34]

In the summer of 1859, while enemies of the inquest in Wisconsin awaited the next session of the legislature to propose their constitutional amendment, the fourth constitutional convention for the Territory of Kansas convened at Wyandotte. Previous constitutions drawn up at Topeka, Lecompton, and Leavenworth had each included a provision guaranteeing the right to indictment by a grand jury in all "capital or otherwise infamous crimes." The Wyandotte

---

[33] "Report of the Judiciary Committee of the House of Representatives on recommending passage of the bill to provide for the trial of offenses upon information," *Michigan House Document No. 4* (1859); *Michigan House Journal*, 1859, p. 237; *Michigan Senate Journal*, 1859, p. 567; *Laws of Michigan*, 1859, number 138, sections 1 and 7.

[34] *Milwaukee Sentinel*, February 1, 12, 1859.

convention adopted the Ohio constitution as its model, but the Committee on the Bill of Rights omitted the article referring to the grand jury and gave no reason for its action. In a territory deeply engrossed in the slavery controversy this move went unchallenged. Five years later it was comparatively easy to put a bill through the legislature providing that grand juries were not to attend state courts unless specially summoned by a judge.[35]

When the Wisconsin legislature convened in 1860, Senator Robert Hotchkiss proposed and the Senate adopted a resolution asking the Judiciary Committee to investigate the expediency of abolishing the grand jury system. Madison and Milwaukee newspapers hailed this as "a good omen of reform." The *Wisconsin Daily Patriot* urged immediate abolition and sounded the rallying cry, "Down with the old rotten fabric." The Senate committee reported favorably on a constitutional amendment. When the resolution reached the floor for debate, several senators questioned the power of states to tamper with the grand jury in view of the fifth amendment to the United States Constitution, but only a series of anonymous letters appearing in the *Milwaukee Sentinel* came openly to the defense. The writer, who signed himself "Invariable," predicted that "gross injustice and oppression on the one hand and bribery on the other," would inevitably follow if prosecution was left at the mercy of one man. The Senate passed the resolution calling for a constitutional amendment, but its action went for nothing. The Assembly buried the resolution in committee.[36]

With the outbreak of civil war, the necessity for concentrated prosecution of the war effort pushed the grand jury question into the background. Furthermore, as in all times

[35] Ariel Drapier (Reporter), *Proceedings and Debates of the Kansas Constitutional Convention* (Wyandotte, Kansas, 1859), 68, 288, 676–678; *Laws of Kansas* 1864, chapter 64, sections 1 and 7.

[36] Madison, *Wisconsin Daily Patriot*, January 17, 1860; *Milwaukee Sentinel*, February 1, 12, November 30, 1859; January 19, 30, February 17, 1860; Monroe, *Wisconsin States Rights*, April 20, 1859; *Wisconsin Senate Journal*, 1860, pp. 43, 71, 277; *Wisconsin House Journal*, 1860, p. 407; Madison, *Wisconsin State Journal*, January 16, February 15, 17, 18, 1860.

of crisis, the value of the institution was enhanced under the arbitrary arrests and military governments of wartime. Yet, opponents of the system made one more attempt to curb it. In July, 1864, the convention framing a constitution for Nevada became the scene of a bitter dispute. But, Nevada was still very much a frontier and the grand inquest had proved its value in territory after territory as America moved west. Jury protagonists finally convinced the delegates that a popular tribunal was better fitted than a public prosecutor to handle the problems of law enforcement on the frontier, and Nevada came into the Union under a constitution that guaranteed its citizens the right to indictment by a grand jury.[37]

In 1864, John N. Pomeroy, a professor of law at New York University, stated that the grand jury in the United States was "an insuperable barrier against official oppression" and that "the innovating hand of reform has not as yet touched the long-established proceedings in criminal actions . . . the grand jury [is] carefully preserved by our national and state constitutions."[38] The professor's conclusions were more hopeful than realistic. Most American legal scholars, many of them insistent that it had survived all possible usefulness, had joined their British brethren in the crusade to abolish the system. In Pennsylvania, Vermont, and Tennessee judicial decisions had seriously curtailed the activities of the juries. Agitation had already begun in some states to follow the lead of Michigan and abandon the use of the institution, while the legislatures of Illinois, Indiana, Oregon, and Kansas were free of all constitutional restrictions on the question. The reformers had made long strides, and they had only begun.

[37] *Official Report of the Debates and Proceedings in the Constitutional Convention of Nevada, 1864* (San Francisco, 1866), 24, 60, 196–198.

[38] John N. Pomeroy, *An Introduction to Criminal Law* (New York, 1864), 126.

Chapter 6

The Trans-Appalachian Frontier

JUST AS THE EARLY COLONISTS had done, settlers moving into the trans-Appalachian wilderness took the grand jury with them as an accepted part of local government, and few imported institutions proved as adaptable to the spirit of the frontier as did the grand inquest.[1] The grand jury served as an agency of law and order in the West, and while it may have lacked the efficiency and singleness of purpose of the public prosecutor, it made up for this deficiency by emphasizing democratic participation in law enforcement. Grand juries sat in frontier communities from the earliest days of government, but they were more than institutions devised to police the community. They served as constantly changing and ever watchful bodies of citizens possessed of sufficient authority to suggest policies and laws and to look after the general welfare of the community. During the territorial period they constituted the first and in some instances the only representative bodies.

Both the Northwest Ordinance and the act providing for territorial government in the area south of the Ohio provided for "judicial proceedings according to the common law." This included the right to indictment by grand jury. Enabling acts creating territories in the West vested the judicial power in the district courts and a supreme court, presided over by judges named by the president. The lawmakers did not set qualifications for jurors but left the matter up to the territorial legislatures. Frequently, there

---

[1] The bulk of the material in this chapter originally appeared in the author's "The Grand Jury on the Frontier," in *Wisconsin Magazine of History*, 40:3–8, 56 (Autumn, 1956), and is used with permission.

were no separate federal and territorial courts. The district courts simply gave over the first days of each session to the trial of cases arising under federal laws and the federal Constitution. Following this, they took the remainder of the session to try cases coming under laws of the territory. In some territories the same grand jury passed upon persons arrested for violation of federal or territorial laws, while in others the court impaneled separate indicting bodies.[2]

Court facilities on the frontier were generally crude. For the first few years a settler's cabin or the public room of a tavern often served as the seat of justice. Occasionally judges held court in the open under the shade of a tree. Where there was no courthouse, grand jurors retired to the woods to deliberate in private. In cold weather they huddled around a fire while they weighed the testimony and evidence, discussed local problems, or prepared presentments for the court. Even after counties constructed courthouses, juries often deliberated outdoors. Early courthouses were apt to be little more than crude log cabins, at times unheated and unfurnished. A typical frontier courthouse consisted of a hewed log structure about twenty feet long and twelve feet wide, with a split shingle roof. Inside was a single room with the judge's platform at one end, and separated from the main cabin by a rail bannister. Furnishings included a clerk's table, a sheriff's box for prisoners, and split log benches for the petit and grand jurors. If they deliberated inside during cold weather, juries usually met at one end of the room.[3]

[2] *United States Statutes at Large*, 1:51 (1787), The Northwest Ordinance; 1:123 (1790), Territory South of the Ohio; 1:549 (1798), Territory of Mississippi; 2:58 (1800), Territory of Indiana; 2:283 (1803), Territory of Louisiana; 2:309 (1805), Territory of Michigan; 2:514 (1809), Territory of Illinois; 3:493 (1819), Territory of Arkansas; and 5:10 (1836), Territory of Wisconsin.

[3] Reuben G. Thwaites, *Early Western Travels, 1748–1846* (Cleveland, 1904–1907), 4:158, 202; William F. English, *The Pioneer Lawyer and Jurist in Missouri* (Columbia, Missouri, 1947), 19; Thomas D. Clark, *The Rampaging Frontier* (Indianapolis, 1939), 179; Samuel Haycraft, *A History of Elizabethtown, Kentucky and Its Surroundings* (Elizabethtown, 1921), 34; Alma O. Tibbals, *A History of Pulaski County, Kentucky* (Bagdad, Kentucky, 1952), 10–11; Nina M. Biggs and Mabel L. Mackay, *History of Greenup County,*

Jury duty on the frontier as elsewhere was not entirely a solemn and serious occasion. County and circuit court days became gala affairs in many western communities. Whole families from the area around the county seat observed the occasion by coming to town. The country people welcomed the excuse to leave the routine work of the farm. They brought picnic lunches and remained for the day, visiting with neighbors and meeting old friends. While the women gossiped and minded the children, the menfolk swapped horses or traded farm produce, watched athletic contests, threw dice, settled the political issues of the day, or had a few rounds with friends at the local tavern.[4]

The crowds gathered around, watching the horseshoe contests or the tug-of-war; the small clusters of men deep in political argument, as well as the throngs of drinkers who lined the town bars, were likely to include men who had come to town to serve on the grand jury. Jurymen were indistinguishable from other persons gathered at the county seat to trade and enjoy themselves. The only thing that set them apart from their neighbors was the summons they had received from the sheriff, telling them to appear for grand jury duty at the approaching session of court. In most western territories and states the clerk of court chose the grand jurors by lot from a list of eligible persons. In some states the county supervisors prepared the list, while in others this task was the duty of the judges of election in each township. All qualified electors were eligible for jury duty in most western areas. In only a few states was land ownership a prerequisite. However, as in the Colonial period, the re-

Kentucky (Louisville, 1951), 21; Joseph Wells, *History of Cumberland County* [Kentucky] (Louisville, 1947), 55; Samuel C. Williams, *Beginnings of West Tennessee* (Johnson City, Tennessee, 1930), 138; Zella Armstrong, *The History of Hamilton County and Chattanooga, Tennessee* (Chattanooga, 1931), 223; *Pioneer History of Geouga County, Ohio* (n. p., 1880), 23; George A. Dupay, "The Earliest Courts of the Illinois Country," in *Illinois State Historical Society Transactions,* 11:48 (1906).

[4] William E. Connelley and E. Merton Coulter, *History of Kentucky* (Chicago, 1922), 2:791–792; Clark, *Rampaging Frontier,* 164–165; *Cincinnati Chronicle,* December 8, 1827.

quirements were not high. Preëmption claimants and those who had made their first payment on government land were regarded as landowners.[5]

Some prospective jurors were reluctant to leave their farms or businesses for an indefinite period, while others were eager to bask in the limelight that the role of grand juror would cast upon them. A few had served as grand jurymen in the past and could assume the air of old hands in the matter, while others looked forward to their initial experience as a member of the grand inquest. They usually received $1.00 to $1.25 for each day of service, plus three to six cents per mile for travel to and from the county seat. In Arkansas the court also reimbursed jurymen for any tolls they had paid in traveling to the court. In some western states grand jurors received their pay in scrip that could be used for county taxes or was redeemable in cash if the county treasurer had sufficient funds. An Indiana judge solved the problem of insufficient funds by giving each juror a credit of one day's work on the roads in lieu of pay. In some instances western courts, like their colonial predecessors, found it necessary to impose fines upon those who failed to appear for jury duty. Fines generally ranged from three to five dollars, but judges in Iowa Territory could impose up to twenty dollars. Jurors often brought with them equipment with which to camp out and provisions sufficient for the duration of the session. Even if the jurors could have afforded to stay at the local tavern for $1.25 a day, few village taverns could have accommodated the crowd that accompanied each court. Several justices, about ten traveling attorneys, eighteen grand jurors and twenty-four petit jurors, plus the litigants and their witnesses, often ran the total participants to well over fifty persons.[6]

[5] *Revised Laws of Illinois*, 1833, pp. 378–379; *Revised Statutes of Wisconsin*, 1849, chapter 97, sections 1, 3, 7, 10; *Laws of Alabama*, 1823, pp. 496–497; *Revised Statutes of Arkansas*, 1838, chapter 85, section 5; *Iowa Statutes*, 1860, chapter 115, sections 2720 and 2723.

[6] *Statutes of Kentucky*, 1809, vol. 1, chapter 262, section 27; *Statutes of Ohio*, 1833, pp. 137, 722; *Laws of Iowa Territory*, 1838, p. 298; *Revised Sta-*

When they were not hearing witnesses or deliberating, the jurors were free to enjoy themselves. Occasionally judges had to discharge those persons who were unable to sober up before the court convened. In some areas it became customary for "freshman" members of a panel to "treat" the rest of the members. In a few instances such a custom resulted in a large bar bill for jurors by the time the session was completed.[7]

Shortly after the opening of court, the judge, following the accepted procedure, appointed a foreman of the grand jury and swore him in. The clerk of court then administered the time-honored oath to the other grand jurors. Each swore to "present no person through malice, hatred or ill will," and not "to leave any person unpresented through fear, favor or affection or any reward." In addition, they bound themselves to bring before the court all persons guilty of crimes or misdemeanors committed within their county. The jury then completed its organization by choosing from among the members of the panel a secretary to keep a record of its deliberations.[8]

After the court had organized the grand jury, the judge addressed the jurymen, telling them of the nature of their duties. Usually, he called their attention to the most common criminal offenses as defined by the state or territorial laws, informed them of any specific duties that the legislature had given them, and advised them of local conditions that needed investigation. Jury charges delivered by frontier judges were not likely to be exhibitions of legal erudition such as those of eastern jurists. Few western judges were sufficiently well versed in the intricacies of the law to go into such matters, and even if they had been, an involved

tutes of Indiana, 1843, chapter 50, section 9; *Acts of the Legislature of Louisiana,* 1835, pp. 240–241; *Acts of the Legislature of Arkansas,* 1845, p. 55; *Laws of Missouri,* 1841, pp. 98–99; Leander J. Monks, *Courts and Lawyers of Indiana* (Indianapolis, 1916), 1:107; Augustus F. Shirts, *Primitive History of Hamilton County, Indiana* (Noblesville, Indiana, 1901), 65.

[7] *Cincinnati Chronicle,* November 24, December 8, 1827.

[8] *Statutes of Ohio,* 1833, p. 121; *Revised Statutes of Wisconsin,* 1849, chapter 97, section 16; *Iowa Statutes,* 1860, chapter 196, sections 4620–4623.

legal discussion would not have been well received. Frontier justices became famous for their colorful and outspoken grand jury charges dealing with homey subjects of local interest and importance. Like their earlier counterparts, they frequently took occasion to deliver a political oration or a lecture on the state of public morality.[9] Judges condemned the practice of carrying concealed weapons, complained of gambling and excessive drinking, and warned against the evils of extravagance and idleness. In 1806, Judge Charles A. Wickliffe of Kentucky denounced with great vigor the alarming increase in vagrancy in the community. In closing his charge, he implored the jurors to bring into court "that vagbonding set, sleek and fat; that never works and yet always has enough money to drink and gamble on."[10]

As was true of all grand juries, those on the frontier held their meetings in secret and heard only witnesses on behalf of the complainant. In most territories and state grand jurors could not be sued for libel for matters that they included in their presentments and were immune from arrest, except for capital crimes, during their term of service. Jurors were free to seek the advice of the county prosecutor regarding matters of law, but they could also ignore him if they chose to do so.[11]

Western panels were keenly aware of their prerogatives and resented any attempt by either judge or prosecutor to dictate to them. As grand jurors, they had the final word as to whether a person would be brought to trial. If the jurors refused to find a true bill, the judge was powerless in the matter and could only impanel a second inquest in hopes that it would indict. Some frontier juries evinced an extreme reluctance to indict, particularly in connection with shooting frays, if they felt that justice had already been

[9] English, *Pioneer Lawyer,* 14–19; Joseph C. Guild, *Old Times in Tennessee* (Nashville, 1878), 114, 366–368; Clark, *Rampaging Frontier,* 170–171.

[10] Haycraft, *History of Elizabethtown,* 63.

[11] *Revised Code of Illinois,* 1827, p. 162; *Revised Laws of Illinois,* 1833, p. 382; *Revised Statutes of Wisconsin,* 1849, chapter 97, section 23.

accomplished by more direct means. The independence of grand juries manifested itself on many such occasions.[12]

Occasionally, grand juries engaged in open conflict with prosecuting attorneys and judges and made use of their powers of presentment to protest what they deemed high handed actions and encroachment upon their privileges. In 1832, a grand jury in Michigan Territory went so far as to protest against the judge's practice of admitting persons to bail where there was evidence that they had committed a capital crime.[13] In the following year the jurors attending the Michigan Territorial Supreme Court objected to the treatment they had received at the hands of the attorney general as "a grievance insulting the whole community." They regarded this as a bold attempt to render the grand jury subservient to the prosecutor "by brow-beating and insulting" the representatives of the people, and warned their fellow citizens to preserve the independence of the grand jury "as the greatest safeguard of our privileges."[14] In 1825, a Tennessee jury boldly indicted the state court of appeals "from the chief justice to the bailiff" for encroaching upon the office of the clerk of the old court of appeals.[15] Jurors of Wayne County, Michigan Territory, dispatched a memorial to President John Quincy Adams and the United States Senate requesting that Solomon Sibly not be reappointed to the territorial supreme court because of his "mental imbecility." The jurors also protested against James Witherall's appointment as chief justice, "due to superannuation."[16] A jury at St. Louis, in 1805, denounced an attempt on the part of the court to make the grand jury

---

[12] Jonas Viles, "Old Franklin: A Frontier Town of the Twenties," in *Mississippi Valley Historical Review*, 9:279 (March, 1923); "The Judiciary of the Territory of Iowa," in *Iowa Journal of History and Politics*, 20:230 (April, 1922).

[13] Clarence E. Carter, ed., *The Territorial Papers of the United States* (Washington, D.C., 1934–1962), vol. 11, *The Territory of Michigan 1820–1829*, p. 328.

[14] *Detroit Gazette*, September 12, 1823.

[15] Millard D. Grubbs, *The Four Keys to Kentucky* (Louisville, 1949), 48.

[16] Carter, *Territorial Papers*, 11:1144–1145.

"a mere passive tool" and accused the judge of having swindled a man out of six hundred acres of land. A Lexington, Kentucky, grand jury jailed three witnesses who had refused to testify during a probe of illegal gambling. The presiding judge told the jurors they had misinterpreted the law, and rebuked them for jailing the witnesses. The jurors countered with a resolution castigating the judge, but he had the last word when he fined and jailed the entire panel for contempt of court.[17]

Indictments of early western grand juries revealed an attempt to bring order and decorum to boisterous frontier communities. They reproved persons for selling spirituous liquors without a license, presented those guilty of fighting and drunkenness, recommended severe penalties for dueling, took special pains to expose horse thieves, and conducted crusades against gambling. Hardly a grand jury met on the frontiers that did not return indictments for "profane swearing." In addition, they gave their attention to more serious crimes such as larceny, assault and battery, and murder.[18] But the problems of law and order did not take the entire time of frontier inquests.

In some territories and states the legislatures directed grand juries to perform specific duties. In Indiana and Illinois every panel had to inquire into the conditions of the local jail and the treatment of prisoners and to report its findings to the court. An Indiana law required the grand inquest to check upon highway supervisors and present any who were delinquent. The jurors also had to investigate local taverns at each session of court. Arkansas grand juries had the task of examining toll roads and bridges and

---

[17] *Ibid.*, vol. 13, *The Territory of Louisiana-Missouri 1803–1806*, pp. 248–251; *Richmond* (Indiana) *Palladium*, November 22, 1834.

[18] Haycraft, *History of Elizabethtown*, 34, 44; Tibbals, *History of Pulaski County, Kentucky*, 10–11; Lexington, *Kentucky Gazette*, September 29, 1800; Maude J. Drane, *History of Henry County* [Kentucky] (n. p., 1948) 11; M. W. Montgomery, *History of Jay County, Indiana* (Chicago, 1864), 133; Leorah M. Chapman, *A History of Johnson County, Illinois* (n. p., 1925), 274; Deborah B. Martin, *History of Brown County, Wisconsin* (Chicago, 1913), 95.

reporting those found to be unsafe or impassable. But even when not specifically instructed to do so, frontier jurors kept a constant check on the condition of roads and bridges and public buildings in their county. They audited the accounts of county officials and did not hesitate to denounce and indict those who were found guilty of malfeasance and corruption.[19]

Grand juries acted on their own initiative to suggest laws and projects they believed would benefit their communities and to petition state and territorial legislatures and Congress for special consideration. In 1806, jurors of Elizabethtown, Kentucky, asked the legislature to declare wolves "outlaws" and set a price on their scalps. An inquest sitting at Natchez, Mississippi Territory, protested that the taxing of boats by the government prevented the freighting of produce from their area to New Orleans. Jurors at Mobile, Mississippi Territory, petitioned Congress for free navigation of the Mobile River and asked that the people of that area be exempted from payments due on government lands "until their produce can find its way freely to the ocean."[20] In 1824, a Madison County, Tennessee, jury decried the unimproved condition of the nearby Forked Deer River and recommended that the people "arouse themselves" and engage an engineer to make surveys. The jurors censured the local inhabitants and their representatives in the legislature for neglecting a project "which would provide a market and an increase in population."[21] In 1825, grand juries of both McNairy and Hardeman counties in Tennessee protested against the judicial system of the state. They complained that the county courts had become mere nullities because litigants could appeal to circuit courts and secure a

---

[19] "The Laws of Territorial Indiana" in *Indiana Historical Collections,* 20:345 (1934); *Laws of Indiana,* 1817, chapter 32, section 7; *ibid.,* 1818, chapter 11, section 11; *Revised Code of Laws of Illinois,* 1827, p. 248; *Acts of the General Assembly of Arkansas,* 1845, p. 56; John D. Caton, *Early Bench and Bar of Illinois* (Chicago, 1893), 141.

[20] Haycraft, *History of Elizabethtown,* 35; Carter, *Territorial Papers,* vol. 5, *The Territory of Mississippi,* 63–66, 479–481.

[21] *Jackson* (Tennessee) *Gazette,* June 5, 1824.

second jury trial. The jurors pointed out that this frequently resulted in high costs for those seeking justice.[22]

At a time when territorial residents had little voice in their government, grand juries boldly proclaimed the needs and desires of western communities and served as agencies of protest. In some areas, where the people had no voting representative in Congress and the territorial officials were non-resident political appointees, grand juries were one of the few means of making known the wishes of the people. In June, 1799, grand jurors in Mississippi Territory complained that outsiders unfamiliar with local conditions had framed the code of laws for the territory.[23] In the same month another jury charged that local residents had no voice in the government of Mississippi Territory and denounced the governor and judges for exceeding their authority. The jurors protested that political and military appointees included persons "hackneyed in Spanish duplicity and drudgery."[24] Several years later, jurors of Washington District, Mississippi Territory, told Congress in a petition that since they were not represented in that body, they were using the grand jury to make known their grievances.[25] In 1815, the inquest of Arkansas County, Missouri Territory, complained to the government in Washington that the residents of their area could not get full benefit from the right of preëmption unless the federal government established an additional land office in the territory. As it was, they pointed out, the distance to the land office in St. Louis was too great. The jurors also deplored the lack of a post office in their county and demanded that the army station at least one company of soldiers among them for protection against marauding Indians.[26]

Political appointees named to territorial offices were frequently unfit, rapacious individuals, less interested in the

[22] *Ibid.,* August 20, September 10, 1825.
[23] Carter, *Territorial Papers,* 5:63–66.
[24] *Ibid.,* 66–68, 89.
[25] *Ibid.,* 479–481.
[26] *Ibid.,* vol. 15, *The Territory of Louisiana-Missouri, 1814–1821,* pp. 87–88.

welfare of the territory than in recouping their private fortunes. Local residents were not pleased to welcome such officials, and like the British colonists, they made their resentment known through their grand juries. Western panels repeatedly remonstrated against the activities of appointed officials and often dispatched petitions to Congress asking for their removal. Land agents were a favorite target for charges of larceny, favoritism, and drunkenness. United States marshals, federal and territorial judges, local army commanders, all came under the watchful eye of the grand jury and had occasion to feel the sting of its reprimand.[27] Jurors convening in Michigan Territory in 1809 censured Governor William Hull for remitting fines imposed by the Supreme Court. The outspoken jurymen rebuked territorial legislators for appropriating funds for the survey of a road from the Miami River to Detroit. Then they turned to the Supreme Court and denounced the almost continual absence of a majority of the judges.[28] Superior Court Judge Harry Toulmin became the target of a Mississippi territorial grand jury in 1811. The angry citizens protested against the judge's conduct, stating that he "has not scrupled to prostitute his dignity and betray the sanctity of his office." Among other things, they charged that he had corresponded with the Spanish government with the object of defeating the designs of the United States upon West Florida.[29] In the same year, an inquest in the St. Charles area of Louisiana Territory declared that the residents should have a greater share in making the laws and levying the taxes of the territory. They protested against the decisions of the land commissioners and demanded equitable relief for those land claimants who had been unsuccess-

[27] *Ibid.*, vol. 6, *The Territory of Mississippi, 1809–1817*, p. 290; Mineral Point (Wisconsin)̃ *Miners Free Press*, September 1, 1840; *Green Bay* (Wisconsin) *Republican*, May 14, 1844; Mary U. Rothrock, *The French Broad-Holston Country: A History of Knox County, Tennessee* (Knoxville, 1946), 51.
[28] *Collections of the Pioneer Society of the State of Michigan*, 8:587–598 (1907).
[29] Carter, *Territorial Papers*, 6:243, 245–246, 268–270.

ful.[30] Jurors in St. Louis held the view of those in St. Charles and urged that all judges be required to have some "permanent interest" in the territory and be compelled to reside there, as a first step toward placing the territorial government in the hands of "those who bear the burdens."[31] A Michigan jury censured the legislative board of the territory for passing measures at the request of a few individuals and for adopting laws when it was not in session. As a remedy, the jurors recommended "a legislature constituted by the people."[32]

Some juries took occasion in their report to the court to endorse local political candidates or comment upon electioneering practices. Jurymen attending court in western North Carolina in 1816 condemned "that deamon among us," the caucus, by which the legislature and the Congress "attempt to impose upon the American people a President not of their own choice." A measure giving congressmen an annual salary brought forth the comment that this "had a terrible squinting at aristocracy," serving to unite wealth with power.[33] In 1823, a Tennessee jury branded as a "nuisance" the practice of candidates treating voters with whiskey at campaign rallies. Such things, the jurors said, had "a direct tendency to contaminate the pure streams of representative government."[34]

Through the variety of their activities and powers, frontier grand juries acted as effective sounding boards in making known the desires of the people and served as a curb upon the activities of public officials. Any and all persons were free to come before them to make known their grievances, against their fellow citizens or their government. The men sitting on the grand inquest changed with each session of court and provided an inquisitorial body that gave no one

[30] *Ibid.*, vol. 14, *The Territory of Louisiana-Missouri, 1806–1814,* p. 495.
[31] *Ibid.*, 525.
[32] *Ibid.*, 11:329.
[33] Cincinnati, *Western Spy*, June 14, 1816.
[34] Mt. Pleasant (Ohio), *Weekly Historian*, September 6, 1823; Wirt A. Williams, ed., *History of Bolivar County, Mississippi* (Jackson, 1948), 39.

group a vested interest in law enforcement. Rotation of grand jury duty placed upon each man in the community the obligation of taking part in his government. Those who served became better acquainted with the operation of local government and gained experience that they could have gained in no other way except by holding office. All public officials came under the surveillance of local grand juries. Jurors commended those whom they found doing a good job, but were unfailing in their criticism of those who were not. They did not hesitate to use the ample powers that they possessed to conduct searching investigations into corruption in government or widespread evasion of the laws. Illegal voting and betting on elections, favoritism in awarding contracts, fraud in land sales, all became subjects of grand jury investigations.[35] States that came into the Union before 1860 each retained the grand jury as an integral part of its legal and governmental machinery, and in those states the representative body that had proved useful in protesting the lack of self government during the territorial period often became equally important as a voice of the people after statehood.

[35] Little Rock, *Arkansas Democrat,* July 17, 1846; *Milwaukee Sentinel,* February 25, May 6, 1851, April 12, 1856; Madison, *Daily Argus and Democrat,* October 14, 1854; Madison, *Wisconsin State Journal,* October 17, 21, 1854; Thomas B. Carroll, *Historical Sketches of Oktibbeha County* [Mississippi] (Gulfport, 1931), 69.

Chapter 7

The Slavery Question

ALTHOUGH NEGRO SLAVERY eventually became an important national issue, it was at bottom a local institution, adopted because of and adapted to local conditions.[1] The grand jury is also a local institution best adapted to the solution of local problems, and few grand juries met in the southern states prior to the Civil War without concerning themselves with some aspect of slavery. They checked upon the enforcement of laws regulating slaves and free Negroes, worried about insurrectionary tendencies, interested themselves in the treatment of slaves, and guarded against the infiltration of abolitionists and their propaganda. Although these problems were common to all the slave states, their relative importance varied with the community involved, and grand juries, summoned to represent each county, understood the needs of their particular localities and were well qualified to suggest appropriate measures to meet them. In the northern states grand juries only rarely concerned themselves with slavery. They did, on occasion, indict persons for violating state laws against kidnapping or charge persons with giving aid to runaway slaves, but, for the most part, inquests concerned themselves only when some specific event made it important to their particular locality. Slavery was not a local problem in the North.

Southern grand juries took seriously the task of maintaining control over slaves and free Negroes. Some were

[1] The bulk of the material in this chapter originally appeared in the author's "Southern Grand Juries and Slavery," in *The Journal of Negro History,* 40:166–178 (April, 1955), and is used with permission.

specifically directed by state legislatures to present "all persons of color" who conducted themselves in a manner dangerous to the peace and order of the state,[2] while others, in the tradition of grand jury powers and duties, simply did it anyway. Inquests regularly called attention to laxity in the enforcement of regulatory measures and suggested additional restrictions. In 1823, grand jurors in Charleston, South Carolina, protested against the large number of schools in the city run by "persons of color." The jurors recommended an ordinance forbidding colored persons from teaching "under severe penalty." Some masters taught their slaves to read and this aroused grand jurors of Sumter County, South Carolina. They warned that such practices could lead only "to consequences of the most serious and alarming nature."[3] Fear of insurrections led to laws prohibiting slave gatherings and juries watched closely to see that they were enforced. In 1827, jurors of Portsmouth, Virginia, presented John Booth for allowing over twenty slaves to assemble in his shop "to drink and make noise."[4] Slaves had no right to profit from their own labor and were not allowed to go into business for themselves. Masters continually violated laws that prohibited slaves from earning money and grand juries reminded citizens that such practices increased the number of free Negroes. The inquest of Wilkes County, Georgia, cited the instance of a local slave named Archy, who bought himself and part of his family by hiring his time. Another slave, Dolphin, made and signed his own contracts, contrary to the law.[5] In 1842 the Maury

---

[2] *Laws of North Carolina*, 1790–1804, p. 11; *Revised Code of Virginia*, 1819, chapter 111, section 87; *Revised Statutes of Missouri*, 1845, chapter 167, article I, section 37.

[3] Howell M. Henry, *The Police Control of the Slave in South Carolina* (Emory, Virginia, 1914), 83, 167.

[4] *Commonwealth vs. Booth*, 27 *Virginia* 669 (1828).

[5] Ralph B. Flanders, *Plantation Slavery in Georgia* (Chapel Hill, 1933), 238. The most important single source in cases concerning slavery is Helen C. Catterall, ed., *Judicial Cases Concerning Slavery and the Negro* (Washington, D.C., 1926–1936), hereafter cited as Catterall. *State vs. Woodman*, 1 Catterall 48 (North Carolina, 1824), allowing a slave to hire himself out; *Common-*

County, Tennessee, grand jury presented a master for allowing his slave to sell liquor for his own profit. Two years later, another Tennessee jury forced a planter to stop one of his slaves from practicing medicine and receiving fees. In 1847, jurors of Boone County, Tennessee, objected that a woman permitted her slave, Clarissa, to hire herself out.[6]

Enforcement of laws prohibiting all trade with slaves without their master's consent became an important duty of grand juries in the South. In 1828, jurors of Sumter County, South Carolina, were very much disturbed over the practice of shopkeepers trading with slaves after dark and asked the legislature to enact a penalty for trading with Negroes at night or on the Sabbath.[7] In Bibb County, Georgia, grand jurors were perturbed over the security of a master's property if any and all persons could do business with his slaves. They pointed out that failure to enforce laws against trading with slaves "materially impaired" their value by leading to unrest among them, and decried the fact that throngs of slaves crowded saloons every night, many of them becoming very intoxicated. In fact, the selling of whiskey to slaves became a frequent cause of grand jury complaint in the South. There were few jury reports that did not call for an end to the practice, and indictments were very common. Jurors of Chatham County, Georgia, suggested a law mak-

---

wealth vs. Gilbert, 1 Catterall 319 (Kentucky, 1831), permitting a slave to go at large and hire out; *Commonwealth vs. Major,* 1 Catterall 340 (Kentucky, 1838), allowing an old slave to run a "tippling house"; *State vs. Glasgow,* 2 Catterall 365 (South Carolina, 1836), allowing a slave to vend liquor.

[6] *State vs. Love,* 23 *Tennessee* 255 (1843); *Macon vs. State,* 2 Catterall 520 (Tennessee, 1844); *Parker vs. Commonwealth,* 1 Catterall 380 (Kentucky, 1847).

[7] Henry, *Police Control,* 166; *State vs. Goode,* 2 Catterall 43 (North Carolina, 1821); *State vs. Scott,* 2 Catterall 339 (South Carolina, 1829) are both indictments for buying goods from slaves; *State vs. Weaver,* 2 Catterall 162 (North Carolina, 1851), buying stolen property from a slave; *State vs. Williams,* 2 Catterall 188 (North Carolina, 1855), buying stolen tobacco from a slave; *State vs. Borroum,* 3 Catterall 330 (Mississippi, 1852), buying cotton from a slave; *Ricks vs. State,* 3 Catterall 40 (Georgia, 1855), trading with a slave; *Dacy vs. State,* 3 Catterall 42 (Georgia, 1855), buying corn from a slave; *Carpenter vs. State,* 3 Catterall 68 (Georgia, 1859), buying hides from a slave.

ing the sale of intoxicating liquor to slaves and free Negroes punishable by confinement in the penitentiary. As an aid to enforcement they recommended that rewards be offered for convicting testimony. In 1839, jurors of Pickens County, Alabama, indicted John Saunders for buying two hundred pounds of cotton from a slave without his master's knowledge. In 1857, inquests of both Spartanburg and Darlington, South Carolina, proposed that the legislature provide that corporal punishment be meted out to anyone caught trading slaves.[8]

Failure to enforce patrol laws frequently disturbed southern jurors. The inquest of Houston County, Georgia, deplored the fact that streets and corners of villages in the county were thronged with Negroes at all hours, from Saturday night until Monday morning. Jurors of Wilkes County in the same state blamed "the indulgence of the slave holders" for laxity in law enforcement. They warned against the frequency with which large crowds of Negroes assembled, "ostensibly for the purpose of religious worship," to be addressed by "Negro preachers or exhorters."[9] In Darlington, South Carolina, grand jurors protested against allowing slaves to own horses and travel about in buggies and wagons. They feared that such practices would lead to "a spirit of insubordination" among the slave population. Similar fears led other juries to report instances when slaves assembled unattended by white persons.[10]

---

[8] Flanders, *Slavery in Georgia,* 272–273; Henry, *Police Control,* 90, 188. *State vs. Saunders,* 3 Catterall 146 (Alabama, 1839); *State vs. Brown,* 2 Catterall 37 (North Carolina, 1819); *State vs. Blythe,* 2 Catterall 71 (North Carolina, 1835); *State vs. Murphy,* 3 Catterall 147 (Alabama, 1839); *Commonwealth vs. Kenner,* 1 Catterall 396 (Kentucky, 1850); *Commonwealth vs. Cook,* 1 Catterall 404 (Kentucky, 1852); *Commonwealth vs. Hatton,* 1 Catterall 418 (Kentucky, 1855); *State vs. Presnell,* 2 Catterall 155 (North Carolina, 1851); *Johnson vs. Commonwealth,* 1 Catterall 238 (Virginia, 1855); *Hately vs. State,* 3 Catterall 35 (Georgia, 1854); and *Reinhart vs. State,* 3 Catterall 72 (Georgia, 1859), are all indictments for selling liquor to slaves.

[9] Flanders, *Slavery in Georgia,* 237, 278.

[10] Henry, *Police Control,* 110; *State vs. Brown,* 2 Catterall 535 (Tennessee, 1847) and *Smith vs. Commonwealth,* 1 Catterall 371 (Kentucky, 1845) are for permitting over ten slaves to assemble and drink.

Free Negroes, like slaves, were often subjects of grand jury inquiry in the South. Many jurors regarded them as a disturbing element in their communities and tried to keep a close check upon their activities. In 1858, members of a jury sitting in Union County, South Carolina, went on record in favor of a law "to clear the state of all free persons of color" in order to strengthen the institution of slavery. Jurors in York County, South Carolina, suggested the use of state funds to send free Negroes to Liberia, giving those who desired to remain the alternative of becoming slaves.[11]

While southern grand juries took seriously the task of maintaining control over slaves and free Negroes, they took just as seriously the task of protecting them from the unpleasant aspects of their position. As early as 1802 the inquest of Alexandria County, Virginia, objected to making the District of Columbia a slave mart for the entire South, "where dealers exhibit to our view a scene of wretchedness and human degradation." The jurors issued a strong protest against the practice of selling free Negroes as slaves and demanded "legislative redress" of their grievances.[12] In 1816, the grand jury of Charleston, South Carolina, called attention to the many instances of Negro homicide committed within their city. They objected to the reflection which such cruel and barbarous treatment of slaves cast upon the reputation of the city. Members of the inquest also condemned the sale of free Negroes who were in jail or in debt.[13]

Throughout the South it became common practice for grand juries to denounce publicly and indict masters who used cruel methods of punishment or did not feed and clothe

---

[11] Henry, *Police Control*, 188; *Commonwealth vs. Scott*, 1 Catterall 229 (Virginia, 1853), indictment of a free Negro for selling liquor without a license. *State vs. Jacobs*, 2 Catterall 226 (North Carolina, 1859) and *State vs. Harris*, 2 Catterall 227 (North Carolina, 1859) are indictments of free Negroes for carrying firearms.

[12] *Register of the Debates in Congress*, 20th Congress, 2nd session, p. 177. The presentment was read before the House of Representatives by Minor of Pennsylvania, January 7, 1829.

[13] Henry, *Police Control*, 16, 116.

their slaves properly.[14] Grand juries in Virginia did not
hesitate to indict owners and overseers alike on charges of
"cruelly beating" or assaulting slaves.[15] In 1843, grand
jurors of Perry County, Alabama, indicted William H.
Jones for murder after he had beaten one of his slaves
to death. In Warren County, Mississippi, jurors charged
Thomas Dowling, an overseer, with murder after he had
struck a slave. In 1847, jurors of Marlborough, South Carolina, brought seven persons to trial for cruelty to Negroes.
Succeeding grand juries returned additional indictments
for cruelty in 1849 and 1855. Members of the inquest sitting
at Darlington, South Carolina, requested that a slave sentenced to two years in jail and five hundred lashes have his
punishment reduced because it would endanger his life.
In Augusta, Georgia, masters had been accustomed to sending their slaves to the guard room of the city hall to be
whipped by the town marshal, until the grand jury protested against the use of the city hall as a place of public
punishment.[16]

It was natural that a local institution so thoroughly em-
broiled in the regulation and protection of slaves as was the
grand jury should become just as thoroughly involved in
questions and controversies concerning the continuation of
the institution of slavery itself. Abolitionist activities early
and regularly came under the consideration of the southern
grand juries.

In Savannah, Georgia, in April, 1804, Judge Jabez Bowen, Jr., raised the issue of emancipation in his charge to
the Chatham County grand jury. The judge instructed the

---

[14] *Commonwealth vs. Howard*, 1 Catterall 200 (Virginia, 1841), beating a
female slave; *Turnipseed vs. State*, 3 Catterall 154 (Alabama, 1844), cruel and
unusual punishment of a slave; *State vs. Bowen*, 2 Catterall 412 (South
Carolina, 1849), denying food and clothing to slaves.

[15] *Commonwealth vs. Cohen*, 1 Catterall 131 (Virginia, 1819); *Commonwealth vs. Booth*, 1 Catterall 139 (Virginia, 1827); *Commonwealth vs. Carver*,
1 Catterall 149 (Virginia, 1827); *Commonwealth vs. Turner*, 1 Catterall 150
(Virginia, 1827).

[16] *State vs. Jones*, 3 Catterall 151 (Alabama, 1843); *Dowling vs. State*, 3 Catterall 304 (Mississippi, 1846); Henry, *Police Control*, 54, 76.

jurors in the nature of their duties and impressed upon them the seriousness of their deliberations. Having done this, he astounded all in the courtroom by launching into a bitter attack upon slavery, denouncing the institution as a barrier to the happiness and welfare of the people of Georgia. In conclusion, the judge ordered the grand inquest to bring in a plan for the gradual emancipation of slaves in the state. The sentiments expressed by Judge Bowen came as a complete surprise to the jurors. Although he had come to Georgia from Rhode Island, the judge had given no indication of his antislavery views before the legislature elected him to the bench.

The grand jurors retired, too astounded by the unexpectedness of the judge's remarks to make an immediate reply, but they talked of nothing else in the course of their deliberations. Finally, they resolved to show their displeasure by ignoring the court completely. Word of Judge Bowen's address had spread rapidly through the city of Savannah and next morning an excited crowd attended court. But, true to their resolve, not one of the twenty-two grand jurors appeared. The judge promptly declared them in contempt of court and fined each of them ten dollars. Thereupon the members of the inquest marched into court in a body and presented a statement of their views. They censured Judge Bowen for uttering remarks that were "injudicial, insulting to our government and repugnant to the general interests of the country," and accused him of disseminating ideas that would foster "domestic insurrection." They refused to proceed with other business and recommended that the judge's charge not be published, but that a copy be forwarded to the state legislature. The action of the grand jurors further aroused Judge Bowen. He committed the entire panel to jail for contempt of court and ordered that his address be published in the local newspaper.

Public sentiment in Savannah was with the grand jurors, and it was not difficult to persuade local justices to issue a writ of habeas corpus for their release. In doing so, they complimented the jurors on the "patriotism, firmness, and dignity" with which they had conducted themselves. The justices also issued a warrant for Judge Bowen's arrest on charges of attempting to incite a slave insurrection. Bowen remained in jail for two weeks until his father posted $80,000 bond. At its next session the Georgia legislature impeached the judge and he returned to Rhode Island.[17]

Local incidents of grand jury concern with abolition were many. In 1818, Jacob Gruber, a Methodist minister from Pennsylvania, denounced slavery before a camp meeting at Hagerstown, Maryland. Gruber characterized the slave trade as cruel and inhuman and attacked the institution as inconsistent with the Declaration of Independence. Grand jurors sitting at Hagerstown indicted the minister for attempting to incite slaves to rebellion.[18] In 1827, a North Carolina inquest charged a northern man with having concealed a mulatto girl on board a ship for the purpose of helping her out of the state to freedom. Five years later another North Carolina grand jury accused three persons of a similar project.[19] In 1835, jurors of Tuscaloosa, Alabama, indicted Robert G. Williams, the editor of the New York *Emancipator,* on charges of sending his paper into Alabama in violation of a law that prohibited the circulation of seditious writings in the state. The indictment came to nothing when Governor William L. Marcy of New York refused to grant extradition.[20] A Kentucky grand jury accused John B. Mahan, one of the founders of the Ohio Anti-Slavery Society, of illegal abolitionist activities within their state. In Alabama, in 1837, the grand jury of Lowdes County uncovered an incipient slave revolt. A local white person, Richard M'Donald, had urged slaves to rise against their masters

[17] Charles C. Jones, *Memorial History of Augusta, Georgia* (Syracuse, New York, 1890), 423–425.

[18] Clement Eaton, *Freedom of Thought in the Old South* (Durham, North Carolina, 1940), 131.

[19] *State vs. Johnson,* 2 Catterall 53 (North Carolina, 1827); *State vs. Edmund,* 2 Catterall 67 (North Carolina, 1833).

[20] James B. Sellers, *Slavery in Alabama* (University, Alabama, 1950), 366–367.

and follow him to Texas, gathering additional slaves as they went. Two years later, jurors attending court at Mobile, Alabama, discovered that a free Negro cook on board the brig *Martha* had secreted a slave in his kitchen in an attempt to take her north.[21]

As abolitionists in the North stepped up the tempo of their attacks upon slavery, southern grand juries took an increasingly active role in trying to prevent antislavery literature and orators from coming into their states. In 1841, the Maryland legislature ordered grand juries to call before them at every term of court all postmasters and deputy postmasters in their jurisdiction to testify regarding inflammatory literature received by free colored persons. Over-zealous grand jurors in Kent County insisted that it was the duty of postmasters to read everything in all newspapers delievered through their post offices. The presiding judge intervened, however, and held that it would be sufficient if they reported upon the general character of each paper received.[22] The grand inquest of Accomac County, Virginia, became incensed over the circulation of the *Christian Advocate and Journal* of New York City through their post office. The jurors declared that the newspaper was clearly designed to persuade Negroes to rebel by denying the property right of masters in their slaves.[23]

Antislavery advocates as well as abolitionist newspapers invaded the southern states and gave grand juries cause for concern. In 1842, jurors sitting in Richmond, Virginia, indicted an abolitionist for attempting to carry a slave north. The defendant and the fugitive got as far as Fredericksburg, Virginia, before they were captured. Two years later the inquest of Fayette County, Kentucky, charged Delia Webster, principal of the Lexington Female Academy, and

[21] Russel B. Nye, *Fettered Freedom* (East Lansing, Michigan, 1949), 200; *State vs. M'Donald*, 3 Catterall 141 (Alabama, 1837); *State vs. Hawkins*, 3 Catterall 146 (Alabama, 1839).

[22] Jeffery R. Brackett, *The Negro in Maryland* (Baltimore, 1889), 225–226; Eaton, *Freedom of Thought*, 128.

[23] *Fond du Lac* (Wisconsin) *Whig*, May 13, 1847.

Calvin Fairbanks, a Methodist minister, with "aiding and
enticing slaves to escape." The court found both of the accused guilty and sentenced them to terms in the state prison.
The following year a grand jury in Hardy County, Virginia, charged Robert Logan with encouraging Felix Smith,
a slave, to escape by furnishing him with clothes, money,
and provisions. In 1846, jurors of Wood County, Virginia,
just across the Ohio River from free territory, indicted
three residents of Ohio for assisting slaves to cross the
river to freedom.[24]

As slavery became the dominant issue in the sectional
controversy, it became more and more common for southern grand juries to summon persons before the courts to
answer charges of harboring runaways or encouraging and
assisting fugitives to escape.[25] In 1840, Samuel Janney, a
Quaker schoolteacher, published a refutation of the Biblical
defense of slavery in a Leesburg, Virginia, newspaper.
Grand jurors of Loudoun County indicted Janney for pub-
lishing an article designed to incite slaves to rebellion. The
court quashed the indictment, but the grand inquest brought
Janney into court a second time and charged him with denying the right of property in slaves.[26] In 1850, the grand in-

[24] *Young vs. Commonwealth*, 1 Catterall 202 (Virginia, 1842); Sellers, *Slavery in Alabama*, 200; John W. Coleman, *Slavery Times in Kentucky* (Chapel Hill, 1940), 196–203.

[25] *Logan vs. Commonwealth*, 1 Catterall 208 (Virginia, 1845); *Commonwealth vs. Garner*, 1 Catterall 210 (Virginia, 1846). Tennessee grand juries indicated persons for aiding slaves to escape in *State vs. Curtis*, 2 Catterall 525 (1845) and *State vs. Craft*, 2 Catterall 528 (1845). Virginia cases were *Cole vs. Commonwealth*, 1 Catterall 216 (1848), for advising a slave to escape, *Morrisset vs. Commonwealth*, 1 Catterall 219 (1849), for stealing two slaves, and *Smith vs. Commonwealth*, 1 Catterall 219 (1849), for concealing a fugitive slave. A South Carolina case was *State vs. Brown*, 2 Catterall 411 (1849), for aiding runaways to reach Ohio. Other cases were *State vs. Groves*, 2 Catterall 173 (North Carolina, 1853), aiding a runaway slave; *State vs. Kinman*, 2 Catterall 441 (South Carolina, 1854), *State vs. Chaney*, 2 Catterall 448 (South Carolina, 1856), and *State vs. Clayton and Carter*, 2 Catterall 459 (South Carolina, 1858), all for assisting fugitive slaves; *State vs. Woodly*, 2 Catterall 190 (North Carolina, 1855), for concealing a slave; *State vs. Burk*, 2 Catterall 202 (North Carolina, 1856), for harboring a runaway; *Sherman vs. Commonwealth*, 57 *Virginia* 677 (1858), for advising a slave to abscond.

[26] Eaton, *Freedom of Thought*, 135–136.

quest of Grayson County, Virginia, charged Jarvis C. Bacon, a local minister, with holding that masters had no property right in their slaves. The indictment resulted from a sermon that Bacon had preached from the New Testament text, "Ye are the salt of the earth." In the course of his message, he related the incident of the overthrow of the money changers in the temple and observed that there were thieves and robbers in church that very day. To illustrate his statement, the Reverend Bacon pointed out that if he stole his neighbor's corn he would be called a thief, but he could steal the labor of another human being with impunity.[27] The following year, jurors of Troup County, Georgia, indicted Thomas Grady of Boston on charges of attempting to induce a slave to commit a crime. Grady had promised twenty dollars to a slave if he would coax two other slaves to leave their master and accompany Grady to Boston. Witnesses testified that he had told the slaves to steal their master's money, even if they had to "cut the damned old rascal's throat."[28]

Finally, as the abolitionist crusade waxed stronger and stronger, many southerners became too touchy on the subject of emancipation to await the slow deliberations of their local courts. More and more, residents of southern communities organized themselves into extralegal committees to deal out summary justice to persons suspected of antislavery activities. As early as 1835 a citizen's committee of Charleston burned abolitionist literature taken from the post office. A Richmond mass meeting asked for a permanent vigilance committee to keep watch over post offices, ships, and hotels. In 1845, a committee of sixty citizens of Lexington, Kentucky, closed Cassius Clay's abolitionist paper, *The True American.* They entered his office by force, dismantled the equipment, and shipped it to Cincinnati. Such Vigilante methods made it entirely unnecessary to wait for the courts and also freed them from the limitations of a

[27] *Bacon vs. Commonwealth,* 1 Catterall 221 (Virginia, 1850).
[28] *Grady vs. State,* 3 Catterall 31 (Georgia, 1852).

legal procedure that excluded slave testimony against white persons. Often such testimony was the only evidence against persons suspected of being abolitionists.[29]

Unlike their southern counterparts, grand juries in the North were only rarely concerned with the slavery question. Only when some event in their own immediate area called for action did local residents use their grand juries to express their position on the institution of slavery, the laws for the regulation of slaves and the slave traffic, or the actions of free Negroes. And, until 1850 and the entrance of the federal courts into the fugitive slave controversy, such cases were rare.

Some northern grand juries became concerned with the problem of the free Negro. As early as 1823 jurors of Philadelphia presented as a nuisance the large number of "tippling houses, dram shops, and cheap dancing halls" in the alleys of the Negro quarter of the city. To curb the constantly growing community of free Negroes, the jurors recommended that the legislature pass a law making it more difficult for them to take up residence in Pennsylvania. In 1842, Negroes of Philadelphia staged an elaborate procession to celebrate the anniversary of the abolition of slavery in the British West Indies. When a crowd of white persons tried to break up the parade, a violent street battle ensued and several individuals were seriously injured. In the evening a mob pushed through the Negro quarter, stoning homes and beating any Negro it could capture. Finally, the crowd vented its anger by burning the newly constructed African Hall and the Colored Presbyterian Church. The grand jury that investigated the riots laid the blame squarely on the free Negro community of the city for providing "undue provocation."[30]

Northern grand juries also indicted persons for abolitionist activities. In 1834, abolitionists rescued two fugitives

---

[29] Nye, *Fettered Freedom*, 56–57, 133; Eaton, *Freedom of Thought*, 31, 97–99, 133; James E. Cutler, *Lynch Law* (New York, 1905), 122–130.
[30] Edward R. Turner, *The Negro in Pennsylvania* (Washington, D.C., 1911), 155–156, 163–164.

from a Pittsburgh, Pennsylvania, jail and the local grand
jury indicated them for violating a state law.[31] James G.
Birney, Kentucky slaveholder turned abolitionist, employed
a mulatto girl as a servant in his Cincinnati home. When
a judge, acting under the Fugitive Slave Law of 1793, declared the girl to be a chattel, grand jurors in Cincinnati
indicted Birney for harboring a slave contrary to Ohio law.[32]
A grand inquest in Massachusetts charged Sophia Robinson,
a leading abolitionist, with kidnapping a five year old Negro
child who had accompanied his master to Boston from
Mobile, Alabama, on a visit.[33] In 1843, a Massachusetts inquest indicted three men for assaulting a Boston constable
while they were attempting to rescue George Latimer, a
fugitive slave.[34] In the same year jurors in Adams County,
Illinois, charged several local residents with "harboring and
secreting" a slave who had escaped from Mississippi.[35]
Members of the inquest of Bureau County, Illinois, returned
an indictment against Owen Lovejoy for assisting a runaway slave to escape.[36]

Grand juries in northern states also brought individuals
to trial for kidnapping free Negroes in violation of state
laws. This became an increasingly important problem, particularly in the border states. In 1836, a Delaware grand
jury charged John Wholey with abducting Robert Richards,
a free colored person, and taking him into Maryland to be
sold as a slave.[37] In the following year, a New Hampshire
jury indicted several persons for kidnapping, and for having sold as a slave a six year old Negro boy bound out under
indenture.[38] In 1837, Edward Prigg, acting as the agent of
a Maryland slaveholder, seized Margaret Morgan, a Negro

---

[31] Nye, *Fettered Freedom*, 199.
[32] William Birney, *James G. Birney and His Times* (New York, 1890), 265;
Birney vs. Ohio, 8 *Ohio* 230 (1837).
[33] *Commonwealth vs. Robinson*, 4 Catterall 501 (Massachusetts, 1837).
[34] *Commonwealth vs. Tracy et al.*, 4 Catterall 510 (Massachusetts, 1843).
[35] *Eells vs. the People*, 5 Catterall 65 (Illinois, 1843).
[36] John D. Caton, *Early Bench and Bar of Illinois* (Chicago, 1893), 122.
[37] *State vs. Whaley*, 4 Catterall 223 (Delaware, 1836).
[38] *State vs. Rollins*, 4 Catterall 540 (New Hampshire, 1837).

woman, and took her and her children to Maryland without
securing the consent of a judge as prescribed by the federal
Fugitive Slave Law. The grand jury of York County, Pennsylvania, indicted Prigg for kidnapping a free Negro in
violation of a state law. The York County Court convicted
Prigg and the Supreme Court of Pennsylvania sustained
the verdict, but the United States Supreme Court held the
Pennsylvania law unconstitutional.[39] In 1841, a Massachusetts jury indicted Elias M. Turner for kidnapping an eight
year old colored boy with the intention of selling him as a
slave in Virginia.[40] On a number of occasions Delaware
grand juries charged persons with violating the state law
by assisting in the abduction of free Negroes to be sold as
slaves in neighboring Maryland.[41]

The Fugitive Slave Law of 1850 brought federal grand
juries into the slavery controversy. The Fugitive Slave Act
of 1793 had made no provision for criminal proceedings
against those who assisted runaways, but the new law made
such persons liable to a fine of $1,000 and six months' im-
prisonment, upon indictment by a grand jury and conviction.[42] Furthermore, abolitionist crusaders bitterly attacked
the new law from the start and made opposition to it the
mark of loyalty to the cause. In these circumstances attempts at enforcing the law created a situation in which
several dramatic "rescues" of fugitives by mobs and resulting efforts to punish the mob leaders placed federal grand
juries squarely in the middle of the battlefield.

In Boston, in February, 1851, federal marshals arrested
a Negro named Shadrach as a fugitive slave. The United
States commissioner postponed the case, but before Shadrach could be led back to his cell, a mob broke into the courtroom and rescued him. President Millard Fillmore issued

---

[39] *Prigg vs. Pennsylvania,* 14 *United States Court Reports* 417 (1842).

[40] *Commonwealth vs. Turner,* 4 Catterall 509 (Massachusetts, 1841).

[41] *State vs. Whitaker,* 4 Catterall 227 (Delaware, 1840); *State vs. Jeans,* 4
Catterall 231 (Delaware, 1845); *State vs. Updike* and *State vs. Harten,* 4 Catterall 232 (Delaware, 1847).

[42] *United States Statutes At Large,* 1:302–305 (1793) and 9:462–465 (1850).

a proclamation directing that all "aiders and abettors" be prosecuted, and Judge Peleg Sprague warned grand jurors attending the district court in Boston, that it was imperative that they enforce the criminal provisions of the new Fugitive Slave Law. Sprague denounced those who appealed to a "higher law" to justify their actions, as persons "beyond the scope of human reason and fit subjects either of consecration or a mad-house." The grand jurors returned three indictments for the rescue of Shadrach, but all three of the men presented by the grand inquest were acquitted by the trial jury.[43]

A Pennsylvania grand jury was next to become involved. In September, 1851, a Maryland slaveholder, Edward Gorsuch, and his party, accompanied by a United States marshal, went to Christiana, near Lancaster, Pennsylvania, to reclaim two fugitive slaves. The slaves had received advance warning of the approach of the Gorsuch party and had locked themselves, with a supply of weapons, in the home of William Parker, a free Negro. A bloody encounter ensued when the fugitives refused to surrender and armed men from the neighborhood gathered to assist the slaves in resisting capture. The Negroes, and those who aided them, killed Gorsuch and severely wounded his son before the party from Maryland withdrew. The United States marshal returned later, and with the assistance of fifty federal soldiers, arrested thirty-six persons for aiding the fugitives. On September 29, 1851, Judge John Kane reviewed the facts in the Christiana rescue for the benefit of grand jurors attending the circuit court in Philadelphia and told them that charges made against those in jail would be sufficient to establish the crime of treason if they could be proved. The judge denounced those who had been arrested as "fanatics of discord" who were bent upon stirring up resistance to

[43] *United States vs. Scott,* 27 *Federal Cases* 990 (1851); "Charge of Judge Sprague to the Grand Jury," in 30 *Federal Cases* 1015 (1851); Boston, *The Liberator,* February 21, April 18, June 13, November 14, 1851; Wendell P. Garrison and Francis J. Garrison, *William Lloyd Garrison* (New York, 1885–1889), 3:325–327; Henry S. Commager, *Theodore Parker* (Boston, 1936), 220.

the law and announced that they should be held accountable
for any treasonous acts they had instigated.[44] The abolitionist press greeted Judge Kane's charge to the grand jury
with a storm of protest and ridicule. William Lloyd Garrison declared that it was now evident that Judge Kane was
"a lineal descendant of that Cain who slew his brother
Abel." The *National Era* of Washington, D.C., rated the
judge for reviving the "loathsome doctrine" of constructive
treason and blamed his charge upon "that strange infatuation which . . . has given to slavery a controlling interest in
our halls of legislation and courts of justice."[45]

Grand jurors deliberating on the Christiana affair returned thirty-eight treason indictments, charging those indicted with traitorously combining against the United
States. The jurors expressed hope that "the bloody tragedy
of Christiana" would serve as a lesson by imparting modera-
tion to abolitionist zealots.[46] In the treason trials that followed, Thaddeus Stevens acted as chief defense counsel.
The trials dragged on for several months, but each of the
defendants was found not guilty.[47] Nine of those tried and
acquitted in the federal court in Philadelphia returned to
Lancaster County to face proceedings by the state. The
district attorney framed bills of indictment charging them
with riot and murder. In the meantime, however, antislavery
men went before the Lancaster grand jury in an attempt
to have them indict Deputy United States Marshal Henry
H. Kline for perjury. The grand jurors took no part in the
controversy, ignoring both the charges against Kline and
the district attorney's bills of indictment.[48]

[44] W. U. Hensel, "The Christiana Riot and the Treason Trials of 1851," in
Lancaster Historical Society Papers, 15:18–27, 57–58 (1911); "Charge of Judge
Kane to the Grand Jury," in 30 *Federal Cases* 1047 (1851).
[45] *The Liberator,* October 10, 24, 1851; Washington, *The National Era,*
October 9, 1851.
[46] *The National Era,* November 27, 1851; Hensel, "Christiana Riots," 58.
[47] *United States vs. Hanway,* 26 *Federal Cases* 105 (1851); *United States vs.
Williams,* 28 *Federal Cases* 631 (1852); Hensel, "Christiana Riots," 88; Richard
Current, *Old Thad Stevens* (Madison, 1942), 93.
[48] New York, *National Anti-Slavery Standard,* November 4, 1852; Hensel,
"Christiana Riots," 91, 98.

Early in the month following the Christiana affair, the "Jerry Rescue" took place at Syracuse, New York. William Henry, popularly known as Jerry, was a Missouri slave who had fled to upper New York several months earlier. On October 1, 1851, Jerry's owner arrived in Syracuse, warrant in hand, to claim his property. On the same day, visitors crowded the city for the Onondaga County Fair where Gerrit Smith and a group of abolitionists were holding a convention of the Liberty Party. Deputy United States Marshal Henry W. Allen arrested Jerry and took him before United States Commissioner Joseph F. Sabine. When word of Jerry's arrest reached the abolitionists, they hastily adjourned their meeting, and the convention set out en masse to liberate the fugitive. The crowd attacked Sabine's office and rescued Jerry, only to have federal authorities recapture him. That evening, Gerrit Smith, the Reverend Samuel J. May, Charles A. Wheaton, and several other prominent antislavery leaders met to map their course of action. Smith convinced the group that a forcible rescue, accompanied by a vigorous "popular demonstration" would do wonders to aid the abolitionist cause. That night the abolitionist leaders led a crowd of sympathizers which stormed the jail, rescued Jerry from his captors, and hurried him off on the road to Canada and freedom.

The morning following Jerry's rescue, federal authorities arrested some of those who had taken part in the action and the United States attorney drew up bills of indictment to lay before a grand jury. At the October, 1851, session of the circuit court at Buffalo, Justice Samuel Nelson reviewed the events of the incident before the grand jury, heaping scorn upon those "disorderly and turbulent men, the common disturbers of society" who had been responsible for "this outrage against the United States Constitution." He warned the jurors that the northern states would be held to a strict enforcement of the Fugitive Slave Law and asked them to help their state "redeem herself from the odium of suffering the Constitution to be trampled underfoot." The jurors approved twenty-four indictments laid before them and the court bound the accused over for trial. Abolitionists raised the cry of "jury packing" and pointed out that the United States marshal had allowed "volunteers" to sit on the grand jury. But at the trial, all efforts on the part of the defense to quash the indictments on these grounds failed. Shortly after indictment of the Jerry rescuers, Gerrit Smith suggested to local abolitionist leaders that they prosecute Deputy Marshal Allen on charges of kidnapping. They followed Smith's suggestion and laid the matter before the grand jury of Onondaga County. The sympathetic jurors returned a true bill. A trial jury acquitted Allen, but his trial gave abolitionist leaders one more opportunity to denounce the Fugitive Slave Law. Trials of the rescuers in federal court were no more successful. After they secured only one guilty verdict in four trials, federal authorities dropped the remaining cases.[49]

Rescues of fugitive slaves also took place in the West. On March 10, 1854, Benjamin Garland of St. Louis, assisted by two deputy marshals, recaptured Joshua Glover, his runaway slave, in Racine, Wisconsin. Garland took the fugitive to Milwaukee and placed him in jail pending a hearing before the United States commissioner. That evening, a large crowd, swelled by large numbers who had come from Racine by boat, gathered before the jail. Abolitionist orators played upon the sympathies of the people. Finally, the mob stormed the jail, released Glover, and placed him on a ship bound for Canada. United States Commissioner Winfield Smith issued a warrant for the arrest of Sherman M. Booth and John Ryecraft, both prominent local abolitionists, but the pair secured their release on a writ of habeas corpus issued by the Wisconsin Supreme Court. The court declared the Fugitive Slave Law unconstitutional because it did not pro-

[49] Ralph V. Harlow, *Gerrit Smith, Philanthropist and Reformer* (New York, 1939), 297–301; W. Freeman Galpin, "The Jerry Rescue," in *New York History*, 26:19–34 (January, 1945); *The Liberator*, October 10, 1851; "Charge of Justice Nelson," in 30 *Federal Cases* 1013 (1851); *United States vs. Reed*, 27 *Federal Cases* 727 (1852).

vide a jury trial for fugitive slaves and because it conferred judicial powers upon court commissioners.[50]

Federal authorities rearrested Booth and Ryecraft. The Wisconsin court refused to interfere and the matter went before a federal grand jury in January, 1855. Antislavery leaders charged that the jury was picked to include persons hostile to abolitionists. The clerk of the federal court refused to furnish a list of grand jurors for publication, which prompted the *Milwaukee Sentinel* to charge, "Such a court, with its staff quartered upon us, striving to fine and imprison our citizens, is but the tool of the slave power." Federal Judge Andrew J. Miller countered by asking the grand jurors to indict the publishers of the *Sentinel* for libeling the United States court and its officers. The jurors indicted Booth and Ryecraft for violating the Fugitive Slave Law but only rebuked the abolitionist press for threatening the court and instructed the federal attorney to institute proceedings if the libels persisted. The trial jury found Booth and Ryecraft guilty. Judge Miller fined them and sentenced them to short jail terms, but again the Wisconsin Supreme Court intervened and released them on habeas corpus. Execution of their sentences awaited appeal to the Supreme Court of the United States.[51]

Several months after the Milwaukee mob successfully liberated Joshua Glover, Boston abolitionists received word that Anthony Burns had been arrested in their city as a fugitive slave. Burns, a slave preacher who had left Virginia and made his way north, was a favorite of the abolitionists. They called a mass meeting at Faneuil Hall for the evening of May 26, 1854, to protest the capture. The time was favorable for such a gathering: abolitionists and women's rights

[50] *Milwaukee Sentinel,* March 14, 16, 17, 22, 30, 1854; Mason Vroman, "The Fugitive Slave Law in Wisconsin," in *Wisconsin State Historical Society Proceedings,* 1895, pp. 124–144; *In Re Sherman M. Booth,* 3 *Wisconsin* 1 (1854); Joseph Schafer, "Stormy Days in Court—The Booth Case," in *Wisconsin Magazine of History,* 20:89–110 (September, 1936).

[51] *In Re Booth and Ryecraft,* 3 *Wisconsin* 145 (1854); *Milwaukee Sentinel,* January 5, 6, 8, 9, 15, 24, 1855; *United States vs. Booth,* 21 *Howard* 506 (1858); *United States vs. Ryecraft,* 27 *Federal Cases* 918 (n.d.).

leaders crowded the city, attending conventions. Wendell Phillips and Theodore Parker delivered fighting speeches, exhorting the crowd in Faneuil Hall to oppose enforcement of the hated Fugitive Slave Law. Over and over again they shouted, "What are you going to do?" With this challenge ringing in their ears, the inflamed crowd moved into the street and marched on the courthouse where Burns was incarcerated. The mob was too late, however. Federal troops had arrived and repulsed the attack. The following day, Bostonians draped their stores in mourning and watched silently as federal troops led the manacled Burns down State Street on his way back to Virginia.[52]

On June 7, 1854, Justice Samuel Curtis directed grand jurors attending the federal district court at Boston to indict those persons who had attempted to obstruct justice in the Burns rescue. The justice announced that those who had incited others to commit the offense were equally guilty and subject to indictment. In spite of all judicial urgings, the grand inquest refused to return indictments in the matter. Theodore Parker rejoiced that the jurors had not "disgraced the state by such meanness" as indicting. But he did express some regret, stating ruefully, "I should have loved the occasion for a speech."[53] Federal officials did not give up after their rebuff at the hands of the grand jury, however. At the October term of court they determined to try again, this time selecting the grand jury with greater care. Justice Curtis' brother-in-law appeared on the new jury, and this brought charges that federal officials had used illegal methods to secure "a more pliant" panel. Edmund Quincy, prominent antislavery leader, charged that Curtis cared little for convictions in the Burns case, but only wished to enhance his character "in the Southern market" so he could become chief justice. The new jury did not disappoint those who had

[52] Garrison, *William Lloyd Garrison*, 3:409–410; Commager, *Theodore Parker*, 232; Hazel Wolf, *On Freedom's Altar* (Madison, 1952), 105.

[53] "Charge of Justice Curtis," in 30 *Federal Cases* 983 (1854); *The Liberator*, November 18, 1854; Garrison, *William Lloyd Garrison*, 3:410–411; Commager, *Theodore Parker*, 243–246.

selected it. It returned indictments against Parker and Phillips as well as against others who had addressed the Faneuil Hall meeting. But, when the cases came to trial the court quashed the indictments on a technicality and Parker lost a second opportunity for an abolitionist oration. He did the next best thing and published his prepared attack on "judicial tyranny" in book form.[54]

The manner in which grand juries in the North and in the South dealt with the question of slavery reflected the basic local nature of the grand inquest. In the South, slavery, the free Negro, and the threat of abolitionist interference were ever-present problems in every community. As a result, grand juries attending the county courts took it upon themselves to enforce laws relating to slavery and to suggest solutions to other aspects of the problem. When the abolitionist tide rose, a southern institution was under attack and southern grand juries assumed an important role in its defense. In the North, however, the question of slavery was not one that touched the everyday lives of the people. Although federal juries entered the slavery controversy, they became involved because they were charged with enforcing a specific law. Grand juries summoned to attend local courts in the North did not concern themselves with slavery unless some specific event in their communities brought it to their attention. They did not enter the abolitionist crusade as active participants. To have done so would have altered the basic nature of the grand inquest.

[54] *United States vs. Stowell,* 27 *Federal Cases* 1350 (1854); *The Liberator,* November 18, 1854; Garrison, *William Lloyd Garrison,* 3:410–411; Commager, *Theodore Parker,* 243–246.

Chapter 8

The Civil War and Reconstruction

THE AMERICAN CIVIL WAR, like other crises in American history, again demonstrated the value of local democratic institutions like the grand jury. The juries served as sounding boards for both judicial and lay opinion on the aims and conduct of the war and as more or less effective checks to official and military excesses brought on by wartime conditions. Grand juries attended local and central governmental courts in both North and South throughout the course of the conflict, and, true to their traditions, they reflected the opinions and interests of the communities in which they sat. Some allowed their enthusiasm for the war to lead them to denounce fellow citizens. Wartime hysteria drove others to return wholesale treason and conspiracy indictments. In areas where the war was less popular, grand juries occasionally protested against usurpation of authority by the central government and questioned the high handed tactics of military officials. However, throughout the period state grand juries did not lose their concern for local affairs. They remained important law enforcement agencies and continued to propose solutions to the everyday problems of their communities.

During the secession crisis and the days just preceding the opening of the war, while the sections were readying themselves for armed conflict, federal judges throughout the North hastened to deny the South's right to form a new nation. As judges had in the past, they chose their charges to grand juries as a means of making themselves heard. Judge David A. Smally told jurors at New York City, in January, 1861, that the South may have had some cause for complaint, but he denied its right to secede. In March, 1861, Judge Peleg Sprague reminded federal jurors sitting in Boston that the United States was not a confederacy of states and that the southerners had no right to secede. He declared emphatically that the Constitution provided for complete supremacy of the federal government. Judge Nathan Hall took advantage of his address to a grand jury in Rochester, New York, to warn the rebels that "the pretended right to secession has no foundation in reason or the Constitution." He defined treason and cautioned the jurors not to distrust the government in its efforts to suppress rebellion. In Ohio, Judge Humphrey Leavitt delivered a heated charge to Cincinnati jurors in which he sought to arouse support for coercion of the southern states. Leavitt denounced the rebel leaders and argued that "for the unmitigated atrocity of its design, and the madness and infatuation of those who began the rebellion, it has no parallel in history."[1]

In the hectic spring of 1861, when days were crowded with news of secession, most federal jurists included a definition of treason in their charges to grand juries. Some sought to discourage support of the rebels by defining treason very broadly. Other judges took a more conservative view and confined it to the actual waging of war against the United States. Grand juries found it difficult to reconcile the many conflicting interpretations. Judge Sprague told jurors in Boston that mere rebellion absolved no man from his allegiance to the United States, while Justice Samuel Nelson stated in New York that persons who adhered to an insurrectionary regime were not enemies and that trade with them was lawful. Judge John Cadwallader informed grand jurymen attending the federal district court at Philadelphia in May, 1861, that any conduct which might tend to

[1] "Charge to the Grand Jury," in 30 *Federal Cases* 1032 (1861); "Charge to the Grand Jury," in 30 *Federal Cases* 1039 (1861); "Judge Hall's Opinion on Habeas Corpus," in *Rebellion Pamphlets* in the Wisconsin State Historical Society, 26:106–107; "Charge to the Grand Jury," in 30 *Federal Cases* 1036 (1861).

give aid or comfort to the insurgents should be regarded as treasonable. Members of the Philadelphia grand inquest, however, appeared more interested in investigating frauds against the government and indicted brokers for furnishing worthless coffee at exorbitant rates.[2]

Throughout the war federal judges in the North used addresses to grand juries as occasions to denounce the enemy and encourage support of the war. Speaking in Boston in 1863, Judge Sprague delivered an extended attack on "the deadly heresy" of states' rights. He defined the theory of national supremacy with such clarity that the Union League published his charge for general distribution. Justice David Davis warned the people of southern Illinois to give strict obedience to the federal government. Justice Stephen Field called upon loyal citizens in California to strengthen the hand of the national government. He denounced as unfounded all apprehensions that executive power threatened the people's liberties.[3]

From the beginning, federal grand jurors were active in matters growing out of the war. A jury at Baltimore investigated the burning of bridges on the North Central Railroad and the mobbing of troops in April, 1861. The inquiry began in June, continued through the summer, and ended with treason indictments against eleven persons. In July, 1861, federal grand jurors in New York City ordered the officers and crew of the captured Confederate privateer *Savannah* held as pirates. A St. Louis federal inquest charged David H. Caldwell with treason for recruiting troops for the Confederacy.[4] Anti-war newspapers attracted the attention of grand jurymen in New York City in August, 1861. The jurors issued a public warning that the New York

[2] "Charge to the Grand Jury," in 30 *Federal Cases* 997 (1861); 30 *Federal Cases* 1034 (1861); *New York Tribune*, June 27, 1861; *Baltimore Sun*, May 27, 1861; *Philadelphia Press*, May 21, June 3, 1861.

[3] Peleg Sprague, "What is Treason?" in *Rebellion Pamphlets*, 28:1; *New York Tribune*, June 16, 1863; Stephen Field, "Charge to the Grand Jury," in *Rebellion Pamphlets*, 26:28.

[4] *Baltimore Sun*, June 21, September 18, 21, 28, 30, October 15, 1861; *New York Tribune*, July 17, 1861; *St. Louis Democrat*, August 26, 1861.

Journal of Commerce, the *New York News,* and the *Brooklyn Eagle* were all three guilty of "encouraging the rebels now in arms against the federal government." Their protest prompted federal authorities to exclude the three papers from the mails on the ground that they were "disloyal."[5] In the following month, federal grand jurors at Trenton, New Jersey, complained that the *Newark Evening Journal* and several other New Jersey papers were actively "fomenting rebellion." The jurymen recommended a novel but effective punishment. They asked loyal citizens to withhold all patronage from newspapers that did not give their unqualified support to the national government.[6]

As the war wore on, federal grand jurors frequently turned their attention to instances of desertion, draft evasion, and defrauding the government. In June, 1863, an inquest at New York City indicted forty-one persons for seeking to cheat on government contracts. Two months later, a New York City jury investigated draft riots and indicted eighteen rioters. Confederate General John Morgan's raid into Ohio in October, 1863, produced a flurry of indictments. Federal jurors at Cincinnati charged a large number of persons with helping Morgan to release Confederate prisoners of war. In Baltimore, a United States grand jury indicted fifteen persons for treason, and in Philadelphia grand jurors charged the crew of the Confederate privateer *Petrel* with the same offense. Federal inquests at Cleveland, Indianapolis, and St. Louis returned large numbers of indictments for conspiracy and draft evasion. In the autumn of 1863 grand jurors in Washington, D.C., launched a vigorous campaign to drive prostitution from the district.[7] The city had become a mecca for camp follow-

---

[5] *American Annual Cyclopaedia and Register of Important Events* (New York, 1862–1903), 1:329; *New York Tribune,* August 17, 1861.

[6] *Annual Cyclopaedia,* 1:329–330.

[7] *New York Times,* June 12, 1863; *New York Tribune,* August 5, 1863; *Columbus* (Ohio) *Crisis,* November 18, 1863; James G. Randall, *Constitutional Problems Under Lincoln* (New York, 1926), 85; Margaret Leech, *Reveille in Washington* (New York, 1941), 267.

ers, and vice flourished openly. The inquest spread a dragnet over the city and indicted as many as twenty persons in a single day. In March, 1864, a New York grand jury charged three contractors with furnishing sick horses to the army. In the following month, several residents of Baltimore faced trial for allegedly enticing soldiers to desert.[8]

The Lincoln administration early adopted, and continued to practice, a policy of arbitrarily arresting persons who voiced opposition to the war ór appeared to be politically dangerous. Such a policy enabled the administration to hold dangerous persons indefinitely without preferring charges or bringing them to trial. When the emergency had passed, the government could release them. Indictments, on the other hand, often placed government officials in an embarrassing position. They ran the risk of defeat in prosecuting treason cases or public opposition if success made them appear too vengeful. When grand juries did return indictments for treason, many federal attorneys avoided prosecuting by keeping them on the docket until the next term of court and then dismissing them.[9] The Habeas Corpus Act passed by Congress in March, 1863, directed that federal authorities bring all political prisoners before grand juries and release those not indicted. The act made arbitrary imprisonment illegal after grand juries had passed upon alleged offenses. In practice, however, the new law did not end extralegal imprisonment. Federal officials continued to ignore the courts wherever possible.[10]

State grand juries in the North dealt for the most part with local problems and returned routine criminal indictments, but the arbitrary policies pursued by the administration occasionally brought them into conflict with federal officials. In December, 1862, the grand inquest of Hunterdon County, New Jersey, investigated the arrest of two local persons on charges of interfering with enlistments. The

[8] *New York Tribune*, March 4, May 10, 1864; *Baltimore Sun*, April 12, 1864.
[9] Randall, *Constitutional Problems*, 91, 94, 150–153.
[10] *United States Statutes at Large*, 12:755 (1863); Randall, *Constitutional Problems*, 517–518.

jurors denounced and indicted United States Marshal Abraham R. Harris for his part in the affair. The sheriff arrested Harris and the court placed him under bond to appear at the next term. An Ohio grand jury took similar action when federal authorities imprisoned residents of their county. In Illinois, members of the Macoupin County inquest indicted General John Palmer and four federal officials for the false imprisonment of P. Reader, a local citizen. The jurors protested vigorously against the influx of ex-slaves into their state and accused General Alfred W. Ellet of violating a state law by bringing in free Negroes. Their action led the *St. Louis Democrat* to remark acidly, "Did ever Tory malice take a darker, dirtier shade than this?"[11] In Philadelphia the arrest of Albert D. Boileau, editor of the *Evening Journal,* by military authorities sent the local grand jury into action. Boileau's arrest followed swiftly on the heels of an editorial published January 20, 1863, in which he had compared the annual messages of Jefferson Davis and Lincoln in a manner derogatory of the intellectual capacities of Mr. Lincoln. General Robert Schenk, military commandant of the district, ordered the editor arrested and imprisoned at Fort McHenry. News of the incident prompted grand jurors attending the Philadelphia Court of Quarter Sessions to drop all other business and investigate the affair. The jurors issued a presentment rebuking General Schenk and announced that they intended to preserve "the liberty of the citizens in our keeping." Judge H. Alison, however, censured the jurymen for their action and denounced it as "wrong, unwise, and unnecessary." The judge deplored any collision between the state courts and the national government. Under these circumstances, the Philadelphia inquest took no further notice of military arrests. Editor Boileau secured his freedom after apologizing for his editorial.[12]

[11] *St. Louis Democrat,* December 8, 31, 1862; *Annual Cyclopaedia,* 2:516.
[12] *New York Tribune,* February 2, 3, 1863; *Columbus Crisis,* February 4, 1863; *Annual Cyclopaedia,* 3:470–472.

On May 18, 1864, both the New York *World* and the New York *Journal of Commerce* published a spurious presidential proclamation calling for 400,000 additional troops and setting aside a day for public humiliation and prayer. Acting on orders from the War Department, General John A. Dix closed the two newspapers and arrested the editors. When Governor Horatio Seymour of New York learned of the arrest he ordered District Attorney Abraham Oakey Hall to bring the matter before a grand jury. Judge A. D. Russell read Governor Seymour's letter to the grand jurors, lectured them on the rights of freedom of speech and the press, and assured them that they had "the right to inquire whether acts done in the name of the central government are really built upon the Constitution." The inquest refused to act in the matter, however, and reported to the court that it thought it "inexpedient to inquire into the subject." Governor Seymour rebuked the grand jurors for refusing to do their duty and told the district attorney to bring the matter of the arrests before a magistrate.[13]

Northern grand juries distant from the disputed ground dealt with disloyalty where they found it, but it was in the border states, where sympathies were divided and where the fortunes of war constantly changed jurisdictions, that disloyalty and traitorous acts regularly and vitally concerned the grand inquest. In the early years of the war United States grand juries in the border states returned large numbers of treason indictments against persons who had cast their lot with the Confederacy. Jurors attending the federal district court at Frankfort, Kentucky, in November, 1861, charged thirty-two prominent Kentuckians, including former Vice-President John C. Breckinridge, with treason. In the same month, an inquest deliberating at Wheeling in western Virginia returned true bills against Governor Henry A. Wise, former Secretary of War John B. Floyd,

[13] *New York Tribune,* May 21, June 14, 27, 1864; *New York Times,* May 24, 25, June 14, 1864; *Annual Cyclopaedia,* 4:389–391; *Columbus Crisis,* July 6, 1864; James D. McCabe, Jr., *The Life and Public Services of Horatio Seymour* (New York, 1868), 172–178.

and eight hundred other Virginians who gave their allegiance to the Confederacy. The chief justice of Colorado Territory reported late in 1861 that over ninety persons faced trial there on counts of treason, enlisting with the rebels, and conspiracy. In April, 1862, grand jurors at Nashville, Tennessee, indicted Governor Isham G. Harris, General Gideon J. Pillow, and former United States Judge West H. Humphreys for treason. Confederate Sequestration Receiver Sterling R. Cockrill aroused the jurors' anger for his activities on behalf of the rebel government and was indicted. The grand inquest of Bourbon County, Kentucky, placed thirty-four residents under indictment for having joined the Confederate army. In nearby Fayette County, citizens serving in the southern forces received similar treatment at the hands of local jurors.[14]

In areas where it was beyond the power of United States officials to apprehend persons charged with treason, the indictments served as a means of denouncing important Confederates and also helped maintain enthusiasm for the war. But where individuals charged with treason could be arrested, wholesale indictments frequently presented difficulties. The punishment for treason was too terrible to enforce indiscriminately and over-zealous grand juries, caught up in the excitement of civil war, sometimes construed treason very broadly. In May, 1862, Benjamin H. Smith, the federal attorney in western Virginia, asked federal courts at Clarksburg and Wheeling not to summon grand juries for the spring term, because he feared they would return too many treason indictments.[15]

In the border states the loyalty of grand jurors themselves was sometimes questioned. In April, 1862, Senator Garrett Davis of Kentucky introduced a bill in Congress designed to insure it. The measure required jurors to swear

[14] Lewis Collins, *Historical Sketches of Kentucky* (Covington, 1874), 1:97, 102; Randall, *Constitutional Problems,* 85; E. Merton Coulter, *The Civil War and Readjustment in Kentucky* (Chapel Hill, 1926), 141; William M. Robinson, *Justice in Grey* (Cambridge, 1941), 296.
[15] Randall, *Constitutional Problems,* 85.

that they had never directly or indirectly aided persons in rebellion against the government. Some members of Congress doubted the wisdom of requiring an additional oath, but Davis insisted that it was essential to the maintenance of justice in the border slave states. The important issue, he observed, was "Will traitors excute the law of treason against traitors?" A majority of the members of Congress answered Davis' question in the negative and the loyalty oath for grand jurymen became law in June, 1862.[16]

Federal officials and military commanders often attempted to use grand juries to coerce residents of the border states or of areas recently captured from the Confederate armies. Sometimes coercion of the jurors was also necessary. Wholesale arrests accompanied elections in Kentucky in the summer of 1862. A swarm of provost marshals descended on the state and their activities drove many to the Confederacy. In September, President Lincoln suspended habeas corpus for all those engaged in disloyal practices, regardless of where they were in the country. The total of political prisoners was swelled by General Braxton Bragg's invasion of Kentucky in August and September, 1862. A great wave of arbitrary arrests followed the Confederate retreat, and juries in Fayette and Bourbon counties together indicted over four hundred persons for treason. The indictments were of little practical import, however, because most of those named were well beyond the reach of the court. In some counties recaptured from the Confederates, military authorities dispersed judges and grand juries suspected of being secessionists, and required all federal court officials and jurors to take the special oath. Union forces occupied Memphis, Tennessee, in June, 1862, after the battle of Shiloh. In November, General William T. Sherman authorized Judge J. T. Swayne to reconvene the Memphis Criminal Court. When the court opened, Judge Swayne told the jurors to give their attention to violations of state laws re-

[16] *United States Statutes at Large*, 12:430 (1862); *Congressional Globe*, 37th Congress, 2nd session (1862), pp. 1772, 2394, 2479, 2507–2509, 2619.

garding slavery. Provost Marshal D. C. Anthony countered
with an order forbidding all attempts to enforce state laws
which conflicted with presidential orders, and General Sherman warned the Memphis jurors that if they dared to indict
persons for the hiring or assisting of runaway slaves, they
"would learn a lesson in politics that would last them to their
dying day."[17]

In the South a new nation had come into being, but a new
court system was not necessary. The Confederate States of
America simply took over the United States courts. In many
instances the judges and complete court staffs carried over
and the Confederate tribunals took over the court rooms, the
pending cases, and the laws of their predecessors. Frequently southern courts did not even bother to choose new
grand jurors but merely directed the marshal to summon
those persons drawn at the last term of the United States
court. The Confederate Constitution, using language borrowed from that of the United States, guaranteed the right
to indictment by a grand jury in all criminal cases.[18]

Confederate grand juries, like their counterparts in the
North, had occasion to face problems growing out of the
impending war. In June, 1861, the grand inquest at Mobile
indicted three Italian fruit dealers for treason on charges
of supplying the United States squadron off Pensacola with
fresh fruit and vegetables. At Charleston grand jurymen
accused Marine Captain Frederick Sandvrie of mutiny
aboard the ship *Jefferson Davis*. Jurors attending the Confederate district court at Richmond returned indictments
against several persons for counterfeiting treasury notes.
At Savannah, members of the federal inquest advised the
Confederate Congress to enact a rigid sequestration law.[19]

[17] William B. Hesseltine, *Lincoln and the War Governors* (New York, 1948),
246–247; Coulter, *Civil War and Readjustment in Kentucky*, 141, 149–154;
Joseph H. Parks, "Memphis Under Military Rule," in *East Tennessee Magazine of History*, 14:46–47 (1942).

[18] Robinson, *Justice in Grey*, 123, 133–134; Constitution of the Confederate
States of America, Section 9, Number 16, in James D. Richardson, ed., *Messages and Papers of the Confederacy* (Nashville, 1905), 1:37.

[19] Robinson, *Justice in Grey*, 176, 184–185, 231.

In the South as in the North, military officials arbitrarily arrested persons suspected of disloyalty and usurped the function of grand juries. Revolt in east Tennessee late in 1861 brought a declaration of martial law in the area around Knoxville and military authorities sent many Unionists to detention camps in Alabama. The isolated mountain regions of western Virginia and North Carolina also proved strong centers of disaffection. In the Ozark region of northern Arkansas a roundup of alleged traitors resulted in hundreds of arrests.

In areas where disloyalty was a less serious problem, southern grand juries continued to function and concerned themselves with other problems growing out of the conflict. While the city of Richmond was under martial law during the Peninsular Campaign of 1862, the Confederate district court continued in session and grand juries returned indictments. Charges against counterfeiting became commonplace in the returns of southern juries. In November, 1862, jurors at Knoxville uncovered a ring of fifteen persons engaged in passing spurious treasury notes. The Tennessee jurymen also submitted to the court a list of "alien enemies" in the district whose property they believed should be confiscated. The Confederate inquest at Mobile indicted counterfeiters in December, 1862, and also protested against the numerous frauds perpetrated against the government. They discovered that many individuals and companies had connived to ship private property at government expense. George B. Clitherall of New Orleans had sent $150,000 worth of privately owned sugar and molasses to Montgomery under the pretense that it was for the army. The jurors expressed regret that no law covered such fraudulent practices and asked Congress to remedy the situation. In eastern Tennessee, a grand jury indicted a Confederate finance officer for forgery and embezzlement. In Georgia, jurymen attending federal court at Savannah warned individuals who disparaged the Richmond government that they had better close "their impudent and imprudent mouths." The panel went on to denounce persons who speculated in depreciated currency and called upon the people to treat them as enemies.[20]

Occasionally state grand juries in the South gave their attention to federal matters and returned indictments for counterfeiting and harboring deserters. But for the most part, like those in the North, county inquests confined themselves to local matters. They kept a close watch over slaves and free Negroes as they had before the war, and they indicted masters who allowed slaves to work for themselves. Individuals who insisted upon trading with colored persons provided a constant source of irritation.[21]

As the war moved into its final year, grand jury presentments in the South reflected the accumulated problems and hardships of three years of conflict. Grand jurors at Milledgeville, Georgia, created a good deal of excitement in their community when they took it upon themselves to scrutinize the returns for the state's income tax. They protested indignantly that some persons who had made fortunes in business during the war reported only fifteen per cent of their annual income. In March, 1864, Judge Iverson L. Harris asked the Milledgeville inquest to look into the problem of high food prices. He noted that farm commodities were out of reach of many soldiers' families. The jurymen did so, but they disagreed with the judge and issued a presentment "to correct the misapprehension and evil reports in certain quarters concerning the price of provisions." They justified higher prices on the basis of poor crops and contended that farm products were higher in many other counties. Turning from the matter of high prices, the jurors protested against

[20] *Ibid.*, 143, 185, 204–205, 250, 276–278, 292, 293, 385–389; Georgia Lee Tatum, *Disloyalty in the Confederacy* (Chapel Hill, 1934), 148–151.
[21] *State vs. Lewis,* 60 *North Carolina* 300 (1864), harboring a deserter; *Young vs. State,* 39 *Alabama* 357 (1864), buying wheat from a slave; *Wilson vs. State,* 38 *Alabama* 411 (1863), enticing a slave from his master; *State vs. Brown,* 60 *North Carolina* 448 (1864), allowing a slave to go at large; *State vs. Duckworth,* 60 *North Carolina* 240 (1864), allowing a slave to keep herself as a free person; Oliver P. Temple, *East Tennessee and the Civil War* (Cincinnati, 1899), 388–411.

the "loose manner" in which laws relating to slaves were enforced. The panel members condemned the practice of allowing slaves and free Negroes to sell wood, butter, eggs, and other products without a permit. They exhorted patrol commissioners to do their duty, warning that "no enforcement of the patrol laws can be too rigid." Milledgeville grand jurors were not exceptional in urging strict enforcement of laws regulating the conduct of Negroes. Jurors attending the city court of Montgomery, Alabama, indicted several white persons for enticing slaves from their masters. Other inquests preferred criminal charges against individuals for trading with slaves and selling them liquor. In April, 1864, the grand jury at Atlanta denounced the activities of Confederate conscription officials. They protested that an officer and twelve soldiers on conscript duty broke down the door and fired into a house which they believed harbored deserters. The jurors indicted the soldiers for "aggravated riot." An inquest sitting in west Florida returned indictments against persons in the community who harbored deserters. In March, 1865, after Sherman and his troops had passed through their city, grand jurors at Milledgeville still called for more rigid enforcement of laws controlling colored persons. They inveighed against "the great and growing evils" of slaves hiring their own time, living apart from their owners, and trading on their own account. As for the war, the jurors deprecated disputes between the state and Confederate governments and warned all citizens to pull together in order to win the war or to suffer the consequences of "Yankee domination."[22]

The defeat and dissolution of the Confederacy brought federal grand juries back to the South, and Radical Republican policies regularly received their support. But local juries remained much the same and continued to act as criminal accusers and spokesmen of the people. Few south-

---

[22] Milledgeville (Georgia), *Southern Recorder*, March 8, 1864, March 14, 1865; *Caldwell and others vs. State*, 34 *Georgia* 10 (1864); Robinson, *Justice in Grey*, 203; *Martin vs. State*, 39 *Alabama* 523 (1865); *Amos vs. State*, 34 *Georgia* 531 (1866); *Young vs. State*, 39 *Alabama* 357 (1864).

erners believed Negroes ready to sit on juries, and in the period before the southern states fell under military rule only white persons served.[23] Even when under military domination southerners sought and often found effective methods for keeping Negroes and Radicals off the juries. Thereby the local white people retained control of this vital institution. And, throughout the Reconstruction period local juries struggled against Radical policies and the supporters of them. Carpetbaggers also felt the wrath of the panels.

Even before Radical Reconstruction got under way many communities found themselves overrun with treasury agents and subject to the whims of military officers. Local grand juries spoke out forcefully against the intruders. In Kentucky, where the Emancipation Proclamation did not apply, Major General John M. Palmer began a campaign to assist slaves to leave the state. Opposition to Palmer's methods grew until the Louisville grand jury indicted him, in November, 1865, for violating state laws.[24] Military interference in elections also proved a fruitful source of grand jury protest in Kentucky. In Campbell County, jurymen accused two United States army officers of intimidating voters. Jurors in Fayette County denounced military officials for stationing troops at polling places. In Powell County, Senator Henry C. Lilly and a local judge faced charges of destroying the freedom of elections.[25]

The conduct of United States treasury agents seeking out Confederate cotton brought forth bitter protests from southern grand juries. At Jefferson, Texas, jurors returned three indictments against agent R. L. Robertson, charging him with stealing cotton. Robertson appealed to military authorities and secured his release, only to be rearrested.

[23] Charles W. Ramsdell, *Reconstruction in Texas* (New York, 1910), 125; Thomas S. Staples, *Reconstruction in Arkansas* (New York, 1923), 107; J. G. de Roulhac Hamilton, *Reconstruction in North Carolina* (Raleigh, 1914), 166–167.

[24] *Cincinnati Commercial,* November 13, 1871; Collins, *Historical Sketches of Kentucky,* 1:165.

[25] Coulter, *Civil War and Readjustment in Kentucky,* 284–285; Collins, *Historical Sketches of Kentucky,* 1:170.

Finally, a squad of soldiers forcibly rescued the treasury agent and General E. R. Canby issued an order that state courts had no authority to investigate the title to cotton held as captured property. Local officials did not abandon attempts to prosecute Robertson until General Canby threatened to arrest the judge. Whereupon the judge adjourned court and announced that if he could not punish cotton thieves, he would not punish anyone.[26] In May, 1866, federal grand jurors sitting at Mobile reported that treasury agents had stolen a hundred and twenty-five thousand bales of cotton belonging to the federal government. They charged that the bulk of captured cotton shipped from Mobile found its way into private hands through the connivance of federal officials. The jurymen denounced federal agents who seized cotton in private hands on the pretext that it had belonged to the Confederate government, and then refused to release it unless it was sold to S. E. Ogden and Company at half its value. The jurors called attention to fraudulent practices of agents Thomas Dexter and James M. Tomeny, but regretted their inability to return indictments because of what they termed "the wilful absence and concealment of witnesses."[27]

In New Orleans, Democratic leaders turned to the grand jury in an effort to prevent Radicals from inaugurating Negro suffrage. In July, 1866, the Radicals reconvened the Louisiana Constitutional Convention of 1864. Their intention was to give colored persons the vote and to disenfranchise whites. Judge Edmund Abell responded by asking the grand jury to investigate Radical leaders. Before the jurors acted in the matter, street warfare broke out between a white mob and Negro guards stationed to protect the assembled convention. A three hour battle resulted in ninety killed and over two hundred wounded. Judge Abell charged that the riot had resulted from "an attempt to

---

[26] Ramsdell, *Reconstruction in Texas*, 44, 81.
[27] Walter L. Fleming, *Civil War and Reconstruction in Alabama* (New York, 1905), 297; *New York Times*, June 2, 1866.

subvert the government" and ordered the grand jury to conduct a full investigation. General Philip Sheridan realized the danger of such an inquiry and closed the courts in New Orleans. In his report to President Johnson, he characterized Abell as "one of the most dangerous men."[28]

In Galveston, Texas, occupation troops broke into stores and set buildings on fire, causing $130,000 damage. An army investigation whitewashed the affair, but the county grand jury looked into the riots and indicted an army officer on charges of arson and burglary. However, when military authorities intervened, prosecution proved impossible.[29]

In Milledgeville, Georgia, in September, 1866, the grand inquest lamented the fact that the community "has been infested with cotton stealers and treasury rogues" as well as gangs of thieves banded together to rob and plunder. The jurors did not express regret for the war, but announced that they remained "firmly persuaded that we were right— still believing in the justice of our cause." They deplored any attempt to repudiate the war debts because it would set a bad example for the "debtor class."[30]

It did not take long for native southerners and Radicals alike to realize the importance of grand juries in any contest for control of the defeated South. The group that dominated the local inquests controlled the power of indictment. By indicting their enemies or refusing to indict their friends, grand jurors could wield very persuasive powers. They could make life difficult for intruders and thus provide an excellent means of combatting outside interference. Agents of the British Crown had discovered this fact before and during the American Revolution, as had unwel-

[28] "Report of the Select Committee on the New Orleans Riots," *House Report No. 16,* 39th Congress, 2nd session (1866–1867), serial 1304, pp. 275–277; Willie M. Caskey, *Secession and Restoration of Louisiana* (Baton Rouge, 1938), 211–230.

[29] Ramsdell, *Reconstruction in Texas,* 128.

[30] Milledgeville, *Southern Recorder,* September 4, 1866; James W. Gardner, *Reconstruction in Mississippi* (New York, 1901), 167–170; Hamilton J. Eckenrode, *The Political History of Virginia During the Reconstruction* (Baltimore, 1904), 81.

come territorial appointees and meddling abolitionists. The Reconstruction era reemphasized the importance of the grand jury to the people of a colonial area. As had American colonists and territorial citizens before them, southerners used their grand juries to discredit and harass officials of the central government and to drive out the intruders.

The triumph of the Radicals in Congress and the establishment of military rule in the South in March, 1867, extended the influence of the army over southern courts. Trial by military commission augmented or replaced civil trials in many areas. Radicals, trying to take over southern grand juries by making colored persons eligible and excluding whites, received support from the military. When local judges balked at accepting Negroes on grand juries, military authorities closed the courts. In Alabama, General John Pope effectively excluded most white persons from juries when he ordered them to take the "test-oath." General Griffin followed suit in Texas and, because state laws prohibited Negroes from serving, many courts closed, unable to find qualified jurors. General Daniel Sickles ordered civil authorities in North Carolina to revise jury lists to include all persons who paid taxes. Military authorities removed Judge Augustus Reese from the Georgia superior bench when he refused to accept a jury of Negroes.[31]

The special grand juror's oath passed by Congress during the war enabled Radicals to exclude Democrats from federal grand juries in the South, but they were less successful with the state grand juries. In some sections grand inquests were partly black after 1867, but in many areas white residents were able to circumvent laws aimed at placing Negroes on juries. Sheriffs became important officials and the complexion of juries frequently hinged on which party controlled the office. In counties where local officers were Democrats, the names of colored persons seldom reached the jury

---

[31] Fleming, *Civil War and Reconstruction in Alabama*, 480, 487; Ramsdell, *Reconstruction in Texas*, 155, 158; Hamilton, *Reconstruction in North Carolina*, 207–208; *State vs. Holmes*, 63 *North Carolina* 18 (1868); C. Mildred Thompson, *Reconstruction in Georgia* (New York, 1915), 177–178.

lists. In June, 1869, the Republican attorney general of Georgia reported to Governor Rufus B. Bullock that the "insurrectionists are determined to control the office of sheriff and through it the summoning of jurors."[32] When Democrats regained control of the Alabama legislature in the 1874 election, they enacted a measure to assure themselves of control of grand juries throughout the state. The legislature authorized the governor to appoint a jury commission to choose grand jurors for any county. Where Negroes were in the majority or Republicans retained control, the governor could take the selection of jurors out of the hands of local officials. Radical politicians told Congressional investigators that Democrats succeeded in getting control of local grand juries in Mississippi. Congress met this threat by making it a federal offense to disqualify any person from jury service because of race or color.[33] In spite of the federal law, however, fewer and fewer colored persons served on local grand juries in the South.

In counties where southern whites managed to retain or regain control of the grand juries, they became agencies of protest against Negro and carpetbag rule. When the Reconstruction legislature of Alabama met for its first session, twenty of its members found themselves under indictment for crimes ranging from adultery to murder. But the legislature met the threat by passing a law relieving members from the penalties of most major crimes. The grand inquest of Perry County, Alabama, charged the clerk of the circuit court with horse stealing. In Dallas County, Alabama, the year 1868 saw almost every Radical official un-

---

[32] William W. Davis, *The Civil War and Reconstruction in Florida* (New York, 1913), 595; Francis B. Simkins and Robert H. Woody, *South Carolina During Reconstruction* (Chapel Hill, 1932), 144–145; Gardner, *Reconstruction in Mississippi,* 305; Thompson, *Reconstruction in Georgia,* 354; Milledgeville, *Southern Recorder,* March 2, 1869; "Conditions in Georgia," *House Executive Document No. 288,* 41st Congress, 2nd session (1869–1870), serial 1426, p. 24.

[33] "Investigation of Alabama Elections," *Senate Report No. 704,* 44th Congress, 2nd session (1876–1877), serial 1732, pp. 103, 154, 203; "Mississippi Election of 1875," *Senate Report No. 527,* 44th Congress, 1st session (1875–1876), serial 1669, p. 1036; *United States Statutes at Large,* 18:336 (1875).

der indictment. Grand jurors at Milledgeville, Georgia, condemned "the reckless expenditure of state funds in advertising in newspapers," and reproved Governor Bullock for
his indiscriminate exercise of executive clemency in pardoning persons convicted of "outrageous crimes." The jurors
warned that such a policy could lead to mob rule. Another
Milledgeville jury denounced the state government for keeping the people "burdened and ground with heavy taxes,
which are to become worse instead of better." Florida grand
jurors frequently protested against the waste of tax money
by carpetbag officials and their failure to keep roads in
repair. A Louisiana grand jury returned fourteen indictments charging George Wickliffe, the state auditor of public
accounts, with extortion. In Georgia Foster Blodgett, Radical supervisor of the state-owned Western and Atlantic
Railroad, plundered the line until a grand jury called a halt
to his activities. The road showed a deficit of $750,000 as a
result of his graft. Jurors of Floyd County, Georgia, demanded that state officials reduce expenditures. In Leon
County, Florida, a Negro state senator Charles Pearse,
faced trial on bribery charges while in Alabama the solicitor
of Dallas County left town because there were so many
indictments against him. The grand jury charged his successor with bribery and he also took to his heels. At Montgomery, Alabama, jurors reported "great irregularities"
among justices of the peace who failed to remit fines they
collected. In South Carolina, grand juries resorted to indictments on a large scale to remove unwanted public officials. Two trial justices and three county commissioners
faced charges of bribery in Newberry County. Officials in
Charleston and Williamsburg counties found themselves
in the same position. In Abbeville County, five Negro and
Radical officers stood accused of corruption. In North
Carolina, Polk County, grand jurors indicted their Republican sheriff for assault on a local citizen.[34]

[34] Fleming, *Civil War and Reconstruction in Alabama*, 739, 742, 746; Milledgeville, *Southern Recorder*, September 7, 1869; September 6, 1870; Davis,

In New Orleans, Radical leaders recruited Negroes when they reorganized the city police force, and antagonism soon developed between colored patrolmen and white residents. Southerners claimed that it was impossible to get Negro policemen to arrest criminals of their own race and that they frequently assaulted white persons. New Orleans grand juries took up the cause of white citizens and harassed police officials with indictments for assault, false imprisonment, and murder.[35] In January, 1872, Judge Abell called the attention of New Orleans grand jurors to rampant corruption in their state. He depicted Radical rule as one in which "the people have suffered themselves to be literally robbed before their own eyes and the money plundered from them to be devoted to licentiousness, bribery and corruption." The panel announced that it found flagrant corruption in payments made by the Board of Liquidation and warned Radical Governor H. C. Warmouth that he did not enjoy the confidence of the people of Louisiana. The *New Orleans Republican* denounced the grand jury for daring to criticize the Radical administration and suggested that such activities could lead to abolishing the institution in Louisiana.[36] Other grand juries followed the lead and took action against extravagance and corruption in government. Members of the grand inquest at Milledgeville, Georgia, recommended reducing the county treasurer's commission by half. In East Feliciana Parish, Louisiana, jurors indicted the local tax collector for embezzlement. The Republican tax collector at Natchitoches met a similar fate. A road contractor fled Washington County, Mississippi,

---

Civil War and Reconstruction in Florida, 681; Thompson, *Reconstruction in Georgia*, 221, 243; Ella Lonn, *Reconstruction in Louisiana after 1868* (New York, 1918), 47; "Report of the Committee on Condition of Affairs in the Southern States," *House Report No. 22*, 42nd Congress, 2nd session (1871-1872), serial 1530 (North Carolina), part 2, p. 314, serial 1531 (South Carolina), part 3, p. 57, serial 1532 (South Carolina), pp. 806–807, serial 1534 (Georgia), part 6, p. 636, and serial 1537 (Alabama), part 7, pp. 1153–1154; *State vs. Pearse*, 14 *Florida* 153 (1870); *Diggs vs. State*, 49 *Alabama* 311 (1873).

[35] *New Orleans Republican*, January 12, February 12, August 17, 23, September 23, 26, 27, 1871; Lonn, *Reconstruction in Louisiana*, 254.

[36] *New Orleans Republican*, January 17, 31, February 8, 9, 1872.

following indictments charging him with fraud and conspiracy. The same jury indicated the Radical sheriff for falsifying records.[37]

Even though many persons named by local grand juries did not stand trial, the indictments served their purpose if they drove unwanted individuals from the community. Toward this end, juries frequently declared bonds of Radical officials insufficient and if that did not work, brought criminal charges against them. In Tallahassee, Florida, the county inquest indicted two state senators and a member of the governor's cabinet for bribery. At Vicksburg, Mississippi, five white grand jurors were unable to get the twelve colored members of the panel to launch an investigation into corruption in the county. Judge George F. Brown denounced the jurors who refused "to do their duty" and dismissed the inquest. Succeeding grand juries at Vicksburg did not hesitate to probe corruption and indicted the clerk of court, his deputy, and the chancery clerk on charges of embezzlement and forgery. Jurors attending the city court at Montgomery denounced the county commissioners for their "shameful disregard of law and public treasure." They reported finding fraud and extortion in the payment of county claims, illegal manipulations on the part of the county treasurer, and offenses against the tax collector "too numerous to mention." The jurors noted that his reports "have put Munchausen to shame." They also indicted a former Union soldier appointed notary by the governor and accused the judge and sheriff of misdemeanors in office. In April, 1874, an Alabama grand jury indicted justices of the peace for falsifying records, censured the probate judge, and warned that county bankruptcy could be the only result unless wasteful spending ended. Rome, Georgia, jurors indicted Justice Algernon S. Hawkins for malpractice. In Clay County, Mississippi, the grand inquest accused Republican

---

[37] Milledgeville, *Southern Recorder,* March 5, 1872; "Presidential Election of 1876," *House Miscellaneous Document No. 31,* 45th Congress, 3rd session (1878–1879), serial 1865, part 3, pp. 144–145; Lonn, *Reconstruction in Louisianna,* 353; "Mississippi Election of 1875," serial 1669, pp. 1464, 1469.

supervisors of issuing fraudulent warrants and indicted the sheriff for "wilful neglect of duty." Democratic judges encouraged the jurors. Judge Henry D. Clayton pleaded with an Alabama inquest in December, 1874, to punish those who had fastened Radical government on the state, urging the jurors to "find them out, gentlemen; expose them, strip them to public gaze, indict them, make them quit, break them up, they have nearly broken you and your country." By the end of 1874, entire slates of Radical officials faced criminal charges in many southern counties. In Amite County, Mississippi, all members of the Radical board of supervisors were under indictment while in Dallas County, Alabama, indictments had sent many carpetbaggers hurrying north.[38]

As the Reconstruction period drew to a close southern grand juries did not slacken their campaigns to drive Republicans from office. In March, 1875, jurors convening in Washington County, Mississippi, excluded the Radical district attorney from their sessions and refused to indict white persons arrested for intimidating Negroes. Republican Judge Charles E. Shackleford refused to allow them to continue their deliberations and adjourned the court. Grand jurors in Noxubee County, Mississippi, attacked public officials for their management of county affairs. They disclosed that the clerk of court had received $3,000 in unlawful claims and rebuked the country supervisors for their lavish spending. In South Carolina, ex-State Treasurer Niles G. Parker faced a prison term after conviction on charges of using state funds for illegal purposes. Grand juries indicted James A. Bowley, Negro chairman of the House Ways and Means Committee of the Legislature and John B. Dennis, superintendent of the penitentiary, for accepting bribes. In Mississippi, the Clay County inquest

[38] Davis, *Civil War and Reconstruction in Florida,* 665; "Vicksburg Investigating Committee," *House Report No. 265,* 43rd Congress, 2nd session (1874–1875), serial 1659, pp. 302–303, 461–463; "Affairs in Alabama," *House Report No. 262,* 43rd Congress, 2nd session (1874–1875), serial 1661, pp. 258–265, 699, 795, 839, 841; *Hawkins vs. Georgia,* 54 *Georgia* 653 (1875); "Mississippi Election of 1875," serial 1669, pp. 256–258.

named carpetbaggers in larceny indictments and jurors in Issaquena County indicted the entire board of supervisors for increasing the tax rate. Many persons who faced indictments fled beyond the borders of southern states and southerners made no attempt to extradite them. In some areas, Democrats and Republicans reached compromises and agreed to drop state and federal prosecutions against indicted persons.[39]

In July, 1877, following a Democratic victory, grand jurors at Greenville, South Carolina, rejoiced that "we have entered upon a new era; the government has changed hands." The judge encouraged the jurors to present all persons "engaged in oppressing your people" and they replied with violent criticism of the methods used by federal agents to enforce internal revenue laws. The jurymen also presented the county auditor and the jury commissioner for continuing to perform their duties after Governor Wade Hampton had removed them. In Columbia, South Carolina, the grand jury began a cleanup of corruption and indicted the president of the State Senate, the speaker of the Assembly, clerks of both houses of the legislature, the state treasurer, and several legislators for bribery and fraud.[40]

Southern grand juries not only protested against Radical corruption and harassed Negroes and carpetbaggers with indictments but also consistently refused to enforce laws giving colored persons the vote. Radical legislatures passed laws against the Ku Klux Klan but found them virtually impossible to enforce. Major General Alfred Terry told several congressional investigators that most judges were impartial, but that they could not control the grand juries and compel them to indict. In 1869, the Republican judge of Green County, Alabama, loosed a vigorous attack upon Klan

[39] "Mississippi Election of 1875," serial 1669, pp. 75, 248–249, 587–589, 644, 1472–1473, 1501–1503; Woody and Simkins, *South Carolina during Reconstruction*, 169, 476, 543.

[40] *Greenville* (South Carolina) *Enterprise and Mountaineer*, April 4, July 4, 11, November 21, December 5, 1877; *State vs. Cardoza*, 11 *South Carolina* 195 (1878); *State vs. Smalls*, 11 *South Carolina* 262 (1878).

activity and instructed the grand jurors to investigate the murder of the Radical prosecuting attorney. The mixed black and white inquest examined five hundred witnesses but reported that it could not find evidence sufficient to indict. In Jackson County, Florida, a band of armed men escorted a carpetbagger out of town. When instructed to investigate the incident, the grand jury reported that it could find no evidence of kidnapping. Fear of reprisals kept some juries from indicting Klan members. After a Radical judge had asked Fayette County, Alabama, jurors to suppress the Klan, masked riders staged a mass parade and left a picture of a coffin at the courthouse with the message, "Go slow, K.K.K."[41] Few local grand juries interfered with Klan activities in their communities. In January, 1871, jurors at Rome, Georgia, deplored the actions of masked riders and asked all persons to cease such activities. Local residents greeted the presentment in a hostile manner and the two succeeding grand juries took great plans to deny the existence of any organized group. Jurors in Blount County, Alabama, found indictments against a large number of persons for opposing the Klan. In South Carolina, a courtroom audience broke into cheers when the inquest refused to charge Klan members with intimidating colored persons. Fear kept some jurors in line; Negroes and some white persons were warned not to appear for jury duty.[42]

Failure of the Radicals to gain control of state grand juries and secure indictments against Klan leaders led to pressure for federal laws. Congress responded in May, 1870, with an act aimed at the Ku Klux Klan. It gave federal courts the power to try persons accused of keeping Negroes from voting. The law extended federal jurisdiction over all

[41] "Civil and Political Conditions in Georgia," *Senate Executive Document No. 3*, 41st Congress, 2nd session (1869–1870), serial 1405, p. 3; Stanley F. Horn, *Invisible Empire: The Story of the Ku Klux Klan, 1866–1871* (Boston, 1939), 123, 136–137; Davis, *Civil War and Reconstruction in Florida*, 604.

[42] "Conditions in Georgia," serial 1534, pp. 84, 639, 879; "Conditions in North Carolina," serial 1530, pp. 110, 303, 393; "Conditions in Alabama," serial 1537, pp. 733–736; "Conditions in South Carolina," serial 1531, p. 28.

elections and gave Radicals an opportunity to fight back against extralegal organizations that threatened their control of southern states. Federal grand juries, from which most whites were easily excluded, proved less reluctant to indict Klan members. The federal inquest at Raleigh, North Carolina, investigated a Klan raid upon the town of Rutherford and indicted over seven hundred and fifty persons for taking part. Although most of those indicted never came to trial, the Republicans hoped that wholesale indictments would discourage Klan membership.[43] Continued Klan activity throughout the South and the threat it posed to Radical control prompted Congress to enact additional legislation. The Federal Election Act of February, 1871, and Ku Klux Klan Act of April, 1871, increased the penalties provided by the earlier law and authorized federal judges to exclude all accomplices from grand juries. As a result, federal courts gained broad powers to try persons accused of criminal conspiracy.[44]

Carefully screened federal grand juries soon crowded dockets with indictments. In October, 1871, President Grant proclaimed that "unlawful combinations and conspiracies" existed in nine South Carolina counties and suspended the writ of habeas corpus. Federal troops moved into the area and arrested over fifteen hundred persons. A federal grand jury composed of six whites and twenty-one Negroes indicted over seven hundred and fifty persons for violating the enforcement acts. The jurors concluded their session with a demand for more vigorous prosecution of persons indicted over seven hundred and fifty persons for violating the and character of the outrages."[45] In Mississippi, the first in-

---

[43] *United State Statutes at Large,* 16:140 (1870); Horn, *Invisible Empire,* 209; "Report on Affairs in the Southern States," serial 1541 (Florida), part 13, p. 104.

[44] *United States Statutes at Large,* 16:433; 17:13 (1871). William W. Davis, "Federal Enforcement Acts," in *Studies in Southern History and Politics* (New York, 1914), 215–217.

[45] "Report on Affairs in the Southern States," serial 1529, part 1, pp. 47–48; Horn, *Invisible Empire,* 235–240; Woody and Simkins, *South Carolina During Reconstruction,* 463–464.

dictments under the new enforcement acts stemmed from the murder of a Negro in Monroe County by a group of men wearing Klan outfits. Federal grand jurors at Oxford named twenty-eight persons in criminal indictments. By April, 1872, almost five hundred persons in the state faced trial. In North Carolina ninety-eight indictments embraced over nine hundred persons.[46] In April, 1873, a federal jury charged one hundred Louisianans with violation of the enforcement acts. The charge resulted from alleged intimidation of Negroes in the November, 1872, congressional election. In the eastern area of North Carolina over eight hundred persons faced trial in federal courts, while almost three hundred individuals in northern Mississippi had indictments against them. Well over thirteen hundred cases crowded the dockets of federal courts throughout the South by the end of 1873.[47] In 1874, United States grand juries added another three hundred and fifty indictments. The number of trials for violation of the enforcement acts did not correspond with the large number of indictments. It was not expedient to try all accused persons, and United States attorneys prosecuted only the leaders. This did not lessen the importance of wholesale indictments, however. Radical leaders recognized their value as a means of quieting opposition.[48]

Election frauds regularly took the attention of both state and federal grand juries in the South during Reconstruction. Investigations by federal juries served a useful purpose for the Radicals. Grand jury reports of violence and atrocities made excellent campaign propaganda and indictments served as a club to keep southerners in line. Since southern whites controlled the state juries and the Radicals

[46] Davis, *Civil War and Reconstruction in Florida*, 218; Gardner, *Reconstruction in Mississippi*, 351–353; *Annual Report of the Attorney General of the United States*, 1872, pp. 10–13.

[47] *United States vs. Cruikshank et al.*, 92 *United States Court Reports* 542 (1875); *United States vs. Hammond*, 26 *Federal Cases* 99 (1875); *Report of the Attorney General*, 1873, pp. 28–29.

[48] *Ibid.*, 1874, pp. 26–27; *United States vs. Petersburg Judges of Election*, 27 *Federal Cases* 506 (1874); "Affairs in Alabama," serial 1661, pp. 1029–1032.

the federal, they sometimes arrived at different conclusions. In Lexington, Kentucky, both initiated investigations of an election riot which took place in August, 1871. Disorder broke out when a crowd of Negroes and whites heard that the Republican legislative candidate was in the lead. Three colored persons lost their lives and many were injured in the fighting that ensued. Fayette County grand jurors reported that they were unable to discover who to blame for the affair. But a federal jury indicted six persons, including several city officials and officers of the state militia.[49] In July, 1876, federal jurors at Oxford, Mississippi, reported that they had uncovered "fraud, intimidation and violence . . . without parallel in connection with the election of 1875" and recommended that the national government intervene to insure free elections. A United States inquest in western Tennessee charged twenty persons with conspiring to prevent Negroes from voting. State grand juries, on the other hand, often denied charges of violence and intimidation. When Republican Governor D. H. Chamberlain of South Carolina proclaimed a state of insurrection in October, 1876, grand juries in five counties answered him with reports that no disturbance existed before or after the election. Members of the Chester County jury observed that "armed bodies of United States soldiers" were the only intimidating influence present at the polls.[50]

The election of 1878 brought with it threats of additional investigations by federal grand juries. However, Democrats offered to drop cases in state courts in return for dismissal of those in United States courts. If the Radicals refused, they threatened to match each federal arrest with two of their own. Comparatively few indictments resulted from

[49] *Cincinnati Commercial,* November 6, 1871; *New York Times,* November 6, 1871.
[50] "Mississippi Investigation," serial 1669, part 4, pp. 150–151; *United States vs. Harris,* 106 *United States Court Reports* 629 (1882); "Report of the Committee on South Carolina Elections," *Senate Miscellaneous Document No. 48,* 44th Congress, 2nd session (1876–1877), serial 1727, pp. 891–892; serial 1728, pp. 668–669; serial 1729, p. 573.

inquiries into the election. Radicals had already resigned themselves to losing political control of the South and more and more southern whites appeared on federal grand juries. At Charleston in 1878 federal jurors refused to return indictments in election fraud cases. A few Republican leaders even advised repealing the loyalty oath for federal grand jurors. Some persons had found other uses for it: a New Orleans distilling firm charged with whiskey frauds had tried to set aside its indictments on the ground that two of the jurors should have been disqualified as ex-rebels.[51]

In North and South alike, the role of the grand jury remained essentially unchanged during the course of the Civil War. Federal grand juries, as instruments of the central governments in both sections, concerned themselves with treason, desertion, and other questions stemming from the conflict, but the role of local inquests was far less spectacular. They acted in much the same manner as they had before the war, taking notice of wartime problems only when these touched their communities. Except in a few instances where they became involved in clashes between federal and state authorities, throughout the war local grand juries remained more interested in the basic problems of their local areas. During the Reconstruction period local grand juries played an important role in rescuing southern counties from Radical rule. In some areas, they were the only means by which the southern people could protest against outside interference. Using their power of indictment as a potent weapon, the juries discredited carpetbag officials and helped drive them from their communities. The Reconstruction experiment again demonstrated the importance of grand juries to a colonial area under the domination of an unsympathetic central government.

[51] "Elections of 1878 in South Carolina," *Senate Report No. 855*, 45th Congress, 3rd session (1878–1879), serial 1840, p. 499; *New York Tribune,* December 17, 1878; *New York Times,* December 23, 1878, and June 13, 1879.

Chapter 9

Tradition and Reform, 1865–1917

THE PEOPLING OF LARGE AREAS of the trans-Mississippi West, the rise of the city, and the growth of big business were only the most spectacular and therefore the most noted of the "new" developments in America after the Civil War.[1] Many institutions changed with the times and survived and many were outmoded and discarded. The grand jury suffered both fates: it consistently met the challenge of new community problems and it was discarded so regularly that by the time of American entrance into World War I vast areas in the country had ceased to use it. To the enemies of the grand jury the war between the states was but a short breathing space. Taking encouragement and tactics from the continued English struggle and seeing their Canadian neighbors take up the campaign, the American attackers increased the intensity of their effort. They gradually shifted the basis of their opposition from lay interference to inefficiency, and they gained victory after victory. By the beginning of the war "to make the world safe for democracy" the grand jury did indeed seem to be a dying democratic institution.

In England, the anti-jury campaign waged for over thirty years by leading judges and lawyers was crowned by partial success in 1872, when Parliament provided that grand juries no longer attend courts in the London metropolitan district. Whether or not they were to be summoned in special cases was left entirely to the discretion of the magis-

---

[1] The bulk of the material in this chapter originally appeared in the author's "The Grand Jury Under Attack, Part Two," in *Journal of Criminal Law, Criminology and Police Science*, 46:37–49 (May–June, 1955), and is used with permission.

trates.[2] Not content with this victory, English lawyers continually pressed for abolition of the grand jury system throughout the country. Urged by presiding magistrates, juries themselves continually presented their activities as "a waste of time and expense." In October, 1888, E. E. Meek read a paper before the Incorporated Law Society at Newcastle and summed up the opinion of many members of the British bar. He remarked that the institution no longer served a useful purpose but only served to cause "expense and trouble." Meek pointed out, as many Americans had done, that the liberty of the citizen was amply secured and no longer required the intervention of grand juries.[3] In 1913, when a Parliamentary commission composed of judges and legal experts studied the causes of delay in English courts, it reported that the grand jury system "uselessly puts the country to considerable expense and numerous persons to great inconvenience." The commissioners regarded the grand inquest as "little more than an historically interesting survival" which had "outlived the circumstances from which it sprung and developed." They recommended that Parliament take action to eliminate it from the English court system. At least one judge, L. A. Atherly-Jones of the London City Court, warned those who sought reform at the expense of popular government that "the bold hand of the innovator" should not touch those institutions which guard personal liberty.[4] But Americans who opposed grand juries commented approvingly on the English report. The *New Jersey Law Journal* predicted that it would be only a question of time before they would cease to exist.[5]

[2] *Statutes at Large of England,* 35 and 36 *Victoria* chapter 52 (August 6, 1872).

[3] John Kinghorn, "Ought Grand Juries to be Abolished?" in *Law Magazine and Review,* fourth series, 7:36–37 (November, 1881); E. E. Meek, "On Grand Juries," in *Law Times,* 85:395–396 (October 20, 1888).

[4] "Second Report of the Royal Commission on Delay in the King's Bench Division," in *Reports of Commissioners to the House of Commons* (London, 1914), 37:22; London *Times,* January 6, 8, 10, 1914; *Boston Evening Transcript,* January 17, 1914.

[5] "Editorial Notes," in *New Jersey Law Journal,* 37:97–98 (April, 1914); "Evils of the Grand Jury System," in *Law Notes,* 17:218 (February, 1914).

The strong movements for abolition in England and the United States soon found their triplet, in Canada. The question of retaining the grand jury became a favorite subject of debate among Canadian lawyers and jurists. From time to time lawyers, judges, and members of Parliament went on record as favoring or opposing the institution. The *Upper Canada Law Journal,* voicing the sentiments of the Toronto bar, took notice of the abolition movements in England and the United States. The journal came out against an institution "which affords great facilities for gratifying private malice." This opinion received legislative approval in 1860, when the Legislative Council passed a bill to end the use of inquests in the Recorders' courts of Upper Canada.[6] In October, 1890, Minister of Justice S. D. Thompson circulated a questionnaire on the grand inquest. Thompson's poll indicated that legal leaders in Canada were well divided on the subject. Forty-eight favored abolition, forty-one opposed, and twelve refused to commit themselves. At first the poll seemed a slight victory for those who sought to rid Canada of grand juries, but upon examination it became clear that those judges who served where inquests were on duty overwhelmingly favored retaining them. Most jurists who favored abolition served in the northwest territories or in the rural counties of Ontario, areas where grand juries were little used. In their replies, opponents echoed arguments which had often served to sway delegates in constitutional conventions in the western United States. They stressed the expense and delay attending grand juries and called for a less cumbersome and more efficient method of bringing offenders to trial. Justice John W. Gwynne of the Canadian supreme court summarized their views when he stated, "there exists no reason whatever in my judgement, for the continuance of the grand jury system. . . . It could be abolished with positive advantage to the speedy and inexpensive adminstration of the criminal law."

[6] *Upper Canada Law Journal,* 5:21–52 (March, 1859); 6:274–275 (December, 1860); *Journals of the Legislative Assembly of Canada,* 1860, pp. 77, 82, 415.

Canadian judges who favored retention emphasized the democratic nature of the institution. Judge James Reynolds of Ontario hailed it as a "great educator of the people," while another Ontario jurist said the choice was between a democratic and a bureaucratic system. Chief Justice M. B. Begbie of British Columbia announced that jury service was often the only means by which aliens could become acquainted with "the forms and spirit of British criminal law." He stressed the importance of inquests as spokesmen for their particular localities, calling attention "with great boldness" to their needs and grievances, speaking "with an authority which no other body possesses." Other judges felt that grand juries exercised a "salutary influence" over public officials and were important as a means of exposing dereliction of official duty.

Although the minster of justice had not resquested it, twelve grand juries sitting in Ontario volunteered their advice. Three favored eliminating inquests from Canadian courts, while the other nine expressed vigorous disapproval of any attempt on the part of public officials to usurp the prerogatives of the grand jury. Inquests in Northumberland and Durham counties denounced plans to replace them with crown prosecutors. They thought such a move "a gigantic innovation" which "would furnish more fat berths for office seekers, a class which is very numerous in the county." The Law Association of Hamilton, Ontario, characterized the grand jury as an important emblem of the people's sovereignty. It viewed the inquest as "a channel for the communication of suggested reforms."[7]

Canadian legal circles greeted the results of the jury poll with mixed reaction. In January, 1891, the *Canada Law Journal* of Toronto commented editorially that the opinions of grand jurors were not entitled to much weight in the matter because they were unaccustomed to legal procedure and

[7] "Correspondence between the Department of Justice and the Judges in Canada Respecting the Expediency of Abolishing the Grand Jury," sessional paper no. 66, pp. 5–8, 11–12, 18, 26, 55, 60–61, 64–69, in *Sessional Papers of the Dominion of Canada,* 7th Parliament, 1st session (1891).

untrained in the law. The editorial concluded that it would have been better to take the word of the crown prosecutors. The *Canadian Law Times,* however, thought that legislators should give greater weight to the opinions of the jurors, because they, more than all the judges in the Dominion, represented the people. The *Times* opposed reforms based solely on the recommendations of "expert authorities who are frequently theorists."

Members of Canadian legal circles argued over the relative value of the grand jury and the public prosecutor, much as their brethren in England and the United States had done and were doing. In 1891, a Westminster, Ontario, grand jury issued a sharp protest when the attorney general refused to prosecute a case in which it found a true bill. The *Canadian Law Times* noted editorially that appointment of a prosecutor to take their place would not have been popular with members of the Westminster grand inquest.[8] A decade later, Judge Neil McCrimmon warned his colleagues that since "the millennium" had not yet arrived, it would be neither wise nor expedient to destroy an institution that had proved a safeguard to the liberties of the people.[9] John A. Kains, an attorney, hastened to answer Judge McCrimmon, maintaining that a public prosecutor could not only protect the interests of the people, but would be "guarded by his professional instincts against irrelevant considerations."[10]

In the United States, efforts to abolish the grand jury assumed almost epidemic proportions in the years following the Civil War. Legal and governmental theorists, speaking in the name of progress, inveighed against the institution as a relic of the barbaric past too inefficient and time-consum-

[8] "Grand Juries," in *Canada Law Journal,* 27:4 (January 16, 1891); "The Abolition of Grand Juries," in *Canada Law Times,* 11:275–277 (November, 1891); J. A. Farin, "The Importance of Grand Juries," in *American Law Review,* 26:416–417 (May–June, 1892).

[9] Neil McCrimmon, "The Grand Jury," in *Canadian Law Review,* 1:127–130 (December, 1901).

[10] John A. Kains, "The Grand Jury," *ibid.,* 1:225–229 (February, 1902).

ing for an enlightened age. They conceded that inquests may at one time have been necessary safeguards against royal absolutism and absentee government[11] but saw no further need for such protection. A few individuals cautioned that a free government might require even more checks than a despotism, but progress seemed to be the enemy of the grand inquest and legal and reform opinion in most areas rapidly came to oppose its continuation.

A few judges strove to curtail grand jury powers to initiate and conduct investigations independently of the court. In Tennessee, the supreme court reinforced its position that inquests could summon witnesses only where specifically authorized by law. Pennsylvania courts reaffirmed the restrictive rule which limited juries to an investigation of matters known to one of the jurors or suggested to them by the judge or the prosecutor. Individual citizens were not free to go before a grand jury nor could jurors summon witnesses whom they believed could assist them in their inquiries. Any attempt by a private individual to circumvent this ruling could be punished as contempt of court.[12] As late as 1904 a Philadelphia grand jury challenged the sixty year old Pennsylvania rule. Members of the jury told Judge William W. Wiltbank they had evidence that certain constables in Philadelphia had used their official position to extort money from newly arrived immigrants. In order to obtain additional information, they asked the judge to summon witnesses in the matter. Judge Wiltbank upheld the Pennsylvania rule and denied their request. In doing so, he stated that victims of the extortion racket could not even go before the grand jury and tell their stories unless the court or the prosecutor saw fit to ask for an investigation.[13]

[11] Elliot Anthony, "Origins of Grand Juries," in *Chicago Legal News,* 1:20–21 (October 17, 1868).

[12] *Harrison vs. State,* 44 *Tennessee* 195 (1867); R. H. Stowe, "Charge to the Grand Jury," in 3 *Pittsburgh Reports,* 174 (1869); *McCullough vs. Commonwealth,* 67 *Pennsylvania State Reports* 30 (1870).

[13] *In re alleged Extortion Cases,* 13 *District Reports of Pennsylvania* 180 (1904).

In the federal courts, however, as in most states, grand juries had always been free to subpoena any and all witnesses on their own initiative. Chief Justice Salmon P. Chase urged jurors, convening in West Virgina in August, 1868, to call before them and examine fully government officials or any other persons who possessed information useful to them. He warned that, "You must not be satisfied with acting upon such cases as may be brought before you by the district attorney or by members of your body."[14] In view of Chief Justice Chase's statement of the broad rule prevailing in the federal courts, it was indeed a strange doctrine that Justice Stephen Field announced in August, 1872. Justice Field was the brother of the well-known legal reformer and codifier, David Dudley Field, who had sought to eliminate use of the grand jury in New York. The justice told a grand inquest at San Francisco, California, that they should limit their investigations to such matters as fell within their personal knowledge or were called to their attention by the court or the prosecuting attorney. He warned in particular against delving into political matters unless instructed to do so. If neither the judge nor the prosecutor placed a matter before them, Justice Field observed, "it may be safely inferred that public justice will not suffer if the matter is not considered by you." He reminded the jurors that the type of government which existed in the United States did not require the existence of a grand jury as a protection against oppressive action by the government. The restrictive charge excluded private persons from the grand jury room and curtailed the freedom of action of jurors. It represented an effort to subordinate the grand jury to the wishes of the judge and prosecutor.[15]

Criticism of the grand jury in legal circles in the United States grew stronger in the 1880's. Seymour D. Thompson and Edwin G. Merriam in their *Treatise on the Organiza-*

[14] "Charge to Grand Jury Delivered by Chief Justice Chase," in 20 *Federal Cases* 980 (1868).

[15] "Charge to the Grand Jury Delivered by Justice Field," in 30 *Federal Cases* 993 (1872); Seymour D. Thompson and Edwin G. Merriman, *A Treatise*

tion, Custody and Conduct of Juries, came out against the system and stated that the praise deserved by a few inquests had been "quite undeservedly accorded to the institution itself."[16] In 1886, Eugene Stevenson, a New Jersey public prosecutor, condemned the grand inquest as an arbitrary, irresponsible, and dangerous part of government which long ago should have come "within the range of official responsibility." He preferred the efficiency and decisiveness of a public prosecutor, observing, "It is difficult to see why a town meeting of laymen, utterly ignorant both of law and the rules of evidence, should be an appropriate tribunal. The summoning of a new body of jurors at each term insures an unfailing supply of ignorance." As a final blow, Stevenson declared that no sane statesman or legislator "would ever dream of creating such a tribunal" if it did not already exist.[17] Later in 1886, members of the American Bar Association heard David Dudley Field reiterate the demand for the efficiency of the expert in judicial proceedings. Field pointed out that the best civilization was the result of division of labor, where each person became an expert in his own specialty. Field observed that the jury system, largely because of "superstitious veneration," ignored the benefits to be derived from specialization.[18] Professor Francis Wharton, writing in an atmosphere of social turmoil in 1889, observed that the importance of grand juries shifted with the political trends of an age. At a time when excessive authority threatened, "then a grand jury, irresponsible as it is, and springing from the people, is an important safeguard of liberty." However, he emphasized that when "public order and the settled institutions of the land are in danger from momentary popular excitement, then a grand jury,

---

on the Organization, Custody and Conduct of Juries, Including Grand Juries (St. Louis, 1882), 668–672.

[16] *Ibid.,* 569.

[17] Eugene Stevenson, "Our Grand Jury System," in *Criminal Law Magazine,* 8:713–714, 719 (December, 1886); Edward Q. Keasbey, *The Courts and Lawyers of New Jersey* (New York, 1912), 3:95.

[18] Titus M. Coon, ed., *Speeches, Arguments and Miscellaneous Papers of David Dudley Field* (New York, 1890), 3:208–211.

irresponsible and secret, partaking without check of the popular impulse, may through its inquisitorial powers become an engine of great mischief to liberty as well as to order." Wharton wrote of Justice Field's "new" federal rule of 1872, "this is the view which may now be considered as accepted in the United States courts and in most of the several states." As proof of this, he cited Pennsylvania and Tennessee decisions, the only states having such a rule. In drawing this conclusion, Wharton accepted as the majority viewpoint a position which coincided closely with his desire to reduce the grand jury to a position of subservience.[19] In spite of Wharton's efforts, state and federal courts were reluctant to adopt Stephen Field's new doctrine. In March, 1891, the Supreme Court of Maryland ruled that grand juries could initiate any type of prosecution, regardless of how it came to their attention. To deny it such powers, the Maryland court insisted, would make juries useless and mere tools of the court and prosecutor. Justice David Brewer spoke the mind of the United States Supreme Court when he announced that accepted practice in America allowed grand inquests to investigate any alleged crime, "no matter how or by whom suggested to them."[20]

Those who wished to curb or eliminate the grand jury soon realized that abolishing the institution by law or constitutional amendment offered a better chance of success than did trying to restrict juries. For many years advocates of abolition had been plagued by those who pointed to the fifth amendment of the United States Constitution as standing in the way. Although state and federal courts had frequently held that the guarantee of the right to indictment in the fifth amendment applied only to the federal government, the matter had invariably come up for debate at constitutional conventions. With the adoption of the fourteenth amendment, there were those who had insisted that the

[19] Francis Wharton, *Criminal Practice and Pleading* (ninth edition, Philadelphia, 1889), 227–235.

[20] *Blaney vs. State,* 74 *Maryland* 153 (1891); *Frisbie vs. United States,* 157 *United States Court Reports* 160 (1894).

phrase "due process of law" included the right to indictment by a grand jury. As early as 1872 the Wisconsin Supreme Court decided that the fourteenth amendment did not prevent states from ceasing to use the indictment, but the question remained a point of controversy until the United States Supreme Court settled it in 1884. The test case arose in California when Joseph A. Hurtado challenged his conviction on the ground that he had been brought to trial on an information rather than an indictment. The high court gave judicial approval to states that desired to get rid of the grand inquest. Citing the Wisconsin decision with approval, the justices announced that "due process of law" included any system of prosecution which preserved liberty and justice and was not limited to indictment by a grand jury. Justice John M. Harlan's vigorous dissent stated the case for those who believed indictment by a jury of his neighbors to be the right of every American citizen.[21]

Concentrating their efforts on eliminating the grand inquest entirely, lawyers, jurists, and reformers emphasized the danger of lay interference in judicial matters and called for efficiency in administering justice. Meetings of professional associations were the most common scenes of attacks on the institution.[22] Speaking before the annual convention of the Ohio State Bar Association in July, 1892, Justice Henry B. Brown of the United States Supreme Court proposed abolishing the grand inquest as a means of simplifying criminal procedure. He saw in public prosecutors a far more efficient means of bringing offenders to trial.[23] O'Brien J. Atkinson, Michigan attorney, told members of the Michigan State Bar Association that he could not conceive of any condition where a grand jury would be desirable "or where its secret methods would not be productive of evil." He warned those states which had not followed Michigan's

[21] *Rowan vs. State*, 30 *Wisconsin* 129 (1872); *Hurtado vs. California*, 110 *United States Court Reports* 516 (1884).
[22] "Grand Juries," in *Law Times*, 91:205 (July 18, 1891).
[23] "Address by Justice Brown," in *Proceedings of the Ohio State Bar Association*, 13:42–43 (July, 1892).

lead in abolishing the institution that an accusing body with power to pry into public and private affairs in a secret manner could become a grave threat to liberty in America.[24] The Territorial Bar Association of Utah met in convention at Salt Lake City in January, 1896. Territorial leaders were preparing themselves for another try at statehood and the forthcoming constitutional convention was uppermost in their minds. In his presidential address, J. G. Sutherland recommended that grand juries be eliminated after statehood. Sutherland denounced inquests as useless, oppressive, and expensive and proclaimed that social and political changes in the United States had made them "undesirable as well as unnecessary."[25] C. E. Chiperfield told members of the State's Attorneys Association of Illinois, in 1897, that the average grand juror possessed few of the qualifications essential to his duties. Lack of legal training, he contended, led jurors to "wander through time and eternity in a curious way," often allowing hard luck stories to influence their deliberations. Chiperfield implored, "In the name of progress which is inevitable, I invoke ... the abolition of that relic of antiquity, the twin sister of the inquisition, the grand jury in Illinois."[26]

Charles P. Hogan used the same line of attack when he took the opportunity of his presidential address to urge members of the Vermont Bar Association to oppose the grand inquest. Characterizing it as "a cumbersome and expensive piece of legal machinery," he announced that there was no reason that it should continue to exist "in this enlightened and progressive age." Hogan suggested discarding the grand jury as the English had discarded the ordeal and trial by fire.[27] In July, 1905, the Committee on Law Re-

[24] "Address of O'Brien J. Atkinson to the Michigan State Bar Association," in *Michigan Law Journal*, 3:259–260, 266 (September, 1894).

[25] *Report of the Second Annual Meeting of the Territorial Bar Association of Utah* (1895), 12–14.

[26] C. E. Chiperfield, "The Abolition of the Grand Jury," in *American Lawyer*, 5:488–490 (October, 1897).

[27] Charles P. Hogan, "The Grand Jury System," in *Reports of the Vermont Bar Association*, 5:85–89 (1898).

form of the Iowa Bar Association recommended and the Association adopted a resolution calling for prosecution upon information. Judge M. J. Wade of Iowa City sought to ridicule members who did not fall into line, when he stated tartly, "there are some persons in this world who are wedded to antiquity, revel in cobwebs, and they simply worship whiskers." Judge Wade tempted his colleagues, saying, "Let us do away with a few things and maintain the law for the benefit of the lawyers who are to convict guilty men."[28] Justice Brown of the United States Supreme Court reiterated his dissatisfaction with the grand jury system in an address to the American Bar Association, in 1905. In January, 1906, George Lawyer, Albany attorney, challenged members of the New York State Bar Association to rid their state of grand juries. To continue to countenance such an institution, he warned, was to concede that under a republican form of government the liberties of the individual were in danger just as they had been under a despotism of the dark ages. Lawyer denounced the "arbitrary power" which inquests exercised to inquire into and criticize the acts of public officials. He insisted that under the American form of government the people "require no shield to protect them from the state's aggressions."[29]

Gradually, critics shifted the basis of their public opposition to the grand jury. They ceased to demand that laymen not interfere in matters in which they were untrained. Such statements had an unpleasant, undemocratic ring and might actually rally support for the institution. Instead, they placed increased emphasis on the waste of time and money that grand juries entailed. H. N. Atkinson, a Houston attorney, told members of the Texas Bar Association that "a useless and unnecessary piece of legal machinery" cost Texas counties between $100,000 and $200,000 each year, in addition to taking men away from their homes and busi-

---

[28] *Proceedings of the Iowa State Bar Association,* 11:58, 141 (1905).

[29] George Lawyer, "Should the Grand Jury System Be Abolished?" in *Report of the New York State Bar Association,* 29:29–43 (January, 1906).

nesses to do work "which one man can do just as well."[30]
Aaron Hahn of Cleveland repeated this argument when
urging that the 1912 Ohio constitutional convention eliminate the grand jury from that state.[31] In June, 1915, William Howard Taft appeared before the Judiciary Committee of the New York State Constitutional Convention and
took the occasion to press home an attack on the grand jury
system. Drawing upon his experience as a judge, the ex-
president criticized it as a "bulky and costly" institution
that served only to relieve district attorneys of responsibility for prosecutions. He heartily endorsed the movement
to substitute a legal expert for an unwieldy body of laymen.
The New York convention considered several proposed
amendments limiting the use of grand juries but did not
adopt them.[32]

At a time when most legal scholars advised abandoning
the grand inquest as an archaic relic of the distant past,
a few defenders appeared. Judge Harman Yerkes of Pennsylvania expressed the belief that the grand juries could
provide a means of extending popular control over government. In September, 1901, he told jurors of Bucks County
that bodies such as theirs representing the people of the community, were not outmoded or useless. In times of great
public peril or in the event of deep-seated abuses, he observed, "the divided, yet powerful and also combined responsibility of the secret session of the grand jury . . . has
worked out great problems of reform and correction." He
pointed out that abolition of the grand inquest would leave
the accused citizen completely at the mercy of "an unjust
or unwise judge or district attorney," or subject to the con-
trivances of an unscrupulous prosecutor. Judge Yerkes dis-

---

[30] H. N. Atkinson, "The Useless Grand Jury," in *Law Notes*, 15:109–110
(September, 1911).
[31] *Journal of the Constitutional Convention of Ohio* (Columbus, 1912), 55.
[32] *New York Times*, June 12, 1915; "Judge Taft and the New York Constitutional Convention," in *Virginia Law Register*, new series, 1:226 (July,
1915); *Revised Record of the Constitutional Convention of New York* (Albany, 1915), 1:221–222.

pelled the often repeated idea that because the United States was not ruled by a tyrannical king, grand juries had ceased to be necessary as guardians of individual liberty. He explained that tyrants even more irresponsible than the despots of old sought to dominate local, state, and national governments. Giant business monopolies restless of legal restraints and party bosses who did not hesitate to break judges and create courts took the place of tyrannical monarchs as a danger to freedom in the United States. Against such ruthless forces Judge Yerkes saw grand juries as powerful agencies of the people, challenging business or boss domination of government.[33] Edward Lindsey, of the American Institute of Criminal Law, hailed broad inquisitorial powers as an essential part of judicial machinery, which could secure information otherwise unobtainable. Lindsey pointed out that prosecutors and police departments were at best feeble substitutes for the powerful grand inquest. Although Lindsey defended the grand jury against those who would have destroyed it, in doing so he adopted the criteria used by its critics. He sought to justify the institution on the grounds of efficiency.[34] On this point the grand jury was particularly vulnerable. Few persons familiar with its operations would have denied that a prosecuting officer could act with greater speed and singleness of purpose.

It remained for a layman well experienced in the work of the grand jury to defend it as a democratic agency. Publisher George Haven Putnam recognized that inquests could be slow and unwieldy bodies which frequently tried the patience of judges and prosecutors, but he did not believe it fair to judge the institution solely on that basis. After serving on grand juries in New York City over a period of thirty-five years, Putnam became convinced that no other institution provided such a degree of popular participation

[33] "Charge to the Grand Jury of Bucks County, Pennsylvania," in 24 *Pennsylvania County Reports,* 164–165 (1901).
[34] Edward Lindsey, "Functions of the Grand Jury," in *Journal of the American Institute of Criminal Law and Criminology,* 4:169–171 (June, 1913).

in government. He openly challenged the advice of ex-President Taft, announcing, "There is no other way citizens can bring criticism directly to bear upon public officials." Putnam viewed inquests as more than mere law enforcement bodies. During their term of office jurors acted as representatives of the people of the county and in that capacity could summon before them any public official, high or low. When such bodies ceased to sit, the publisher observed, the cause of popular government would have suffered a severe blow. In 1915, Putnam and others convinced of the necessity of preserving the institution in America organized the Grand Jury Association of New York County. They sought to publicize the importance of the grand inquest to democratic government and to blunt the attack on lay interference.[35]

But it was not within the province of lawyers, jurists, or publicists either to abolish or to retain the grand jury in the United States. That battle had to be fought in the legislatures and constitutional conventions in the individual states. Throughout the period from 1865 to 1917, in state after state opponents of the grand jury made great strides toward eliminating the system entirely. The rash of postwar conventions to frame and revise state constitutions, as well as the creation of new western states, gave them an opportunity to be heard. In the South, the Radicals made no attempt to eliminate grand juries in the constitutions they drafted, and when the southern Bourbons came to write new constitutions, they did not even consider eliminating an institution that had proved so useful in opposing an unfriendly central government during the Reconstruction period. It was in the West, despite that area's recent experience with the value of the institution on the frontier, that legislators and convention delegates were most receptive to proposals to streamline their judicial machinery. By 1917, only four western states retained the grand jury.

[35] George H. Putnam, *Memories of a Publisher* (New York, 1915), 310–313; George H. Putnam, "Grand Jury of the County of New York," in *Annals of the American Academy of Political and Social Science*, 52:37–55 (March, 1914); *New York Times*, February 28, 1930.

In Wisconsin opponents of the system resumed their pre-war campaign to abolish the institution, pointing to the speed and ease with which prosecutors accused offenders in Michigan, where the grand inquest was dead. In contrast they pictured Wisconsin juries as "secret conclaves of criminal accusers, repugnant to the American system."[36] Assemblyman Andrew J. Turner introduced, in January, 1869, a resolution to amend the state constitution to end the grand jury. Although a majority of the Judiciary Committee favored delay in the matter, a minority group issued a vigorous report denouncing the system and brushed aside all opposition. In the Senate, as in the Assembly, anti-jury forces painted a black picture of the institution and took advantage of their superior unity of purpose to gain the support of doubtful senators. Defenders of the grand jury advised caution, but the spirit of advancement and reform swept away their objections. Governor Lucius Fairchild approved the joint resolution when it passed both houses of the legislature in 1869,[37] and again in 1870.[38] The question then became one for the people of Wisconsin to decide. Apathy and indifference marked the campaign which followed. Interest in state and local candidates overshadowed the proposed amendment. A few Democratic newspapers conducted editorial campaigns against abolition, charging that it was a Republican measure, but they made little headway. The *Grant County Herald* announced that a Republican scheme to get control of criminal prosecutions lay behind the amendment. The *Milwaukee News* warned that killing the grand jury was "another step onward in the concentration of

[36] *Milwaukee Sentinel,* May 3, 1867, January 23, February 17, 1868; Madison, *Wisconsin State Journal,* January 22, 1868; *Janesville* (Wisconsin) *Gazette,* February 19, 1868.

[37] *Wisconsin Assembly Journal,* 1869, pp. 39, 400–440, 565, 944; *Wisconsin Senate Journal,* 1869, pp. 526, 600; *Wisconsin State Journal,* February 19, 25, March 5, 1869; *Milwaukee Sentinel,* March 1, 1869; *General Laws of Wisconsin,* 1869, p. 270, Joint Resolution no. 7; Letter from E. Steele to Governor Lucius Fairchild, November 28, 1868, in Fairchild Manuscripts, in the Wisconsin State Historical Society.

[38] *Wisconsin Assembly Journal,* 1870, p. 535; *Wisconsin Senate Journal,* 1870, p. 67; *General Laws of Wisconsin,* 1870, chapter 118.

power," a process that the recent war had hastened. It cautioned against destroying a popular institution which might be necessary to oppose the tyranny of the federal government.[39] In answer to such attacks, proponents of the amendment assumed the role of reformers, struggling to rid the state of an "expensive, unjust system."[40] In the referendum, on November 7, 1870, the people of Wisconsin voted overwhelmingly for reform. Thereafter, the grand jury was to appear in Wisconsin only when one had been specially summoned by a judge.[41]

While opponents of the grand jury in Wisconsin were struggling to rid their state of the institution, their compatriots in Illinois won a partial triumph. They succeeded in getting the constitutional convention meeting in Springfield in 1870 to give the legislature the power to abolish the system. Such a procedure avoided any direct referendum on the matter.[42] Shortly after adoption of the new constitution a special legislative committee urged the legislators to exercise their new authority and eliminate "so thoroughly despotic and subversive" an institution. Petitions approved the committee's advice, but the legislature failed to act on the proposal.[43]

There followed in the United States a series of constitutional conventions in which the question of retaining the grand jury system became an important issue. Delegates assembled at Charleston, West Virginia, in 1872, refused to be swayed by talk of progress and voted down proposals to

[39] Lancaster (Wisconsin), *Grant County Herald,* October 25, 1870; *Milwaukee News,* October 30, November 5, 1870; *Milwaukee Sentinel,* November 17, 1870.

[40] *Wisconsin State Journal,* October 17, 1870; Oshkosh (Wisconsin) *City Times,* November 2, 1870.

[41] *Milwaukee Sentinel,* January 9, 1871; Wisconsin Constitution of 1848, article 1, section 8, as amended, in Francis N. Thorpe, ed., *The Federal and State Constitutions* (Washington, D.C., 1909), 7:4099.

[42] *Debates and Proceedings of the Constitutional Convention of Illinois, 1869–1870* (Springfield, 1870), 176, 202, 1569–1573; Illinois Constitution of 1870, article 2, section 8, in Thorpe, *Federal and State Constitutions,* 2:1014.

[43] "Report of the Special Committee on the Grand Jury System," in *Reports to the General Assembly of Illinois,* 1873, vol. 4; *Journal of the Senate of Illinois,* 1873, p. 300.

turn all criminal prosecution over to public officials.[44] Advocates of reform were more successful in the Ohio constitutional convention where they deleted the guarantee of a grand jury indictment in all criminal cases. Ohio retained the institution, however, when the people refused to approve the new constitution.[45] In Missouri, in contrast to most states, grand juries actually strengthened their authority, with a direct constitutional mandate to investigate all officials having charge of public funds at least once each year.[46] Anti-jury forces fared better in the western conventions. Nebraska's Constitution of 1875 allowed the legislature to "abolish, limit, change or amend" the grand jury system. Ten years later the legislators exercised this power and inquests became extinct in another state.[47] In 1876, Colorado followed the lead of Nebraska and put the matter up to the legislature, which abolished grand juries shortly thereafter.[48] The California Constitution of 1879 allowed prosecution of criminal offenses upon the information of a prosecutor, but it also stipulated that grand juries attend court in each county at least once a year.[49] In a special referendum held in Iowa in November, 1884, the legislature was given authority to abolish grand juries.[50]

The year 1889 saw six territories come into the Union as states and the virtual disappearance of the grand jury from

[44] *Journal of the Constitutional Convention Assembled at Charleston, West Virginia, 1872* (Charleston, 1872), 37, 58.

[45] *Proceedings and Debates of the Third Constitutional Convention of Ohio, 1872* (Cleveland, 1873–1874), 1:113, 191; 2:1737.

[46] *Debates of the Missouri Constitutional Convention of 1875* (Columbia, 1930–1945), 1:264–265; "Missouri Constitution of 1875," article 2, section 12; article 14, section 10, in Thorpe, *Federal and State Constitutions*, 4:2230, 2269.

[47] Nebraska Constitution of 1875, article 1, section 10, in Thorpe, *Federal and State Constitutions*, 4:2362; *Laws of Nebraska, 1885*, chapter 108, section 1.

[48] *Proceedings of the Constitutional Convention for the State of Colorado* (Denver, 1907), 115, 198–200; "Colorado Constitution of 1876," article 2, section 8, 23, in Thorpe, *Federal and State Constitutions*, 1:476, 477. *Laws of Colorado, 1883*, pp. 160–161.

[49] *Debates and Proceedings of the Constitutional Convention of the State of California* (Sacramento, 1880), 81, 150–151, 308–315; *Statutes of California, 1881*, p. 71.

[50] Amendment to article 1, section 11, in Thorpe, *Federal and State Constitutions*, 2:1157.

large areas of the West. Opponents of the grand jury emerged completely victorious from the constitutional conventions that prepared them for statehood. Idaho, Montana, and Washington abolished the use of the grand inquest except for special occasions, while North Dakota, South Dakota, and Wyoming left the question up to their legislatures. In the Idaho convention the expense of the juries, particularly in thinly settled areas, provided a potent argument in winning delegates to the cause of abolition. Antijury leaders claimed that the average indictment cost the people $600 to $1,000 and predicted savings amounting to thousands of dollars each year if inquests ceased to exist. There was no lack of defenders, however, who warned against handing political officials the power of accusation and stressed the need for a people's body to check on local officials. In spite of their efforts, the proponents of efficiency and economy prevailed in Idaho.[51] Delegates attending the Montana convention at Helena in the heat of July, 1889, faced the same decision. Rallying around the slogan, "Let Montana cut the thread that binds us to the barbarous past," advocates of abolition attacked the grand inquest as an outmoded and even dangerous institution. They cited Wisconsin as a model. Defenders of the jury opposed hasty action as a step in the direction of centralization, the removal of one of the important barriers "which serves to protect the rights of the citizen against the government." Despite such protests, a majority of the Montana delegates favored eliminating the grand jury.[52] It met the same fate on the floor of the Washington constitutional convention. In the three other new states, the stories were similar. Promises of economy and lower taxes prevailed against warnings not to kill a democratic institution. Legislatures in North Dakota, South Dakota, and Wyoming abolished the grand jury.[53]

[51] *Proceedings and Debates of the Constitutional Convention of Idaho* (Caldwell, 1912), 260–270, 2050.

[52] *Proceedings and Debates of the Constitutional Convention of Montana, 1889* (Helena, 1921), 100–105, 112–114, 251.

[53] Washington Constitution of 1889, article 1, section 25, 26, in Thorpe, *Federal and State Constitution,* 7:3975; *Proceedings and Debates of the First*

Reformers had their way in a number of other western states. In Oregon the legislature exercised the privilege given it in the state constitution and substituted the information for the indictment in criminal proceedings.[54] In 1900, citizens of Missouri overwhelmingly approved amendments relinquishing grand jury duties to district attorneys.[55] In November, 1904, residents of Minnesota approved abolishing the system in their state. The referendum on the change in the constitution evoked but little discussion and went almost completely unnoticed in the excitement of a presidential election year.[56] Arizona had abandoned the grand jury even as a territory, and the constitutional convention of 1911 voted to continue the practice of prosecuting upon an information.[57]

Opponents of the grand jury suffered occasional reverses in their effort to drive the institution from the American legal system. In 1902, the people of California, where grand juries had gained a reputation as enemies of municipal corruption, rejected a proposed constitutional amendment to end the use of grand inquests.[58] Delegates who met at Guthrie, Oklahoma, in 1906, to frame a constitution for statehood, agreed to abolish regular sessions of the inquest, but they did not wish to leave the question of summoning a grand jury entirely up to the local judges. The Oklahomans did what no other Americans had ever done: provided that the people could call a grand jury when they thought it necessary. The signatures of one hundred resident taxpayers in a county were sufficient to launch an in-

Constitutional Convention of North Dakota (Bismarck, 1889), 364–365; *South Dakota Constitutional Debates* (Huron, 1907), 2:11, 131; *Journal and Debates of the Constitutional Convention of Wyoming* (Cheyenne, 1893), 716, 726; *Laws of North Dakota,* 1890, chapter 71, sections 1, 9; *Laws of Wyoming,* 1890, chapter 59, sections 1, 14; *Laws of South Dakota,* 1895, chapter 64, sections 1, 9.
[54] *Laws of Oregon,* 1899, sections 1, 100, pp. 99–100.
[55] Walter F. Dodd, *The Revision and Amendment of State Constitutions* (Baltimore, 1910), 322.
[56] *Ibid.,* 320; *Minneapolis Journal,* October 28, 1904.
[57] *Minutes of the Constitutional Convention of Arizona* (Phoenix, 1911), article 2, section 20; article 6, section 6.
[58] Dodd, *Revision and Amendment of State Constitutions,* 297.

vestigation.[59] In January, 1908, William S. U'Ren, Charles H. Cary, and other progressive leaders advocated a return to the grand jury system as a part of their program to increase popular control of the government in Oregon. They made use of the initiative petition to bring the question of a constitutional amendment before the people. The referendum evoked little debate. Opponents of the amendment accused grand juries of being responsible for long delays in justice, while progressive leaders replied with the charge that the information system enabled district attorneys to use criminal prosecutions for political purposes. On June 1, 1908, after nine years without them, residents of Oregon voted two to one to restore grand juries in their state.[60] In New Mexico the people expressed themselves in favor of retaining control over criminal prosecutions. At public hearings conducted by the Committee on the Bill of Rights of the New Mexico Constitutional Convention in 1910, popular opinion favored keeping the grand jury, and the new constitution retained it.[61]

Despite a few reverses, reformers had succeeded, by 1917, in making long strides toward abolishing the grand inquest in the United States and other common law countries. England was on the verge of dropping it, and the majority of Canadian legal opinion was against it. In the United States legal circles were generally anti-jury on grounds of inefficiency, expense, and lay interference in professional matters. Further, vast areas in the United States had done away with it. In the East the reformers had succeeded only partially, in the South hardly at all, and in the West overwhelmingly. Only four western states, Texas, California, Oregon, and New Mexico, summoned jurors regularly.

[59] Thorpe, *Federal and State Constitutions*, 7:4274.
[60] *Portland Oregonian*, May 26, 1908; Charles H. Cary, ed., *The Constitution and Debates of the Constitutional Convention* (Salem, 1926), article 7, section 18, p. 444; Allen H. Eaton, *The Oregon System* (Chicago, 1912), 70, 166.
[61] *Proceedings of the Constitutional Convention of New Mexico* (Albuquerque, 1910), 82–85, 197.

Chapter 10

The Trans-Mississippi Frontier

SETTLERS MOVING ACROSS THE MISSISSIPPI, like earlier settlers moving across the Appalachians, took the grand jury with them.[1] The institution had proved its value on earlier frontiers and the new one was not vastly different in this respect. The jury proved an effective instrument for the preservation of law and order in the newly settled communities and it gave local citizens a voice in their government that they might not otherwise have had. It is true that states in the trans-Mississippi area were quick to abandon the grand inquest once the territorial stage was passed, but this was more a measure of the success of the legal reformers than it was of the failure of the institution in its ancient role of citizen prosecutor and defender of local interests.

In creating territories in the West after the year 1836, Congress followed the pattern set in organizing the Territory of Wisconsin. There were no separate federal courts. Judicial authority was placed in district courts and a supreme court appointed by the president, and the district courts tried cases under both federal and territorial laws. In some territories, courts summoned separate grand juries, while in others they used but one panel. Before 1864 Congress left qualifications and methods of selecting grand jurors to the territorial legislatures.[2] Qualifications were

[1] The bulk of the material in this chapter originally appeared as the author's "The Grand Jury on the Trans-Mississippi," in the *Southwestern Social Science Quarterly*, 36:148–159 (September, 1955), and is used with permission.
[2] *United States Statutes at Large,* 5:10 (1836), Wisconsin Territory; 5:235 (1838), Iowa Territory; 9:323 (1848), Oregon Territory; 9:403 (1849), Minnesota Territory; 9:446 (1850), New Mexico Territory; 9:453 (1850), Utah Territory; 10:277 (1854), Kansas and Nebraska territories; 10:172 (1853), Washington Territory; 12:172 (1861), Colorado Territory; 12:209 (1861),

not high. There were no property requirements. In most cases being a qualified elector in the county was sufficient. In Colorado, "known professional gamblers" could not serve, while in New Mexico the law barred aliens. In Arizona, where there was a Mormon colony, the territory followed the lead of the federal government and prohibited persons who practiced or condoned polygamy from serving on grand juries which might pass upon such offenses. In most territories sheriffs selected grand jurors from a list prepared by the county commissioners. Penalties for failure to answer a summons for jury duty varied from a fine of five dollars in New Mexico to one of twenty-five dollars in Arizona. All territories except Oregon permitted persons to challenge the entire panel on the ground of improper drawing or to challenge the qualifications of individual jurors.[3]

Composed as they were of representative persons from the community, grand juries that attended western courts differed little from those which sat at courts throughout the nation. Only in the territories of Wyoming and Washington did women take their places in the grand jury box along with the men. Dakotans chided residents of Wyoming on their innovation and told of the results of one such jury. It deliberated five days and nights and returned no indictments, but there were alleged to have been five elopements. In Tacoma, Washington, an inquest that included five married women embarked on a campaign to wipe prostitution from the city.[4]

Nevada Territory; 12:239 (1862), Dakota Territory; 12:664 (1863), Arizona Territory; 12:808 (1863), Idaho Territory; 13:85 (1864), Montana Territory.
[3] *Statutes of New Mexico Territory,* 1865, chapter 69, sections 4, 5, 8, 9; chapter 70, sections 1 and 10; *Statutes of New Mexico Territory,* 1855, chapter 30, sections 1, 3, 10; *Statutes of Colorado,* 1867, chapter 49, section 1; *Laws of Oregon,* 1843–1872, chapter 5, sections 31 and 35; *Statutes of Minnesota,* 1866, chapter 107, sections 3, 5, 6, 7, 8; *Laws of the Territory of Idaho,* 1873, pp. 5–6; *Code of the Territory of Washington,* 1881, chapter 152, sections 2078 and 2080; *Laws of Arizona Territory,* 1885, p. 340; *Compiled Laws of Wyoming,* 1876, chapter 69, sections 1, 5, 6, 8, 9, 10; *Revised Codes of the Territory of Dakota,* 1877, chapter 37, sections 778–780; chapter 7, sections 117–160.
[4] Yankton (Dakota Territory), *Daily Press and Dakotaian,* October 9, 1875; *Rosencrantz vs. Territory,* 2 *Washington Territorial Reports* 267 (1884).

Court day in the frontier towns of the trans-Mississippi West, like the same occasion on earlier frontiers, brought with it an air of anticipation and suspense. Local residents who had grievances made plans to lay them before the grand jury; persons in jail waited anxiously to see if they would have to stand trial; and the whole town speculated as to the indictments the grand inquest would return. The trials that inevitably followed a sitting of the grand jury would provide a free show for all who could squeeze into the crude courthouse, while the verdicts would serve as topics for endless debate in the days to come. Social life in the frontier county seat quickened while the district court was in session. New faces could be seen on the streets and in the saloons of the town. The judge and the very mobile bar that accompanied him from county to county brought with them news and anecdotes of trials in other communities. The presence in town of litigants, witnesses, and prospective jurors added to the opportunity of renewing old friendships and meeting newcomers. In the evenings veteran lawyers regaled their younger colleagues with stories of practice on the frontier. Gamblers and swindlers made good use of the occasion to reap a harvest. A lack of accommodations in frontier towns frequently left jurors, as well as other persons attending court, to shift for themselves. Grand jurors attending court at Alma, Kansas, slept in a haymow, while the entire court, jurors, judge, witnesses, prisoners and lawyers, meeting at Sheridan, Dakota Territory, slept in the log courthouse on a mud floor.

Frontier courts met in all manner of buildings: in shanties hurriedly constructed of rawhide lumber, in log courthouses, in private homes, or in saloons. In some localities the crude courthouse also served as a community center where a Methodist circuit rider or a Baptist missionary might hold forth. As in most frontier areas, courts were extremely informal. The judge and attorneys as well as the jurors and spectators chewed tobacco, smoked, or whittled during the sessions of court.

The first order of business after the judge had convened the court was to draw and swear the members of the grand jury. The clerk of court drew the names from a list already prepared by the justice of the peace and the county commissioners. If no one challenged the fitness of any of the men, the judge told the jurors of their duties, advised them of any matters he thought they should consider, and sent them out to hear witnesses and deliberate in secret session. In many cases, since most courthouses were only one room cabins, this meant going outdoors. The grand jury heard the evidence against all persons arrested since the last term of court and returned a true bill when it believed the evidence warranted a trial or refused to indict when it did not. In addition, any individual in the community was free to go before the grand jury and present evidence against any other person. Jurors possessed the authority to call before the inquest all persons who could assist them in their investigations, whether they were private citizens or government officials. These broad powers put them in an excellent position to supervise the activities of public officials and indict or report to the people those guilty of malfeasance or corruption. At the conclusion of their deliberations the jurors gave the judge the indictments they had found and reported to the court on the condition of the county. Frequently these reports set forth community grievances with a request that the judge forward them to state authorities. At the end of the session a celebration, at which the jurors marked the successful completion of their duties, was usually in order. Occasionally the members of the bar entertained the jurors as they did following court in Houston County, Texas in 1838 and a few succeeded in getting the jurors "gloriously drunk."[5]

Judges of early western courts were men of varying character. Political appointees from the East generally pre-

[5] Ikie G. Patteson, *Loose Leaves: A History of Delta County* [Texas] (Dallas, 1935), 21; G. H. Barid, *A Brief History of Upshur County* [Texas] (Gilmer, Texas, 1946), 13; John W. Rogers, *The Lusty Texans of Dallas* (New York, 1951), 67; *History of Ellis County, Texas* (Chicago, 1892), 135–136;

sided over territorial and federal courts, and these men were not always of the highest calibre. Local residents made little attempt to hide their resentment against bad appointees. In 1870, the *Owyhee Avalanche* of Silver City, Idaho Territory, protested indignantly against judges "which the powers that be, commonly select from among the political fungi of the states east of us." The ranks of frontier judges also included such characters as Judge Roy Bean, rough and uneducated, who upheld the law almost single-handed, or "Hanging Judge" Parker, who made his name the scourge of the Indian Territory. Frontier jurists seldom neglected, on the occasion of charging the grand jury, to give a rousing stump speech. Reports of the opening of court at Yankton, Dakota Territory, praised the two hour charge delivered by the chief justice as "elaborate, able and eloquent." Where there were large Mormon colonies judges seemingly never tired of dwelling on the horrors of polygamy and asking punishment of all those who would "substitute the harem for the slave pen." At Fort Smith, Arkansas, the "Hanging Judge," Isaac C. Parker, dismissed grand jurors who opposed capital punishment and warned those who remained against "the tricks and artifices of the guilty." He was ever alert to admonish juries against "sickly sentimentality in favor of crime."[6]

Territorial legislatures frequently imposed specific duties upon grand juries in addition to their broad task of investigating all public offenses. They often directed inquests

Armistead A. Aldrich, *The History of Houston County, Texas* (San Antonio, 1943), 30; George L. Crocket, *Two Centuries in East Texas* (Dallas, 1932), 255–256; Charles H. Carey, *A General History of Oregon* (Portland, 1935), 2:485; Beatrice G. Gay, *Into the Setting Sun: A History of Colman County* [Texas] (Santa Ana, Texas, 1942), 40–41; Guy Waring, *My Pioneer Past* (Boston, 1936), 220–221; William Hase, *History of Dixon County, Nebraska* (Ponca City, Nebraska, 1896), 64; Estelline Bennett, *Old Deadwood Days* (New York, 1928), 36–38; Matt Thomson, *Early History of Wabaunsee County, Kansas* (Alma, Kansas, 1901), 31–32.

[6] Willie A. Chalfant, *Tales of the Pioneers* (Stanford University, 1942), 17; Fred H. Harrington, *Hanging Judge* (Caldwell, Idaho, 1951), 59; Silver City (Idaho), *Owyhee Avalanche*, September 3, 1870; S. W. Harman, *Hell on the Border* (Ft. Smith, Arkansas, 1898), 466, 487, 491–492; *Daily Press and Dakotaian*, November 16, 1877.

to visit and report upon conditions in jails within their county. In Arizona and New Mexico they charged inquests to investigate all "wilful and corrupt misconduct of public officials."[7] But even in those jurisdictions where there was no specific statute, grand juries denounced and indicted officials they found guilty of malfeasance or corruption. The grand inquest attending court at Tucson, Arizona Territory, in November, 1871, denounced bitterly army officers in the region who traded with Indians, giving arms and ammunition in return for game. Such deals, they protested, "sentenced white men to death at the murdering hand of the Apache." The jurors demanded that the army stop allowing Indians to use army camps as rest and supply bases for their raids on the surrounding countryside. They called public attention to widespread corruption among ration officers who profited by selling food designated for distribution to the Indians and accused army officers of giving liquor to the Indians and using Indian women for purposes of prostitution.[8] In March, 1872, the United States grand jury at Brownsville, Texas, declared that a "reign of terror" existed in the area between the Nueces and Rio Grande rivers. It protested that marauding bands from Mexico crossed the border at will, stealing cattle and plundering. The jurors blamed the situation on the lack of an adequate cavalry force and remonstrated against officials in Washington who had ignored repeated requests for assistance. They called upon Texas representatives in Congress to attend to the problem or the people of the area would have to "meet the invaders and despoilers as freemen should, with ball and blade."[9] In September, 1873, the grand jury of Deer Lodge County, Montana Territory, investigated the dealings of the

[7] *Statutes of New Mexico Territory,* 1865, chapter 69, sections 4, 5, 8, 9; chapter 70, sections 1 and 10; *Penal Code of California,* 1872, section 923; *Statutes of Montana,* 1881, p. 308, section 149.

[8] *San Francisco Bulletin,* November 10, 1871; *New York Times,* November 11, 1871.

[9] "Investigation of Indian Frauds," *House Report No. 98,* 42nd Congress, 3rd session (1872–1873), serial 1578, pp. 235–236.

United States Indian agent and uncovered a "ring" that bought and sold goods sent for distribution to the Indians. The inquest at Cheyenne, Wyoming Territory, indicted the federal Indian agent stationed there for stealing twenty thousand pounds of sugar.[10]

County officials were also subject to scrutiny by the probing eye of the grand jury. In Wasco County, Oregon, jurors charged the county judge and the county clerk with receiving illegal fees. The inquest of Kimble County, Texas, sought to oust the local judge and sheriff because they failed to enforce the laws. An inquiry in Custer County, Montana Territory, resulted in indictments against three officials for contriving to defraud the county. A like investigation in Richland County, Dakota Territory, turned up corruption on the part of a county commissioner. In Phoenix, Arizona Territory, a grand jury took the initiative in uncovering graft among county officials. It not only uncovered corruption, but awakened the community to the need of a thorough housecleaning.[11] The grand inquest of Fremont County, Iowa, called the attention of the community to extravagance, "and in some cases something worse," in connection with expenses of the county court. It reported that the county judge had not accounted for all fees paid to him. Jurors in Gage County, Nebraska, indicted the treasurer for the embezzlement of $547, while in Ormsby County, Nevada, the inquest told the court that Robert Logan had failed to account for $1,918 received while he was county tax collector. In Deer Lodge County, Montana, the grand jury denounced a justice of the peace for demanding fees not allowed to him by law.[12]

[10] *United States vs. Ensign,* 2 *Montana* 86 (1876); *United States vs. Upham,* 2 *Montana* 113 (1874); *McCann vs. United States,* 2 *Wyoming* 274 (1880).

[11] *State vs. Packard,* 4 *Oregon* 157 (1871); *State vs. Perham,* 4 *Oregon* 188 (1871); Ovie C. Fisher, *It Occurred in Kimble* (Houston, 1937), 212; *Territory vs. Garland,* 6 *Montana* 14 (1886); *State vs. Bauer,* 1 *North Dakota* 273 (1890); *Phoenix* (Arizona Territory) *Weekly Herald,* April 9, 1896.

[12] *Rector vs. Smith,* 11 *Iowa* 302 (1860); Hugh J. Dobbs, *History of Gage County, Nebraska* (Lincoln, Nebraska, 1918), 323; *State vs. Logan,* 1 *Nevada* 510 (1865); *Territory vs. McElroy,* 1 *Montana* 86 (1868).

Law and order was one of the most serious concerns of grand juries throughout the West. At almost every session frontier grand juries returned bills for illegal gambling, selling liquor on Sunday or to Indians, and cattle and horse stealing. Local residents often regarded horse and cattle stealing, claim jumping, theft of gold or silver ore, as grounds for hanging, if not always at the hands of the law, then under the direction of a vigilance committee. In regions where grazing was important, hardly a grand jury met that did not indict for cattle stealing, and persons sitting on grand juries were frequently members of vigilance associations formed to deal with cattle thieves. In Colorado the supreme court held that such persons were free to serve on inquests. But in 1855 the inquest sitting at Yamhill County, Oregon Territory, indicted a large number of persons for vigilante activity. They had taken the law into their own hands and administered a whipping to a recalcitrant member of the community. The first grand jury to attend a court in the Territory of New Mexico returned bills of indictment against seven persons for murder, two for treason, five for stealing, and three for receiving stolen goods. Subsequent juries in New Mexico often required the services of an interpreter because so few members could understand English.[13] Some inquests took into consideration the unsettled

[13] *United States vs. Tom,* 1 *Oregon* 26 (1853); *Fowler vs. United States,* 1 *Washington Territory* 3 (1854); and *Palmer vs. United States,* 1 *Washington Territory* 5 (1854) are for selling liquor to Indians. *Wood vs. Territory,* 1 *Oregon* 223 (1846); *State vs. Sweet,* 2 *Oregon* 125 (1865), for the illegal sale of liquor. *State vs. Johnson,* 2 *Oregon* 115 (1864), for horse stealing; *Territory vs. Perkins,* 2 *Montana* 469 (1876), for assault to commit murder; *Territory vs. Stears,* 2 *Montana* 325 (1875), for murder; *Territory vs. Perea,* 1 *New Mexico* 625 (1879), for murder by shooting; *Boyle vs. People,* 4 *Colorado* 176 (1878), in which grand jurors were members of a vigilance association; *Christ vs. People,* 3 *Colorado* 394 (1877), for larceny of cattle; *State vs. Brown,* 8 *Nevada* 208 (1873), for cattle stealing. *Territory vs. Big Knot on Head,* 6 *Montana* 242 (1878); *Scales vs. State,* 5 *Texas Court of Appeals* 498 (1878); *Crockett vs. State,* 5 *Texas Court of Appeals* 526 (1879); and *People vs. Garns,* 2 *Utah* 260 (1878), are all for cattle theft. *Newby vs. State,* 1 *Oregon* 163 (1855), for vigilance activity; *Territory vs. Mackey,* 8 *Montana* 353 (1888), for claim jumping; *Territory vs. Copely,* 1 *New Mexico* 571 (1873), for keeping a gaming table known as "monte"; *People vs. Goldman,* 1 *Idaho* 714 (1878), for keeping a gambling house. *United States vs. Sacramento,* 2 *Mon-*

nature of conditions on the frontier and did not seek rigid enforcement of all laws. In 1856, Judge William L. Welch told jurors attending territorial court at Preston, Minnesota, that in a new country where there were few jails and quarrels grew easily out of land claims, they were not expected to deal severely with offenders. The grand jurors followed the judge's broad hint and declined to indict two men accused of first degree murder.[14] But many inquests were not reluctant to bring persons to trial. At the first session of the district court in Johnson County, Texas, the jurors sat only two days but indicted three persons for murder, two for adultery, six for assault and battery, two for gambling, and two for perjury.[15]

The extent of lawlessness in some areas of the West kept grand juries busy indeed. In 1861, it took the inquest of Alameda County, California, three days to hear all witnesses who wished to testify. It returned eleven indictments for murder, manslaughter, and grand larceny. In December, 1861, the inquest attending the Confederate District Court in Arizona Territory charged six persons with murder and two with assault to commit murder. Jurors summoned to attend a territorial court in New Mexico took the occasion to indict Judge Kirby Benedict and every lawyer in attendance for illegal gambling. Throughout the West, indictments for murder, assault with a deadly weapon, and other crimes of violence were commonplace.[16] Some inquests

---

tana 240 (1875); and *United States vs. Smith*, 2 *Montana* 487 (1876), are for sale of liquor to Indians. Francis T. Cheetham, "The First Term of the American Court in Taos, New Mexico," in *New Mexico Historical Review*, 1:28 (January, 1926); Edward D. Tittmann, "The Last Legal Frontier," *ibid.*, 2:221 (July, 1927).

[14] Franklyn Curtiss-Wedge, *History of Fillmore County, Minnesota* (Chicago, 1912), 1:529.

[15] *History of Johnson and Hill Counties, Texas* (Chicago, 1892), 94.

[16] Joseph E. Baker, ed., *History of Alameda County* [California] (Chicago, 1914), 159; Edward D. Tittmann, "Confederate Courts in New Mexico," in *New Mexico Historical Review*, 3:353–355 (October, 1928); Arie W. Poldervaart, *Black Robed Justice* (Santa Fe, 1948), 56; *State vs. Darling*, 4 *Nevada* 413 (1868), for robbery; *State vs. Lowry*, 4 *Nevada* 162 (1868), for assault with a "dirk knife"; *Territory vs. Drennan*, 1 *Montana* 41 (1868), for assault.

were more conscientious than others and earned a local reputation for the number of indictments for serious crimes that they returned. In 1883, an Arizona jury brought in forty "true bills," one-third of them for murder. Jurors meeting in Crosby County, Texas, in March, 1888, won the epithet "the bloody grand jury" for the number of persons they charged with murder.[17]

Occasionally, grand jurors were subject to threats by the friends of persons indicted. In Boise City, Idaho, a notorious gang leader, David Opdyke, succeeded in being elected sheriff in 1865. When the local grand jury indicted him for embezzlement, he resigned but swore revenge upon the members of the panel. The Opdyke gang warned several jurors that they would not live to walk the streets of Boise City.[18] Men who served on frontier juries, however, were prepared for such eventualities. They frequently came to court armed. Chief Justice William F. Turner told grand jurors in Arizona Territory that he addressed them with some hesitation after he had seen how well armed they were, that they looked more like an armed vigilance committee than they did like a grand inquest.[19]

In many instances the sanction of the law was the difference between a western grand jury and a well run vigilance committee. Their common objective was to remove corrupt officials and drive lawless elements from the community. In Montana, a territorial inquest reported to the court that it would be better to leave the punishment of all offenders to the vigilantes, who always acted impartially and who would not allow criminals to escape justice on absurdly technical grounds.[20] The vigilance committee, led in many cases by ministers, doctors, and other respected members of the community, came to be a regular institution on early frontiers.

---

[17] Francis C. Lockwood, *Pioneer Days in Arizona* (New York, 1932), 278; Nellie W. Spikes and Temple A. Ellis, *Through the Years: A History of Crosby County, Texas* (San Antonio, 1952), 215.

[18] Nathaniel P. Langford, *Vigilante Days and Ways* (Boston, 1890), 2:348.

[19] Thomas E. Farish, *History of Arizona* (Phoenix, 1915–1918), 3:346–347.

[20] Thomas J. Dimsdale, *The Vigilantes of Montana* (Helena, 1915), 15.

In Virginia City, Idaho Territory, a committee of armed citizens hung a man who often threatened to shoot persons on the street. In the town of Gilroy, California, local residents formed a committee to drive "thieves and vagrants" from the town. They elected a captain and two lieutenants and proceeded to call at all saloons and dance halls and warn the patrons to leave the city. Finally, they escorted nine men well beyond the city limit.[21]

Occasionally, in the face of corrupt judges and law enforcement officials in league with outlaws, grand juries found it difficult to bring criminals to justice. Such a situation existed in San Francisco in 1851. Juries indicted offenders only to see the cases dismissed or if the men were tried and convicted they were pardoned. Robbery and murder stalked the streets of the city, unmolested by local officials. Finally, the particularly brutal murder of C. J. Jensen, the owner of a local dry goods store, aroused the citizens to action. Since the grand jury appeared blocked by the actions of city officials, on June 9, 1851, a vigilance committee was organized. Action followed rapidly after the organization of the extralegal tribunal. Within twenty-four hours the committee arrested, tried, and hanged John Jenkins, an Australian immigrant, for robbing a safe. The following month, James Stuart, a notorious outlaw, followed Jenkins to the gallows for the murder of Jensen. Following the execution of Stuart, Judge Alexander Campbell charged the San Francisco grand jury that every person who in any manner assisted in hanging Stuart was guilty of murder. He characterized the vigilantes as an illegal group of armed men who "have undertaken to trample on the Constitution, defy the laws and assume unlimited authority over the lives of the community." Judge Campbell not only did not sense the feeling of the community, but he was unaware that seven of the sixteen grand jurors before him were members of the committee. In its report delivered to the court August 2,

---

[21] Frank H. Bushick, *Glamorous Days* (San Antonio, 1934), 244; *New York Times*, May 2, 1864; *San Francisco Bulletin*, November 9, 1873.

1851, the jury refused to consider charges against the vigilantes and instead expressed its appreciation for their work. The jurors stated that many of the "best and most worthy citizens" of San Francisco had acted on the committee at great sacrifice to themselves, solely to serve the best interests of the community. They reminded Judge Campbell that the people had acted only after all other means of bringing criminals to justice had failed. In conclusion, the jurors censured the judge for delays in important trials and criticized law enforcement officials for their indifferent attitude. During the remainder of the session the vigilance committee and the grand jury co-operated in bringing offenders to trial. The committee furnished information and witnesses that enabled the inquest to return indictments. In September, when the governor pardoned a man convicted of a brutal assault, the grand jury of San Francisco threatened to resign in a body.[22]

Two years later, in June, 1853, the grand jury came under attack by San Francisco newspapers after it had dared to criticize the inefficiency of doctors of the State Marine Hospital. The *Alta California* came to the jury's defense, however, and reminded state and city officials that "the reports of the grand juries of this county are among the best papers ever issued by any branch of the government of California and there has been no great abuse within their reach that they did not strike at manfully. No wrongdoer has been too low for their watchful attention, nor any too high." The editor pointed out that there were no more free and representative bodies in the city of San Francisco than the grand juries and that the conduct of public officials was a most suitable field for their inquiry.[23] In November, 1853, the San Francisco grand inquest, in an attack on corruption in the city, indicted several citizens and city officials.

[22] Stanton A. Coblentz, *Villains and Vigilantes* (New York, 1936), 51, 61–62, 81–86; James A. B. Scherer, *"The Lion of the Vigilantes": William T. Coleman and the Life of Old San Francisco* (Indianapolis, 1939), 96–106, 110–113; Hubert Howe Bancroft, *History of California* (San Francisco, 1890), 7:208–209.
[23] San Francisco, *Alta California*, June 4, 1853.

Several jurors voted for true bills even though threats had been made against their lives.[24]

On the night of November 18, 1855, the news that Charles Cora, a notorious gambler and suspected murderer, had shot and killed United States Marshal William H. Richardson shocked residents of San Francisco. The sheriff arrested Cora but gamblers offered odds that he would never be convicted. Agitation for another vigilance committee to make certain that Cora received justice and to clean the city of gamblers and prostitutes increased throughout San Francisco. James King of William, vigorous reforming editor of the *Evening Bulletin,* demanded that the grand jury wage a war against gambling and vice, "a war to the knife, and knife to the hilt." Pressure to reactivate the vigilantes subsided when the grand jury indicted Cora for murder, but in its final report, delivered December 10, 1855, the inquest evinced little desire to launch an all-out campaign against vice and corruption. When the trial jury could not agree on a verdict, the Cora trial ended without a conviction. With this, King began a determined attack upon crime in San Francisco. The crusading editor asked for laws against the carrying of concealed weapons, demanded the closing of houses of prostitution, and recommended the establishment of a chain gang for the punishment of offenders. As his campaign gained momentum, he loosed vituperative attacks on the San Francisco Board of Supervisors. On May 14, 1856, he branded one supervisor, James P. Casey, an ex-convict. That evening Casey surprised and shot King as he was leaving the *Bulletin* office.[25] News of the assault spread rapidly. Later the same evening the old vigilante leaders of 1851 held a hurried meeting to reactivate their committee. The following day they enrolled over three thousand persons. Gamblers hardly needed a warning to leave town. By the end of the first day, they crowded the

---

[24] Coblentz, *Villains and Vigilantes,* 121–122.

[25] *San Francisco Evening Bulletin,* November 19, 20, 22, 27, 28, December 3, 1855; January 17, February 1, May 15, 16, 1856.

boat to Sacramento. On May 18, the committee defied the sheriff and removed both Cora and Casey from the jail. When James King died, the vigilantes tried, condemned, and hanged both men. With King and Richardson avenged, the committee began a program of arresting public officials for corruption, banishing criminals, and probing election frauds. The vigilantes gained military control of the city, and local and state officials were powerless to intervene until the committee voluntarily disbanded on August 18, 1856.[26]

Instances in which grand juries were unable or unwilling to deal unaided with crime in their locality were rare. In the vast majority of cases inquests played an important role in local law enforcement, constantly suggested means of improving the area of their jurisdiction, and kept a close watch over public officials. Such a case was Silver City, Idaho. Silver City was in many ways typical of the mining towns of the far West. Set high in the Owyhee Mountains of southwestern Idaho, it blossomed into a city of five thousand almost overnight following the discovery of silver in 1863. The area proved fabulously rich, second only to the Comstock Lode. Three years later, Silver City became the county seat of Owyhee County and boasted a hotel and daily newspaper. Makeshift houses and shanties filled the valley and spread up the mountain side.[27] All residents who were qualified to vote were eligible to serve on the grand jury. The county commissioners selected thirty persons from the voting list and the clerk of court drew seventeen names from a box. The pay was only $3.00 per day plus fifteen cents per mile for travel, but a fine of up to $50.00 for failure to attend provided an additional incentive.[28]

The problem of "bogus gold dust" took the attention of the first grand jury to meet in Silver City. The editor of the *Owyhee Avalanche* expressed amazement that they could

[26] Scherer, *"Lion of the Vigilantes,"* 171.

[27] *Idaho, A Guide in Word and Picture* (W.P.A. Writer's Project, Caldwell, Idaho, 1937), 381–384; Cornelius Brosnan, *History of the State of Idaho* (New York, 1948), 146–148.

[28] *Laws of the Territory of Idaho,* 1873, pp. 5–7, sections 1, 3, 7, 28.

get seventeen men, some of whom were not engaged in its manufacture. A presentment protested against gold dust made from lead, but the jurors returned no indictments. In neighboring Ada County, the inquest charged several persons with trying to pass gold of their own making.[29]

As in most territories, grand jurors in Idaho were under obligation to inspect the local jail, and Judge Alexander Smith told Silver City jurors of their duty but added, "I have been prospecting these parts for several days and haven't even found any such shebang! You may find one, however, so look around." In October, 1867, the jurors reported that the local jail was totally inadequate, with locks and hinges of inferior quality. In the following year they recommended that the jail and all county buildings be weatherboarded, asked the legislature to amend the revenue laws so as to provide a cash fund for payment of contingents, and called for an investigation of rates charged on toll roads. Indictments included one against a county officer for malfeasance as well as others for murder, for grand larceny in stealing ore, for attempting to bribe a trial jury, and for illegal gambling.[30]

Silver City inquests demonstrated the breadth of their concern with local problems again and again. In April, 1871, the jurors reported that "jury brokerage" was rapidly becoming an organized business by which trials were often made nothing more than "a broad burlesque." They warned that if not ended such practices would afford an excuse for mob violence and vigilance committees. They also asked for additional seats in the courtroom for spectators and pointed out the lack of sanitary facilities in the jail.[31] Later in the same year, Judge David Noggle asked the grand jurors to do their duty to repress public disorders resulting from

[29] *Owyhee Avalanche,* November 3, 1866; *People vs. Page,* 1 *Idaho* 102 (1867).
[30] Thomas Donaldson, *Idaho of Yesterday* (Caldwell, Idaho, 1941), 195; *Owyhee Avalanche,* October 19, 1867, October 10, 1868, March 12, July 16, 1870; Silver City (Idaho), *Owyhee Tidal Wave,* November 25, 1869; *People vs. Freeman,* 1 *Idaho* 322 (1870).
[31] *Owyhee Avalanche,* April 29, 1871.

street fights. He denounced the law licensing "Chinese bawdy houses" and told the panel that it should feel free to express its opinion on any laws or policies of the territory or county. The judge noted that as an agency of protest the grand jury was often more effective than petitions or public meetings. The jurors returned a presentment against the county hospital, which they found to be "totally unfit for the sick," and they advised that new arrangements be made to care for indigent cases.[32] In May, 1873, the grand inquest noted that the county's handcuffs were unsafe and complained of the need for a separate room and stove for the use of grand juries.[33] In May, 1877, in answer to a request, Judge H. E. Prickett told Silver City jurors that they had full power to inquire into any misconduct or neglect of duty on the part of any public officer. However, he advised the jurors not to stop with that, but to check county and territorial legislation for needed reforms and report such recommendations as they deemed proper. The grand jury meeting in June, 1880, exonerated the sheriff of rumored charges of dereliction of duty, demanded that the county commissioners cover a mine shaft in front of the post office, and protested against the "dilapidated condition" of furniture in the courtroom. In 1881, the jurors noted discrepancies in the books of some county officers. They also insisted that the court take action to remove the carcasses of dead animals from the streets of Silver City. Subsequent inquests asked that the county commissioners order property owners "to remove all filth" from adjoining alleys and streets.[34] Through it all Silver City jurors, like their counterparts all over the West, were simply using the grand inquest in the most common and traditionally very effective fashion, in the defense and for the improvement of the community.

It was in Utah that the grand jury played once again its most spectacular role, guardian of a colonial area against

[32] *Ibid.*, November 18, 1871.
[33] *Ibid.*, May 24, 1873, June 6, 1874.
[34] *Ibid.*, May 12, 1877, June 5, 1880, June 4, 1881, May 20, 1882, May 24, 1884.

outside interference. Mormon Utah, like other areas in the West, was subordinate to the federal government, but in Utah the peculiar institution of polygamy provided an open invitation to outside intervention. After the Mexican cession Congress delayed two years before making provision for civil government in the area. Under the abortive state of Deseret establishd in 1849, Mormon leaders retained their control of civil government, but when Congress refused statehood and gave the area territorial status under the Compromise of 1850, the Mormon colony found itself under the control of an unsympathetic central government.[35]

President Millard Fillmore appointed Brigham Young Governor of Utah Territory but sent two gentiles to preside over federal and territorial courts. Judges Lemuel G. Brandebury and Perrey E. Brochus wasted little time in making known their opinions of the Mormon Church and the practice of polygamy. In September, 1851, they chose the occasion of a special conference of the Mormon Church, to which they had been invited as guests, to rebuke the people of Utah for their religious practices and urge them to overthrow the rule of their church. Following such an affront to the community and an open break with Mormon leaders, the judges found it impossible to perform their judicial duties and soon left the territory.[36]

After their initial experience with gentile judges, church leaders set about establishing their own system of civil and criminal courts. In February, 1852, the territorial legislature ordered a probate court established in each county. The court was to have jurisdiction over all civil and criminal matters. The Legislative Assembly appointed the judges with the consent of Governor Young. The probate judges in cooperation with the selectmen of the counties were to name all grand juries, including those to attend the federal and

---

[35] *United States Statutes at Large*, 9:453 (1850).
[36] Edward W. Tullidge, *The History of Salt Lake City and its Founders* (Salt Lake City, 1886), 85–86; Preston Nibley, *Brigham Young, The Man and His Work* (Salt Lake City, 1936), 165–166.

territorial courts. In this way, Mormon leaders effectively placed this powerful arm of the courts under their complete control. They realized that in any future struggle with agents of the central government control over the power of indictment could prove a potent weapon.[37]

President Fillmore appointed new judges to replace those originally named. One of the new appointees, Justice W. W. Drummond of Illinois, soon incurred the displeasure of the Mormon community for his denunciations of their laws and institutions. He announced almost immediately that he would not recognize decisions of the Mormon-controlled probate courts. Drummond's companions on the territorial bench, Chief Justice John F. Kinney and Justice Leonidas Shaver, had both tacitly recognized the jurisdiction of these courts. Mormon leaders moved to meet this threat through their juries. In January, 1856, the grand jury attending the probate court at the capital, Fillmore City, indicted Judge Drummond and his Negro servant for "assault and battery with intent to murder." The charge grew out of a street scuffle in which the judge had been involved, and gave the grand jury a long awaited opportunity to strike at him. Samual W. Richards, a member of the territorial legislature, wrote his brother in England that members of the legislature knew that Drummond would be indicted even before the jury returned the true bill. Richards made it plain that the real reason for the jury's action was the judge's attempt to "rule our probate courts out of power with his decisions." Drummond tried to retaliate by exhorting grand jurors in Carson County to indict church leaders for practicing polygamy, but they refused to respond. In February, 1857, Judge Drummond left unannounced for California where he submitted his resignation and launched a tirade of abuse against the Mormon colony, charging that federal authority had been flouted and his life threatened.[38]

[37] *Laws of Utah Territory,* 1850–1855, chapter 1, sections 23, 29, 34, 40.
[38] Tullidge, *History of Salt Lake City,* 144–145; Hubert Howe Bancroft, *History of Utah* (San Francisco, 1889), 490–491; Washington, *National Intelligencer,* December 23, 1856.

Drummond's accusations strengthened the new president, James Buchanan, in his determination to enforce federal authority in Utah. He dispatched Alfred Cumming, a non-Mormon, accompanied by a force of twenty-five hundred, commanded by Albert S. Johnston, to replace Brigham Young as territorial governor. Mormon guerrilla bands harassed the federal force, but in the summer of 1858 United States troops entered Salt Lake City and Young agreed to accept the new governor. President Buchanan followed with pardons for all leaders of the "rebellion." In the meantime, news of the "Mountain Meadows Massacre" had reached the East and added to the growing feeling against the Mormons. The tragedy had taken place in September, 1857, when a hundred and forty Arkansas settlers bound for California were massacred as they paused to rest and regroup before pushing across the mountains. Non-Mormons placed the blame on the Mormon leaders and implicated Young and other high church officials.[39]

Federal judges immediately undertook to punish Mormon officialdom. In November, 1858, Justice C. E. Sinclair opened the first session of the territorial court to be held after the arrival of the army. He began with a heated charge to the grand jury. He demanded that it indict leaders of the church for treason, intimidation of the courts, and polygamy. The jurors absolutely refused to return true bills. In March, 1859, Justice John Cradlebaugh addressed grand jurors at Provo and presented evidence that implicated Young and other Mormon leaders in the Mountain Meadows Massacre. Cradlebaugh spared nothing in his effort to secure indictments. He railed at the jurors, accusing them of being "the tools, the dupes, the instruments of a tyrannical church despotism," ready and willing to murder at the command of their leaders. In closing his charge, the judge challenged the inquest to "knock off your ecclesiastical shackles" and

<hr>

[39] Robert E. Riegel, *America Moves West* (New York, 1947), 404–407; Frank J. Cannon and George L. Knapp, *Brigham Young and His Mormon Empire* (New York, 1913), 276–279; Allan Nevins, *The Emergence of Lincoln* (New York, 1950), 1:320–323.

bring Mormon leaders to trial for their crimes. Members of the inquest refused even to consider indictments against their leaders. Blocked in his attempt to prosecute Young, Judge Cradlebaugh not only discharged the grand jury but closed the court and remarked angrily that he would not re-open it until the people agreed to punish offenders among their leaders. He warned the populace, "if this cannot bring you to a proper sense of your duty, it can at least turn the savages held in custody upon you." With this, the judge released all prisoners. Chief Justice D. R. Eckles opened court at Fort Bridger on April 5, 1859. He lectured the grand jury on the moral and social evils of plural marriage and urged them to indict those guilty of the practice. As they had done in other Utah courts, the jurors turned a deaf ear to the judge's pleas. Again, it was the grand jury that defeated the efforts of federal appointees to assert their power in Utah.[40]

Mormon leaders had to contend with defection in their own ranks as well as interference from outside. A Mormon, Joseph Morris, claimed that he had received revelations telling him that Brigham Young was leading the church astray, and he established a separate community north of Salt Lake City. When a split developed in the Morrisite community, a group appealed to Mormon leaders to free them. The federal marshal, accompanied by a Mormon posse, destroyed the Morrisite settlement, but only after a three day struggle. The grand jury sitting in Salt Lake City indicted the survivors for resisting a federal posse and in the ensuing trials held in March, 1863, seven were convicted. The convictions went for naught when Territorial Governor Stephen S. Harding immediately issued pardons for the convicted Morrisites.[41]

At the same session of the Utah Court that tried the Morrisite leaders, federal authorities arrested Brigham Young

---

[40] Tullidge, *History of Salt Lake City*, 226–227, 238; Cannon and Knapp, *Brigham Young*, 311; William A. Linn, *The Story of the Mormons* (New York, 1902), 514.

[41] Linn, *Mormons*, 538–543; Tullidge, *History of Salt Lake City*, 318–319.

and released him on bail to await the action of the grand jury. They charged Young with violating the anti-polygamy law passed by Congress in July, 1862. Non-Mormons in Utah hoped to use the new statute against the church leaders, but they reckoned without the Mormon juries. The jurors refused to indict the church leader for polygamy, but instead turned their wrath upon Governor Harding for pardoning the heretical Morrisites. They reported to Chief Justice Kinney, himself a Mormon, "We present his excellency Stephen S. Harding, Governor of Utah, as we would an unsafe bridge over a dangerous stream, for jeopardizing the lives of all who pass over it, or as we would a pestiferous cesspool . . . breeding disease and death." The inquest denounced Harding's action, the turning loose of "convicted criminals," as dangerous to the community. Judge Kinney commended the jurors for discharging their duty fearlessly and calling attention to executive misconduct. The federal government recalled Kinney in June, 1863, and it became increasingly clear that federal courts in Utah could not be made effective until federal authorities controlled the selection of grand juries.[42]

The administration in Washington had little time to devote to affairs in Utah during the Civil War and the struggle for control of the territory subsided, but only temporarily. President Grant's appointment of James B. McKean of New York as territorial chief justice brought to Utah a man who understood the steps necessary to make the federal courts effective. Led by McKean, the Territorial Supreme Court removed Territorial Attorney General Zerrubbabel Snow and Territorial Marshal John D. McAllister from office and decided that the United States district attorney and the United States marshal were the proper persons to enforce territorial laws and impanel grand juries.[43] In September, 1871, Justice McKean went a step further

[42] *United States Statutes at Large,* 12:501 (1862); Tullidge, *History of Salt Lake City,* 320–324.
[43] *Snow vs. United States,* 85 *United States Court Reports* 317 (1873).

and ordered the federal marshal to ignore the method of selecting jurors prescribed by the Utah statute and use his own discretion in selecting them. In addition, when the grand jury attended court, McKean dismissed seven members who stated that they believed polygamy to be a revelation of the church. The result was an inquest that would be certain to bring Mormon leaders to trial. Following a spirited address in which the chief justice called upon the jurors to indict high church leaders, the grand jury on October 2, 1871, returned true bills against Brigham Young, D. H. Wells, Mayor of Salt Lake City, and others for "lewdness and improper cohabitation." On October 28, 1871, the same inquest indicted three other prominent Mormons for murder in connection with the death of one Richard Yates, who had been hanged as a spy during the Mormon War.[44]

What appeared for the moment to be a decisive victory for the agents of the federal government became in the hands of the United States Supreme Court a cause for Mormon celebration. In April, 1872, before Young or the other Mormon leaders could be brought to trial, the court held that under the organic act creating Utah Territory the method of selecting and impaneling a grand jury was to be decided by the territorial legislature. The high court held that a grand jury chosen by the federal marshal was invalid, as were all the indictments it returned.[45] The court followed, in 1873, with a decision limiting the authority of United States officials in Utah to cases in which the federal government was concerned.[46]

By returning control over grand juries to the Mormon leaders, the United States Supreme Court returned Utah federal courts to their helpless position. But the opponents of the church had learned that the grand jury was the key, and they meant to have it. On February 14, 1873, President Grant told Congress in a special message, "Several years of

---

[44] *Owyhee Avalanche*, October 7, 14, 1871, May 4, 1872; Linn, *Mormons*, 568–569; Tullidge, *History of Salt Lake City*, 517–519.

[45] *Clinton et al. vs. Englebrecht*, 80 *United States Court Reports* 434 (1872).

[46] *Snow vs. United States*, 85 *United States Court Reports* 317 (1873).

unhappy experience make it apparent that the territory of Utah requires special legislation . . . to maintain the supremacy of the laws of the United States." He asked Congress to take the selection of grand and petit jurors out of the hands of Mormon officials. Congress responded with the Poland Act, passed in June, 1874. It provided that United States marshals were to draw jurors by lot from a list prepared by the clerk of the district court and the judge of probate in each county. As an added safeguard, persons who upheld polygamy were not to sit upon grand juries considering such cases.[47]

Judge Jacob S. Boreman impaneled the first grand jury to be summoned under the Poland Act. He requested the jurors to investigate the Mountain Meadows Massacre and indict the guilty parties. They returned indictments for conspiracy and murder against John D. Lee and other Mormons, but Young and members of the church hierarchy were not included. After two trials, a jury found Lee guilty and federal officials executed him at the site of the massacre. It now became possible for the first time to secure a grand jury which would indict persons for polygamy. Indictments and convictions followed rapidly. The power of the central government had finally triumphed in Utah, but not until its agents had taken the grand jury out of local hands.[48]

As the frontier receded so did the use of the grand jury, but when settlers streamed into Oklahoma in 1889 the institution became an integral part of the local government, as it had on earlier frontiers.[49] Grand juries returned indictments for the usual crimes of violence but also flooded the courts with charges of perjury and fraud in connection with land entries.[50] In October, 1893, the inquest sitting at

[47] James D. Richardson, ed., *Messages and Papers of the Presidents* (Washington, D.C., 1898), 7:208–210; *United States Statutes at Large*, 18:253 (1874).
[48] Bancroft, *History of Utah*, 564–571, 772–773; *United States vs. Reynolds*, 1 *Utah* 226 (1875).
[49] *Statutes of Oklahoma*, 1890, chapter 72, pp. 977–980.
[50] *Fisher vs. United States*, 1 *Oklahoma* 252 (1892); *Stanleg vs. United States*, 1 *Oklahoma* 337 (1893); *Rich vs. United States*, 1 *Oklahoma* 354 (1893); *Finch vs. United States*, 1 *Oklahoma* 396 (1893).

Guthrie launched a thorough investigation of the federal land office and reported that there was evidence to substantiate "the most radical charges of fraud." Bribed land office officials had sold certificates and connived with persons to make "back door" filings in order to defeat those standing in long lines. In Perry County, grand jurors found that a company of soldiers had kept people off some blocks in the proposed city until "certain politicians" arrived and took possession. The jurors revealed that Harry Bacon, Oklahoma City Democratic leader, had conspired with government officials, before the territory was opened, to locate county seats for their own benefit. After investigating for over a month, the jurors indicted those who were within their jurisdiction and called for a congressional inquiry into land offices in Oklahoma.[51]

Land frauds revealed in Oklahoma in 1893 proved only a preview. Ten years later sensational grand jury disclosures were made throughout the West. Most spectacular, both in the scope of the frauds and in the importance of the persons implicated, was the grand jury investigation of timber stealing in Oregon. The first public disclosure that widespread corruption existed in connection with public lands came on October 26, 1903, when the federal jury at Portland indicted Asa B. Thompson, the receiver of the land office at La Grande. In their investigations, assisted by special agents of the Treasury Department, the jurors found evidence that Thompson had accepted bribes to approve homestead claims. Additional indictments followed on October 27, 1903, when the jurors accused Mary L. Ware, former land commissioner of Eugene, and four other persons of conspiring to forge fictitious names to homestead applications.[52] In the following month a federal grand jury in northern California charged three persons with subornation of perjury in connection with taking up valuable timber lands.[53]

---

[51] Milwaukee, *Evening Wisconsin,* October 28, November 21, 22, 1893.
[52] Portland, *Morning Oregonian,* October 27, 28, 30, November 2, 14, 1903.
[53] *New York Times,* November 13, 1903.

In March, 1904, another grand jury in Portland took up the investigation of Oregon land entries and reported that stockmen in the eastern part of the state had obtained large holdings by conniving with persons to take up homesteads. The jurors named Charles Cunningham, millionaire sheep rancher, a county judge, and six other persons in conspiracy indictments.[54] As grand jury probes continued, the trail of bribery led beyond the state to land officials in Washington, D.C. It remained for the federal grand jury that assumed its duties in Portland in December, 1904, to bring in the leading personages involved in the land steals. The jurors remained in session for four months and returned twenty-six indictments involving over a hundred persons. A cloud of suspicion surrounded Senator John H. Mitchell when he left Oregon in December, 1904, to be on hand for the opening of Congress. The day after he left Portland, the grand inquest confirmed what had already been widely rumored. They charged Mitchell with having accepted a bribe of $2,000 to expedite fraudulent land entries. They also indicted Binger Hermann, Commissioner of the General Land Office in Washington, for knowingly allowing false claims. On January 31, 1905, the jurors named Mitchell and Hermann on additional counts of conspiracy to defraud the government and charged Mayor William Davis of Albany, Oregon, with signing false affidavits to secure land. Through February, 1905, the jurors kept up their barrage of indictments. Judge A. H. Tanner faced perjury charges for testifying falsely before the grand jury in an effort to save his former law partner, Senator Mitchell. State Senator George C. Brownell awaited trial on charges of filing false land claims. Mitchell remained in Washington to defend his name on the Senate floor, but new evidence produced additional accusations against him. The grand jurors concluded their four month investigation in April, 1905, with indictments against former Congressman Willard N. Jones for attempted bribery and State Senator

[54] *Morning Oregonian,* March 22, 23, 26, 1904.

Robert A. Booth, his brother, and five other persons for seeking to secure land through false affidavits. Booth owned a lumber company and had sought to get valuable yellow pine lands.[55]

The spectacular disclosures in the Oregon land probe set off a series of grand jury inquiries throughout the western states. In June, 1905, a federal jury at St. Paul returned indictments for conspiracy to defraud the government of eighteen thousand acres of land in South Dakota by means of fraudulent homestead entries.[56] Montana juries had already brought sixteen men to trial for land frauds when the inquest sitting at Helena in January, 1906, charged Joseph P. Woolman, its foreman, with illegally fencing public lands. Federal grand juries in other jurisdictions returned a total of five hundred and seventy-five indictments for stealing land and timber under the terms of the Timber and Stone Act and the Forest Reserve Lieu Land Act.[57] In December, 1905, an Oregon jury began another full scale inquiry into suspected irregularities in taking up yellow pine lands. After five months of public suspense they broke their silence on May 3, 1906, with criminal charges against five prominent Oshkosh, Wisconsin, lumbermen. They accused the five of obtaining a hundred and sixty thousand acres of virgin timber by inducing persons to file upon it and then turn the land over to them for a sum of money. The clerk of Klamath County, Oregon, and the agents of the Oshkosh lumbermen also faced trial for their roles in securing fraudulent entries. The grand inquest concluded its probe in May, 1906, with indictments against twenty-one lumber dealers of Michigan, Minnesota, and Arkansas, who, operating through their representatives in Oregon, had obtained over two hundred thousand acres of timber land by purchasing claims from "dupes" who had been induced to file. The grand jury cited over four hundred fraudulent claims under

[55] *Ibid.*, December 31, 1904, January 1, February 1, 2, 12, 14, April 9, 1905; *New York Times,* January 1, 1904, January 4, 1905.
[56] St. Paul, *Pioneer Press,* June 9, 1905.
[57] *Evening Wisconsin,* January 6, 1906.

the Timber and Stone Act, involving timber valued at over a million dollars.[58] Grand jurors in Denver, Colorado, summoned representatives of eastern syndicates in May, 1907, to explain how extensive coal and timber land had passed into their hands. After two months of hearing testimony, members of the inquest charged eight men with having conspired to obtain coal lands through fraudulent means.[59]

By the beginning of World War I grand juries attended state courts in only a few western areas. Beyond the Mississippi federal inquests continued to meet and had done much to prosecute those who looted the public lands, but they did not concern themselves with local problems. Before their abolition, county grand juries had served well the communities in which they sat. At a time when territorial residents had little voice in their government, inquests had boldly proclaimed the needs and desires of their areas. In Utah they had played the central role in the bitter struggle for control of the territory. Throughout the West they had kept public officials under constant scrutiny and had made excellent use of their ample powers to begin investigations of corruption in government. The passing of the grand jury in the West left a void that a public prosecutor would find difficult to fill.

[58] *Morning Oregonian,* May 4, 1906; *Oshkosh* (Wisconsin) *Northwestern,* May 4, 1906.
[59] *San Francisco Chronicle,* May 13, July 7, 1907

Chapter 11

Municipal Corruption

THE GRAND JURY had always been effective in dealing with community problems, and the rise of the city often presented it with a most pressing one. As American urban centers grew in population and importance in the period following the Civil War, municipal corruption grew as well. In many large cities municipal governments ceased to represent the people, and controlled elections and well-organized political machines made it difficult to oust corrupt groups from control. Public officials banded together to loot city treasuries. Powerful financial and political interests worked together to buy and sell valuable gas, street railway, and other franchises. It was in the grand jury that the people often found their most potent weapon in the struggle to reclaim their cities.

In 1872, a New York City jury, working in secret session for over four months, succeeded in accomplishing what all other attempts at reform had failed to do. It broke the corrupt Tweed Ring. Tweed, and other politicians who had brazenly defied all efforts to end their pillaging, cringed in fear when the grand jury began to unearth their manipulations. It was not easy for the grand inquest to destroy the well entrenched machine built up over a period of years. As early as 1869 Tweed and his cohorts had gained complete control of the city government. The Boss himself acted as street commissioner, while Peter B. Sweeney became city chamberlain and Richard B. Connolly comptroller. Tweed dictated the nomination of city and county officers and manipulated the elections to assure victory. Controlled judges presided over the courts in the interests of the Ring. Tweed succeeded in having himself elected to the State Senate where he inaugurated a campaign to make New York City completely independent of the legislature. When the legislators gave City Comptroller Connolly authority to issue bonds in settlement of claims against the city, members of the Ring reaped a gigantic harvest. They pocketed over fifty per cent of all claims paid. In March, 1870, Tweed secured a new city charter from the legislature. New York City gained almost complete autonomy and the machine gained ever greater freedom to plunder. A special board of audit composed of Tweed, Connolly, and Mayor A. Oakey Hall became the true ruler of the city and the aldermen became mere figureheads. Following this victory, corruption expanded tremendously. Fictitious institutions enabled Ring members to pocket large sums. All who did business with the city paid handsomely for the privilege. Officials squandered money on city and county printing and reaped an enormous harvest. A new courthouse proved the most lucrative source of corruption. The total cost of the building reached twelve million dollars, half of which went to Tweed and his followers. Tight control of financial affairs plus the power to issue bonds made it easy for the plunderers to keep their raids on the treasury secret. Comptroller Connolly ingeniously manipulated statements of the city's financial condition to hide the rapidly growing deficit.[1]

In 1870, a reform movement attempted to unseat the Tweed regime in the fall election, but the machine was too well entrenched and Mayor Hall won re-election handily. The following year, opponents of the Ring organized a council of political reform and called a protest meeting at Cooper Union for the evening of April 6, 1871. Henry Ward Beecher, Judge George C. Barrett, and other reform leaders addressed the meeting in an attempt to arouse public opinion. They showed how the city debt had climbed from

[1] Gustavus Myers, *The History of Tammany Hall* (New York, 1917), 215–229; Alexander C. Flick, *Samuel J. Tilden: A Study in Political Sagacity* (New York, 1939), 197–200; Dennis T. Lynch, *Boss Tweed* (New York, 1927), 360–366; *New York Times*, July 22, 24, 26, 29, 31, August 2, 3, 5, 7, 11, 1871.

thirty-six to a hundred and thirty-six million dollars in a period of two years. However, the mass meeting produced no tangible results toward overthrowing Boss Tweed. The people of New York City did not fully realize the extent of the frauds until July, 1871, when the *New York Times* secured details of the corruption from disaffected members of the machine. Aided by the biting cartoons of Thomas Nast in *Harper's Weekly,* ceaselessly depicting Tweed in the striped garb of a convict, the *Times* brought to light the various methods by which the Ring looted the public treasury. But though newspaper revelations served to arouse city residents, the *Times* was unable to procure sufficient evidence to prosecute those involved. A second public protest meeting held September 4, 1871, attracted a large crowd of indignant citizens bent upon saving their city from bankruptcy. They approved resolutions appointing an executive committee of seventy to gather evidence to oust corrupt public officials. Led by Charles O'Conor and Samuel J. Tilden, the committee obtained an injunction preventing Comptroller Connolly from disbursing city funds. Evidence gathered by the committee enabled them to instigate civil actions against Tweed and Connolly for money unlawfully taken from the city, but the committee lacked the necessary powers to launch a widespread investigation.[2]

The ballot box, a newspaper crusade, public indignation meetings, and a citizens' investigating committee had all been unable to unseat the Ring. It was not until a grand jury began a thorough inquiry into municipal corruption that the Tweed Ring was in real danger. The grand jury's broad authority to subpoena witnesses and books, made effective by its contempt powers and ability to indict for perjury, enabled it to obtain evidence in spite of the elaborate efforts of Tammany politicians to hide their operations. The secrecy that attended all investigating sessions made it

[2] Myers, *Tammany Hall,* 230–240; Flick, *Tilden,* 210–215; *New York Times,* April 7, July 22, 24, 26, 29, 31, August 2, 3, 5, 7, 11, September 4, 5, 1871; Albert D. Paine, *Thomas Nast, His Period and His Pictures* (New York, 1904), 174–187.

possible for witnesses who feared reprisals to disclose safely what they knew. The grand jurors met for the first time on November 6, 1871. Their first step was to summon Charles O'Conor and Samuel Tilden, the leaders of the citizens' committee. The testimony of these and other witnesses convinced the jurors that widespread corruption existed in New York City. After obtaining what assistance they could from reform leaders, they set out to find evidence against city officials without the assistance of experts from the district attorney's office. The jury summoned all manner of witnesses and interrogated them in secret session. To cover all possible sources of information, the twenty-one jurors split up into committees of two and three. These committees visited banks to check on the accounts of public officials, called at the homes of witnesses who were unable to come to the jury, and checked the operations of each of the city departments. Even in their off-duty hours, many of the jurymen tracked down information useful in tracing frauds to the guilty parties. Their task was not always an easy one. Social and political pressures brought to bear by those who feared indictment handicapped their work. When these failed to influence the jurors, offers of bribes and threats of force were used.[3] After pursuing their investigations for over a month the grand jurors had gathered enough evidence to return the first in a series of indictments. On December 15, 1871, they charged Tweed with submitting forged claims to the county for payment. The next day they indicted Comptroller Connolly on thirteen counts of conspiring to defraud the city.[4]

As December, 1871, drew to a close and the grand jury had not completed its graft probe, New York City politicians had a new hope. A technicality in the state law threatened to end the jury's term. Members of the Tweed gang hoped to be rescued by this technicality, but friends of reform in the

[3] "That Grand Jury," in *Scribner's Monthly*, 3:609–619 (March, 1872), written anonymously by one of the jurors; *New York Times*, February 11, 1872.
[4] *Ibid.*, December 17, 1871.

legislature repealed the provision. With their jurisdiction unquestioned, the jurors continued gathering evidence and on February 3, 1872, returned a large group of indictments. As a result, Tweed and twelve other politicians faced charges of grand larceny and conspiracy. In addition to the Boss himself, the jurors preferred criminal charges against Peter B. Sweeney, his right-hand-man, J. H. Ingersoll, a furniture dealer who submitted fraudulent bills to the city and turned thousands into the coffers of the Ring, and Andrew J. Garvey, who charged three million dollars for plastering the courthouse. Members of the grand inquest completed their labors on February 10, 1872. At that time they returned indictments against Mayor A. Oakey Hall and other members of the Ring.[5]

Judge Gunning S. Bedford commended the jurymen on the efficiency of their investigation and observed that they had concluded "one of the most important, extraordinary and eventful sessions that has ever marked the history of an American grand jury." As the jurymen left the courtroom after four arduous months, they had the satisfaction of knowing that their work would end an era of municipal corruption which had proved so costly to New York City taxpayers. Although the trials and legal struggles of Tweed and his henchmen dragged on for several years, the grand jury had effectively ousted them from control of the city. Tweed later escaped from jail and fled to Spain, only to be returned aboard a United States warship to spend his remaining days in the Ludlow Street Prison.[6]

The need for a thorough investigation of municipal government in New York City presented itself again in 1884. In May, members of the grand jury censured the Department of Public Works for not protecting the city against "designing contractors." They disclosed that favoritism, extravagance, and waste prevailed "to a disgraceful extent."[7]

[5] *Ibid.*, January 5, 17, February 4, 11, 1872.
[6] *Ibid.*, February 11, 1872; Harold Zink, *City Bosses in the United States* (Durham, North Carolina, 1930), 110–111.
[7] *New York Tribune*, May 13, 1884.

However, the most extensive corruption existed among the city's elected representatives. A group of thirteen aldermen formed a "combine" within the City Council, to sell street railway franchises to the highest bidder. They received an offer of $750,000 for the Broadway franchise from the Cable Company, half to be paid in cash and the balance in company bonds. The Broadway Surface Railway Company, through its president, Jacob Sharp, offered a bribe of $500,000 in cash. The wary aldermen remained content with the lower bid, fearing that bonds would be too easy to trace. Each of the members of the combine shared in the purchase price and in August, 1884, the Council passed a resolution granting the franchise to the Broadway Company. Mayor Franklin Edson vetoed the resolution but a technicality had already voided the franchise. In November, 1884, the combine again granted the franchise and overrode the mayor's veto.[8] Rumors of bribery in connection with the Broadway line lingered to plague the anxious aldermen, but it remained for the New York grand jury to bring the full story to light. In April, 1886, the jurors began a month-long inquiry into charges of fraud. They ended their work by returning indictments against each of the aldermen who had sold his vote.[9] A subsequent jury investigated the Broadway Company and indicted President Sharp and the other officers of the corporation.[10]

Sometimes it was not necessary to prefer criminal charges against public officials in order to correct abuses. In less serious cases grand juries often confined themselves to public statements setting forth irregularities and suggesting reforms. In October, 1886, jurymen in King's County, New York, complained that medical directors of the Flatbush Insane Hospital were responsible for its poor condition. The jurors blamed difficulties on "political jealousies, personal

---

[8] *People vs. O'Neil,* 109 *New York* 251 (1888); *New York Times,* August 19, November 14, 25, December 6, 1884.

[9] *Ibid.,* April 6, 7, 10, 13, 14, 1886.

[10] *People vs. Sharp,* 107 *New York* 427 (1887); *New York Times,* October 20, 1886.

dissensions, and improper methods."[11] In June, 1888, a special New York County grand jury reported a great many excise cases accumulated in the office of the district attorney. Members of the inquest remarked that such a state of affairs indicated either "a lack of disposition to prosecute or a lack of efficiency" on the part of the district attorney.[12]

The effectiveness with which a grand jury was able to investigate well-organized and large scale corruption was dependent to some extent upon the co-operation of the county prosecutor. He alone could advise the jurors on legal matters and attend their secret sessions. However, prosecutors were often reluctant to have juries embark upon broad inquiries. Sometimes they feared reprisals and occasionally they themselves were deeply involved in grafting. If the prosecuting attorney sought to stifle an investigation, its success depended largely upon the initiative and ability of the foreman and his fellow jurymen. Although grand inquests possessed ample authority to disregard the county prosecutor and proceed without his advice, it took a courageous and independent minded panel to do so. In March, 1900, publisher George H. Putnam headed an inquest that inaugurated a probe of gambling in New York City. Before long, it became evident that the Tammany district attorney, A. B. Gardiner, was very cool toward the project. Persons ordered to appear under subpoena of the foreman disappeared from the city, and witnesses hesitated to talk in the district attorney's presence for fear they would go on the Tammany "black list." The jurors began to subpoena their witnesses directly, refusing to go through the district attorney's office. When the reforming minister, Charles H. Parkhurst, appeared before the inquest, Putnam asked Gardiner to leave the room. The prosecutor asserted his right to be present but in the midst of his protest the jurors arose and marched in a body to the courtroom. In the heated session that followed Recorder John W. Goff and the dis-

[11] *Ibid.*, October 30, 1886.
[12] *Ibid.*, June 29, 1888.

trict attorney both became thoroughly aroused. However, Recorder Goff agreed with members of the panel and upheld their right to control their own investigation. The jurors returned to their room and Dr. Parkhurst testified without Gardiner's presence.[13]

Following their disagreement with the district attorney, the jurymen took complete control of their investigations, going directly to the recorder for legal assistance. At the close of its one month term of office, the inquest issued a presentment in which it dealt severely with the district attorney. It protested that every effort to fix the responsibility for criminal neglect on the part of the police department "has been persistently discouraged or headed off." In other matters, the jurors stated that Gardiner had given little effective co-operation and recommended that the governor remove him. Investigation of the police department disclosed "unusual activity" during the period of the grand jury inquiry. Police officials had prepared a list of "suspicious places" to exhibit to the inquest. The jurors refused to indict the "dummies" in actual charge of gambling and prostitution, but instead charged the police department "from the roundsmen up to the commissioners" with criminal neglect of duty. The jurymen noted that such neglect could come only from a direct interest in the maintenance of the illegal establishments.[14] Judge Robert Foster expunged the jury's presentment from the record but Foreman Putnam forwarded a copy to Governor Theodore Roosevelt. The governor appointed a special commissioner to try Gardiner, but he opposed removing the district attorney.[15]

In November, 1900, a grand inquest led by Foreman John P. Faure resumed the struggle with Gardiner. When the jurors indicted Police Chief William S. Devery, the prosecutor termed the action an outrage. In its final report, the

[13] George H. Putnam, *Memories of a Publisher, 1865–1915* (New York, 1915), 319–324; *New York Times,* March 16, 1900.
[14] Putnam, *Memories,* 324–327; *New York Times,* March 31, April 1, 1900.
[15] Elting E. Morison, ed., *The Letters of Theodore Roosevelt* (Cambridge, 1951–1954), 2:1347, 1353, 1870.

panel rebuked the district attorney for his attitude toward it and for inefficiency in conducting his office. In December, 1900, Governor Roosevelt finally removed Gardiner for failing to prosecute violations of the state election laws.[16]

Residents of Cincinnati also discovered the reforming potential of the grand jury. In the 1880's criminals seemed to enjoy a special immunity in Cincinnati. Murder, robbery, and other serious crimes increased in numbers, yet guilty persons managed to escape punishment by bribing trial juries or getting judges to set aside verdicts on frivolous technicalities. Matters reached a climax on March 28, 1884, when a trial jury found William Berner guilty only of manslaughter after he had murdered his employer in an attempt to rob him. The Berner case gave proof for the oft repeated charge that bribery played an important part in judicial proceedings. Residents of Cincinnati took matters into their own hands. Leaders called a mass indignation meeting, but it became an uncontrollable mob. There followed two nights of rioting in which fifty-six persons died and over three hundred suffered injuries. The angry mob left the courthouse a smoldering ruin. A special grand jury met to investigate the riot and heard the stories of over a hundred and eighty witnesses. At the conclusion of their inquiry, they accused officials of unduly provoking the people of Cincinnati by corrupting justice in the city. The jurymen pointed to numerous instances of "fixing" cases to suit influential politicians and lawyers.[17]

In 1906, Cincinnatians again resorted to the grand jury in an attempt to free their city from the stranglehold of a political machine. "Old Boy" George B. Cox had gained undisputed dominion over the city. His control of the courts made difficult any attempted investigation of rampant bribery and corruption. Cox's courts managed to head off a jury inquiry into his handling of city funds, but not before he had

[16] *New York Times,* November 6, 9, 10, 1900; *Ten Months of Tammany* (October, 1901), 72, a pamphlet prepared by the City Club of New York.

[17] *Cincinnati Commercial,* May 8, 10, 13, 1884; Alvin F. Harlow, *The Serene Cincinnatians* (New York, 1950), 272–273.

testified and denied under oath that he had ever received interest on public monies. In 1911, District Attorney Henry T. Hunt and Judge Robert N. Gorman stood alone in the city as anti-machine officials and they worked together in an effort to unseat Cox. Gorman summoned a grand jury to continue the abortive probe begun in 1906. The jurors secured evidence that Cox had pocketed interest on public funds deposited with his Cincinnati Trust Company. The statute of limitations had run out on the offense, but the inquest indicted the Boss for perjuring himself in his 1906 testimony. Cox's control over city courts came to his rescue when the common pleas judge quashed the indictment. But the Supreme Court of Ohio reversed his decision, and in 1913 Cox came to trial on the perjury charge. After a three week trial a Cincinnati judge dismissed the case. Although Cox successfully resisted all attempts to convict him, the grand jury's action helped to arouse public opposition to machine control and Cox's hold was appreciably weakened.[18]

In Chicago, rumors regarding bribery in connection with railway franchises led to public pressure for a thorough grand jury investigation. On March 22, 1892, the second day of its probe, the Cook County grand jury accused seven aldermen of conspiring to accept bribes. The jurors noted that whenever a large corporation had a measure pending before the City Council, several company attorneys were on hand to act as go-betweens. Reluctant witnesses left the Windy City as the investigation gained momentum. Frederick Soule, Secretary of the Chicago and Jefferson Urban Transit Company, fled to Iowa but returned under duress to give damaging testimony. Before its term of office ended, the inquest indicted additional aldermen and reported its findings to the court. The jurymen told the people of Chicago that within one year three important ordinances had been eased through the City Council "by the corrupt use of

[18] Zink, *City Bosses*, 264–265; George K. Turner, "Rise and Rule of George B. Cox and His Overthrow," in *McClure's Magazine*, 38:589 (March, 1912); *State vs. Cox*, 87 *Ohio* 313 (1913); *The Autobiography of Lincoln Steffens* (New York, 1931), 482–488; *New York Times*, July 17, 1913.

money." These included a grant of waterfront land and many miles of roadway to the Northern Pacific Railway, an ordinance to establish a virtual gas monopoly, and a franchise to install compressed air pipes under city streets. Jurors also reported finding bribery and graft in the letting of contracts for the purchase of school equipment.[19]

In Wisconsin a grand inquest was a rarity, but in June, 1905, District Attorney Francis E. McGovern of Milwaukee set in motion a four month grand jury probe of graft in the city and county governments. Three weeks after they began their investigation, the jurors had sufficient evidence to bring criminal charges against eighteen county supervisors. Members of the inquest found that bribery had played an important part in awarding contracts for an addition to the county hospital. Payments to supervisors had also paved the way for the sale of county property to the Electric Railway and Light Company. Additional indictments followed on July 12, 1905, implicating businessmen as well as officials in conspiracies to defraud the county. Turning their attention to other matters, jurors charged the chief of the fire department, Herman A. Clancy, with perjury for false testimony given before the grand jury. Charles J. Pfister, wealthy business leader, faced charges of larceny for allegedly stealing $14,000 given him by a client to obtain the city garbage contract in 1901. The inquest discovered also that the president of the city council had been selling feed to the city and he was named in twenty indictments. The Milwaukee jurymen remained in session from June until the end of September, examining almost two hundred and ninety witnesses and indicting over a hundred and fifty persons. Suppressed excitement pervaded the city hall each time the jurors handed the court a group of indictments. Political leaders looked forward to the jury's final report fearfully, yet hopefully because it would signal the end of its deliberations. The final presentment warned the people of Milwaukee that their elected representatives had organized and

[19] *Chicago Tribune*, March 21, 22, 23, 24, 25, 26, 27, 29, 31, April 3, 1892.

fostered vice and gambling in the city. The jurors condemned as "extortion" Mayor David Rose's methods of forcing municipal employees to join his political organization, the "City Democracy." The sheriff's office came in for severe criticism because of the way in which fees collected for the county disappeared. As one means of ensuring better government, the grand jury recommended what the politicians most certainly did not want, "periodic grand juries."[20]

In St. Louis, in 1902, an unbeatable combination aligned itself against graft and corruption in an effort to clean up the city. An aggressive and crusading prosecuting attorney, Joseph W. Folk, and a grand jury free to act without judicial restraint set about ending the reign of the boodlers. Citizens of St. Louis had long known in a vague way that there was corruption in the Municipal Assembly. It was common knowledge that "Boss" Ed Butler controlled the city and acted as broker in the sale of municipal franchises. However, the people of St. Louis hardly realized the extent of bribery and fraud until the reports of the grand jury made it clear. Members of both houses of the bicameral Municipal Assembly had organized combines and established a scale of prices for the sale of legislation and franchises. Startling disclosures of bribery came in January, 1902, when the grand inquest and Prosecutor Folk launched an investigation of a charter granted to the Suburban Railway Company. They discovered that the company had placed $135,000 in a St. Louis bank for delivery to members of the combine once the franchise became effective. Before the end of their two-month term of service, the jurors indicted three members of the Assembly and two directors of the company. The jurymen recommended continuing the inquiry and called for a law declaring forfeit all charters obtained by bribery.[21]

[20] Milwaukee, *Evening Wisconsin*, June 7, 22, July 1, 12, 22, August 5, 10, 21, September 30, October 2, 1905; *Schultz vs. Strauss*, 106 *Northwestern Reporter* 1066 (1906).
[21] James L. Blair, "The St. Louis Disclosures," in *Proceedings of the Detroit Conference for Good Government* (Philadelphia, 1903), 89; Zink, *City Bosses*, 311; *Autobiography of Lincoln Steffens*, 365–373; *St. Louis Post-Dispatch*, January 26, 28, 29, February 2, 1902.

The jury impaneled in St. Louis in February, 1902, resumed the graft probe begun by its predecessor. Two members of the Board of Health admitted that they had each received $2,500 from Butler to award a garbage contract to one of his clients. The inquest indicted the Boss for attempted bribery. From the garbage contract they moved on to investigate the methods by which Robert M. Snyder had acquired a traction franchise. The jurors found that Snyder had paid a total of $250,000 in legislative bribes. Indictments that followed charged Snyder with bribery and George J. Kobusch, the president of the St. Louis Car Company, with perjury before the grand jury. The municipal legislators received the full force of the grand jury's wrath in its final report. The jurymen told citizens of St. Louis that many of their representatives were men who had "no trace of mentality or morality" while others combined education with "base cunning, groveling instincts and sordid desires." Members of the inquest also denounced businessmen "of seeming respectability" who resorted to bribery.[22]

Beginning in April, 1902, a third panel of St. Louis citizens worked two months at uncovering malfeasance in the police department and exposed additional instances of bribery. They returned more indictments and told the people that each succeeding inquiry revealed a picture of even more "infamous blackness" and added to the many instances of plunder.[23] In September, 1902, another jury discovered that Ed Butler, acting as a broker, had paid $47,500 to municipal legislators in return for a street lighting contract. As a result, he faced trial on a second charge of bribery.[24] At his trial in November Butler was found guilty, but the Missouri Supreme Court freed him on a technicality.[25]

While St. Louis was trying to rid itself of a corrupt administration, rumors of legislative bribery circulated in

[22] *Ibid.,* February 3, 5, 7, 9, 11, April 5, 1902.
[23] *Ibid.,* April 7, 30, 1902.
[24] *Ibid.,* September 11, 12, 21, 1902, October 5, 1903; Blair, "St. Louis Disclosures," 95.
[25] *State vs. Butler,* 178 *Missouri* 272 (1903); Zink, *City Bosses,* 313.

Jefferson City, Missouri. In March, 1903, the Missouri Assembly defeated a resolution calling for an investigation. Political leaders who feared an inquiry breathed easier, but they reckoned without an investigation by a grand jury. Circuit Judge James E. Hazell summoned a special inquest in Jefferson City and told its members to inquire into all charges of alleged legislative wrongdoing. Prosecuting Attorney R. P. Stone's coolness toward the probe led the jurors to ask Attorney General E. C. Crowe to act as their legal adviser. Soon the jurymen reported that the baking powder trust had used "disgracefully corrupt" methods in pushing a pure food law through the Missouri legislature in 1899. Under the guise of protecting the people, the act prohibited the manufacture of food products containing alum. Many small baking powder manufacturers had been forced to move their plants from St. Louis as a result. Testimony before the grand jury revealed that United States Senator William J. Stone had been legislative agent for the trust in 1899. In 1901, when the trust blocked repeal of the alum law, Stone had headed the Public Health Society of Missouri which organized to publicize the evils of alum. Attorney General Crowe asked Circuit Attorney Folk's assistance in St. Louis because many of the bribery payments had been made there. Folk turned the St. Louis grand jury loose on the "alum deal" and summoned local legislators to testify. The legislators implicated Lieutenant Governor John A. Lee, naming him as the person who had worked closely with Daniel J. Kelly, agent of the trust, in distributing bribe money in 1901. Unable to deny the accusation, Lee resigned and fled to Kansas, but returned to testify before both grand juries. On the basis of his testimony, Jefferson City jurors indicted Kelly and six state senators on bribery charges. The St. Louis inquest accused one state senator, but the statute of limitations prevented additional indictments. To remedy legislative bribery, the jurymen recommended open legislative hearings, an extension of the statute of limitations, and higher pay for legislators. The pay increase was recommended in the hope that the legislators might be better able to withstand the temptations of bribery.[26]

Minneapolis, too, was saved from a corrupt municipal organization by the grand jury. Dr. Alfred A. Ames had taken office as mayor in January, 1901, and within the short period of one year, residents of Minneapolis saw their city transformed into a haven for criminals and a center of vice and graft. The mayor's brother, Fred Ames, as chief of police directed the reorganization of that department into an efficient agency for the collection of blackmail and the protection of criminals. Mayor Ames established a "schedule of prices" for the privilege of breaking the law. He delegated supervision of the various groups making "pay-offs" to heads of the city departments. One official collected from the gamblers, another covered the "red light" district, and others saw to it that confidence men and thieves made regular payments. Police officials helped criminals to plan robberies, stood guard to prevent interference, and took their share of the loot.

Such were the conditions that faced grand jurors drawn for the summer term in April, 1902. Foreman Hovey C. Clark, a Minneapolis businessman, determined to break the Ames Ring and won the support of his fellow jurymen. The county prosecutor refused to co-operate, so the panel members hired private detectives to assist them in securing evidence. After scouring the city, they finally found two petty criminals who were willing to testify. Charley Howard and Billy Edwards, known as the "big mitt" men, had acted as collectors in the Ames blackmail system, receiving forty-five per cent of all pay-off money.[27] Consternation and distrust invaded the police department and spread through the city administration as other petty criminals hastened to

[26] *St. Louis Post-Dispatch,* March 3, 4, 16, 23, 24, 25, April 2, 4, 5, 6, 8, 11, 12, 13, 18, 19, 22, 24, 27, May 15, 29, 30, 1903.
[27] *Minneapolis Journal,* May 6, 1902; William A. Frisbie, "The Minneapolis House-Cleaning," in *Proceedings of the Detroit Conference for Good Government,* 110–113; Lincoln Steffens, *The Shame of the Cities* (New York, 1948), 65–69; *Autobiography of Lincoln Steffens,* 374–384.

gain immunity by testifying before the grand jury. The worried faces of city officials belied their heated denials that anything was wrong. Members of the inquest worked steadily, tracing money from the "big mitt" men through the various go-betweens to prominent city officials. On May 12, 1902, the jurors publicly accused two police detectives of having received bribes to protect confidence men. Five days later, they struck higher in the city administration and indicted Police Superintendent Fred Ames for accepting money to protect criminals from arrest. They also named Irwin A. Gardner, the mayor's right-hand man, and Detective Christopher C. Norbeck as go-betweens. The indictments kept harried officials in suspense, giving just enough information to hold those charged, but not enough to disclose how much the jurors knew. It soon became apparent that the jurymen were getting close to the mayor himself. Dr. Ames took no chances and left for a health resort in West Baden, Indiana. But Gardner's trial late in May saw the mayor hurrying back to Minneapolis as his former aide threatened "to do some talking" if the Ames brothers did not testify in his behalf. Dr. Ames spent a very uncomfortable half hour on the witness stand, where he denied all allegations by prosecution witnesses. Brother Fred took the stand and protested that his innocence was "like that of a child." However, their poor memories and studied denials were unable to save Gardner from a guilty verdict and a sentence of six years at hard labor.[28]

When the trial of Detective Norbeck got under way, in June, 1902, foreman Hovey Clark made public additional indictments against six more members of the police force. The grand jurors asked for and received court approval of an indefinite extension of their term of office, and by June seventeenth the inquest had worked its way up to the top of the city administration and indicted Mayor Ames on charges of offering a bribe in an attempt to purchase the votes of county commissioners. On the same day, in the middle of his

[28] *Minneapolis Journal*, May 8, 12, 17, 22, 28, 31, June 5, 7, 11, 1902.

trial, Norbeck fled the state. The mayor ordered a "cleanup" of the city and struck back at the grand jury by blaming conditions in Minneapolis on the "advertising" which it had given the city. Bribery charges against the mayor set off a veritable stampede at police headquarters to turn state's evidence as the administration gave signs of crumbling. Officers secretly got in touch with the grand jury and provided it with evidence for additional indictments. Norbeck's capture climaxed the rush to give evidence when the once defiant detective meekly agreed to tell all that he knew. The burly Norbeck, minus both his handlebar mustache and his "air of offended virtue," spent two hours relating details of city corruption. The result was a new group of indictments charging three police officials with accepting bribes.[29]

Fred Ames' trial late in June, 1902, promised additional excitement in the cleanup of Minneapolis. Norbeck took the stand and told how the mayor had given him specific orders to work under Gardner in collecting protection money. He also testified that Fred Ames told him "to take care of" many persons who complained to the police department of official blackmail. The *Minneapolis Journal* reported Norbeck's appearance on the stand in large red headlines, "The Unloading of Norbeck's Guilty Conscience Involves Ames Brothers in Damning Disgrace." In spite of the evidence against him, the trial jury acquitted Fred Ames on July 8, 1902. His good fortune was short lived, however, for the crusading grand jurors countered the verdict with fresh indictments against him. On July fifteenth the mayor appointed an acting chief of police to take over for brother Fred and then left for West Baden to prepare for the ordeal of his own trial. When Fred Ames tried to resume his position as head of the police department, the grand jury dispatched two representatives to West Baden where they forced the mayor to fire his brother and then resign himself. With Dr. Ames kept out of the city by a barrier of indictments until his resignation became effective, the grand jury

[29] *Ibid.*, June 12, 14, 16, 17, 18, 20, 23, 24, 26, 28, 30, 1902.

assumed the role of a committee of public safety. The jurors named an acting mayor and stood ready to enforce his clean-up orders. They forced the resignation of all remaining Ames appointees in the police department and used the threat of indictment as a club over those who might make trouble about it.[30]

The grand inquest ended its work after a term of six months. Before it did so, however, the jurors made certain that their city had been rescued from corrupt government. Mayor Ames failed to appear in court on the date set for his trial, and the grand jury requested the prosecutor to begin extradition proceedings. Ames left Indiana and it was not until February, 1903, that agents located him in New Hampshire. Dr. Ames returned to Minneapolis under duress and stood trial, but the Supreme Court of Minnesota saved him from a prison term after a trial jury had found him guilty of bribery.[31]

San Francisco had long laid claim to the title, "the wickedest city in the world." It had its "Barbary Coast," famed for dives and gamblers, and its mysterious dimly lighted Chinatown where rival tongs fought bloody wars over the profits of a lucrative vice traffic. In the final decades of the nineteenth century, Boss "Blind Chris" Buckley, working through his gang of henchmen, controlled the municipal government of San Francisco, controlled it in the interests of graft and the Southern Pacific Railroad. As a "paid employee" of the railroad, Boss Buckley saw to it that the Southern Pacific got what it wanted. Buckley had things pretty much his own way in the city until citizens began to complain that taxes were too high and that they received nothing in return.

In December, 1890, the grand jurors voiced the people's opposition to corrupt government. Led by an energetic foreman, Adam Grant, they issued a report denouncing extrav-

---

[30] *Ibid.*, July 3, 8, 9, 15, 21, 23, 24, 25, 28, 30, 31, August 1, 2, 7, 1902.

[31] *Ibid.*, September 8, 11, October 2, 28, 1902; May 1, 8, 1903; Zink, *City Bosses*, 348–349.

agance and fraud in municipal affairs. They called public attention to railway franchises from which city officials had reaped tremendous personal profits while the city had received almost nothing. As an explanation for excessively high taxes, the jurymen pointed to graft in street widening projects, padding of payrolls for political reasons, and purchases of land at exorbitant prices for public buildings. The jurors admitted that they had only scratched the surface and urged the future inquests be permitted to employ detectives in their investigations. The *San Francisco Bulletin* applauded the grand jury for having "put its finger on the true reason why the enormous tribute wrung from our people fails to yield all in the way of public improvements." However, in view of the tight control exercised by the sightless boss and his followers, it was not often possible to obtain a panel that was not dominated by machine men.[32]

In August, 1891, Judge William T. Wallace determined to secure another crusading grand jury in San Francisco. He dismissed from the panel nine persons who were obvious "plants" and appointed an elisor to select additional jurors. Judge Wallace instructed the jurors to make a thorough investigation of all charges against public officials. When it became obvious that they meant to carry on the work begun by their predecessors, many of the local politicians "took to their heels." Buckley left for an extended "vacation" in the state of Washington and finally spent the winter in Montreal, out of subpoena range. Viewing the mass exodus of officials and petty grafters, one San Franciscan observed, "Nothing is more terrific to the boodlers than a grand jury broke loose." But not all persons feared the panel of citizens. Richard Chute, political representative of the Southern Pacific Railroad, backed by the railroad's array of legal talent, sought to kill the grand jury before its probe could get under way. Chute refused to testify about the methods used by the Southern Pacific to defeat a bill in the California

[32] *San Francisco Bulletin,* December 18, 1890; *San Francisco (American Guide Series,* New York, 1940), 105–106, 133–134, 225.

legislature directing reassessment of all railroads for delinquent taxes. When Judge Wallace cited Chute for contempt, Southern Pacific lawyers challenged the validity of the grand jury. Judge Daniel J. Murphy of the Superior Court released Chute on a writ of habeas corpus and declared that the inquest had been illegally chosen.[33] But the people of San Francisco did not sit idly by and let a judge strip their grand jury of its power to act. Three thousand persons crowded into Metropolitan Hall the evening of October 2, 1891, to protest against Judge Murphy's decision. Ben Morgan, a well-known criminal attorney, drew cheers from the packed house when he denounced "the hirelings of the railroad company" who were fighting to throw out the grand inquest. Morgan proceeded to try and convict Judge Murphy of being "a dishonest judge." His verdict received the immediate and whole-hearted approval of the irate crowd. Former Congressman Charles A. Sumner followed Morgan on the platform and accused all recent legislatures of paying tribute to "Buckley and his boodlers." An organizer for the Farmer's Alliance denounced railroad domination of the city and state. The indignation meeting passed resolutions demanding a grand jury clean-up of public affairs. The *San Francisco Bulletin* welcomed the "uprising of the people" for control of their own government and expressed doubt that such a movement would have been possible without a grand jury. In this regard, the *Bulletin* noted, "The germ of justice may be said to be developed in the grand jury. There it expands until it is able to set all the other judicial machinery in motion."[34]

The California Supreme Court refused to pass upon the validity of the San Francisco jury because it had not yet indicted any person who could test its legality. The jurors continued their inquiry, summoning several state senators believed to have been involved in a "legislative combine" to

---

[33] *People ex rel Attorney General vs. William T. Wallace,* 91 *California* 535 (1891); *San Francisco Bulletin,* September 23, 24, 25, 30, 1891.

[34] *Ibid.,* October 2, 3, 1891.

defeat the railroad assessment bill. Stephen T. Gage, agent of the Southern Pacific, refused to testify and Judge Wallace cited him for contempt. Only when the Supreme Court refused to release him on habeas corpus did Gage agree to appear before the inquest.[35] Gage's testimony enabled the jurors to return their first indictments. On October 21, 1891, they charged Elwood Bruner, Chairman of the Judiciary Committee of the California Assembly, with taking a bribe and perjuring himself before the grand jury. Several days later the inquest indicted a second member of the legislature and took steps to extradite boodlers who had fled the state.[36] On November 10, 1891, the jurors charged Chris Buckley and his right hand man, Sam Rainey, with accepting bribes in connection with a railroad franchise. Both men had already disposed of all of their property in San Francisco and had long since left town. Continuing their probe of corruption, the jurymen interrogated members of the legislature and other witnesses during the day and late into the night. On December 12, 1891, they asked the court to remove City Attorney John H. Durst for tampering with the assessment rolls. However, the California Supreme Court announced a decision that put an abrupt end to the graft inquiry. The court ruled that the grand inquest had been chosen in an improper manner and had no standing in the eyes of the law. The jurors reluctantly gave up their investigation and "Blind Chris" returned from his Canadian hideout. Once fearful legislators resumed their seats at Sacramento, and "all boodledom rejoiced." For the time being, the court had destroyed the movement to purge the Golden Gate City and end its claim to being "the wickedest city in the world."[37]

Four years later another San Francisco jury tried to end corruption in municipal affairs. After a six-month investigation, jurors issued a scathing report criticizing city and

[35] *Ibid.*, October 6, 7, 9, 16, 1891; *People ex rel Attorney General vs. Wallace,* 91 *California* 535 (1891).

[36] *San Francisco Bulletin,* October 22, 27, 29, 31, November 4, 9, 1891; *Elwood Burner vs. Superior Court,* 92 *California* 239 (1891).

[37] *San Francisco Bulletin,* November 11, 12, 13, 18, December 12, 14, 1891.

county officials. During the course of their work, they indicted persons for vote frauds, but admitted that "such people are but the tools of crafty masters who manipulate elections and thwart the will of the people." The inquest protested against graft in paving contracts and in city coal purchases and urged a complete reorganization of the police department. Courts did not escape censure. The jurymen warned that individuals with "political pull" had been able to secure indefinite continuances. They observed that "some great power is at work . . . a power which seems to be effective enough to almost paralyze the courts." In reply to a State Supreme Court report clearing a San Francisco police judge of such charges, the jurors retorted, "How such actions can be commended is a mystery." Upon reading the jury's report, the presiding judge stated that he would have committed them for contempt if they had not adjourned.[38]

San Francisco did not witness a thorough investigation of corruption until 1906. Eugene E. Schmitz, representing the Union-Labor Party, had secured the mayor's office in 1901. Abraham Ruef, a San Francisco attorney, managed his campaign. Ruef and Schmitz did not gain control of the Board of Supervisors until 1905, but when they did, Ruef took over as the undisputed boss of the Golden Gate City. He organized a political machine to exploit San Francisco and sell protection to criminals. A citizens' committee headed by Fremont Older, crusading editor of the *Bulletin,* and Rudolph Spreckels, millionaire sugar manufacturer, planned a cleanup, but the earthquake and fire of April 18, 1906, dislocated their plans. In October, 1906, Older and District Attorney William A. Langdon persuaded Judge Thomas F. Graham of the Superior Court to discharge the grand jury, which Ruef had packed, and select a new panel. Older also secured the help of Special Prosecutor Francis J. Heney and detective William J. Burns to assist the new inquest.

[38] *San Francisco Chronicle,* June 13, 1895; "Report of the California Grand Jury on the Administration of Justice in that State," in *American Law Review,* 29:590–594 (July-August, 1895).

Both Heney and Burns had attained national prominence for their work in exposing an Oregon land ring. In mid-October, before the people had learned of the new grand jury, Ruef's henchmen broke up a reform mass meeting. Agitation for a committee of public safety increased and citizens talked of possible vigilance activity. However, announcement of the proposed grand jury inquiry quieted those advocating more direct means of ousting Ruef.[39]

In an attempt to ward off an investigation by a reform minded grand inquest, Mayor Schmitz removed Prosecutor Langdon and appointed Ruef to the post. Judge Graham, however, refused to recognize Ruef as the district attorney and proceeded with the project of selecting a new grand jury. On November 8, 1906, the date set for drawing the panel, a tremendous crowd gathered at the Temple Israel where the Superior Court had convened since the earthquake. Ruef, with an array of stenographers and his bodyguard, stood ready to record all proceedings for the time when he might want to try to invalidate the grand jury. Before the drawing, Heney and Langdon insisted that officers of the court, all Ruef appointees, spread the contents of the box out on a table to make certain that none of the slips were packeted together. Following selection of the panel, Judge Graham impressed upon the jurors the necessity of acting "without fear or favor" and hinted that he would discharge them if they failed to press the inquiry "with vigor, promptness, and decision."[40]

Led by their foreman, B. P. Oliver, the jurymen began their work as soon as they could find suitable rooms in the quake- and fire-ravaged city. On November fifteenth, less than a week after organizing, by returning five extortion indictments against Ruef and Mayor Schmitz, they showed San Franciscans that they meant business. The inquest

[39] Franklin Hichborn, *"The System." As Uncovered by the San Francisco Graft Prosecution* (San Francisco, 1915), 11, 19, 22–30, 67–73; Walton Bean, *Boss Ruef's San Francisco* (Berkeley, 1952), 153–155.

[40] Hichborn, *"The System,"* 85–104; *San Francisco Chronicle,* November 9, 10, 1906.

charged each of them with extorting protection money from owners of French restaurants.[41] It was not easy for the jury-men to obtain information on more important frauds. From November, 1906, to March, 1907, the grand jurors, assisted by Heney and Burns, labored to unearth evidence of bribery and graft. Finally, they succeeded in trapping Supervisor Thomas F. Lonergan into accepting a bribe. When con-fronted by witnesses to the transaction, Lonergan broke down and told the grand jury what he knew of corruption in the city administration. Lonergan related how bribery had secured railroad, trolley, and telephone franchises and kept gas rates at high levels. In return for a promise of immunity, other guilty members of the Board of Super-visors agreed to confess. Their confessions disclosed that they had received bribes totalling over $200,000. On March 20, 1907, armed with the evidence for which they had been searching, the jurors returned sixty-five bribery indictments against Ruef and ten against T. V. Halsey, agent of the Pacific States Telephone Company. Halsey had arranged with Ruef to pay the supervisors $50,000 to oppose a fran-chise to the Home Telephone Company, a rival firm. In the next few days the inquest examined officers and employees of both telephone companies and charged Louis Glass, a vice-president of the Pacific States Company, with ordering payment of the bribes. The jury also indicted Abram K. Detweiller of the Home Telephone Company for attempted bribery. In the meantime, in order to keep from standing trial, Abe Ruef opened a fight to invalidate the grand in-quest, but met defeat in the state courts and failed also in his appeal to the United States Supreme Court.[42]

While the grand jurors were trying to trace the sources of the various bribes paid to the supervisors, they also had to deal with the problem of who was to govern San Francisco. Mayor Schmitz stood indicted and all but a few of the supervisors had confessed to accepting bribes. The

[41] *Ibid.,* November 12, 14, 16, 1906.
[42] *Ibid.,* November 20, 21, 22, 24, 1906; Hichborn, *"The System,"* 132, 155, 170.

people had lost all confidence in the city administration and newspapers began to agitate for the removal of guilty persons. The decision was clearly up to the grand jury, for it alone held the confidence of the citizens and could make the supervisors do its bidding. To be completely unhampered in their investigation, the jurors decided to allow the old supervisors to remain and continue to manage the city's affairs, but the grand inquest continued as "the power behind the throne," holding the municipal legislators in line through threat of indictment. In this manner, they assumed control of executive and legislative as well as judicial affairs in San Francisco. When the Car Workers' Union called a strike against the United Railway Company and a bitter struggle ensued, a committee of the grand jury warned police officials against excessive brutality and threatened to ask the governor for troops if the chief of police could not keep order.[43]

The grand jurors did not allow routine responsibilities of running the city to keep them from tracking down those who had corrupted the city government. Early in May, 1907, the jurors summoned officers of the United Railway Company to explain how they had secured a charter to reconstruct the city's transit system after the earthquake. The opportunity for which the jurymen had been waiting came when Ruef agreed to plead guilty in the French restaurant case and confess all that he knew in return for immunity in the bribery cases. The once powerful political leader told the jurors the details of the trolley franchise deal in which he and Mayor Schmitz had each received $50,000 and the supervisors had split $100,000. He related how the Pacific Gas and Electric Company had paid to keep San Francisco gas rates high and how bribes had obtained a franchise for the Parkside Transit Company. Ruef's confessions created a sensation in San Francisco. They resulted in additional indictments against Ruef and Schmitz and all important

[43] *San Francisco Chronicle,* March 22, May 10, 1907.

officers of the public utilities companies that had been involved in the bribery schemes.[44]

Mayor Schmitz's trial on the original extortion indictment began May 22, 1906, and the grand inquest gave consideration to naming a new mayor. Committees of jurors delved into the operations of each department in the city government. The full panel paused in its graft probe long enough to examine minutely and make recommendations on all budgetary requests. During the course of the Schmitz trial, the grand jurors accused Police Chief Jeremiah Dinan of misconduct in office for trying to tamper with the trial jury. On June 14, 1907, a verdict of guilty automatically ended Schmitz's term as mayor of San Francisco and the Board of Supervisors looked to the grand jury to tell them who should be named as his successor. As a temporary measure the jurors gave the office to James L. Gallagher, one of the supervisors who had confessed his guilt. The *San Francisco Chronicle* headlined the move, "Big Stick Makes a Mayor." When the San Francisco graft probe drew to a close and the grand inquest no longer needed to maintain complete control over the city, it named Dr. Edward R. Taylor, Dean of Hastings College, as mayor. He in turn appointed a new Board of Supervisors.[45] Schmitz and Ruef each received sentences of five years in prison on the extortion charges, but the Supreme Court of California freed both of them. Business leaders who faced criminal indictments tried in every possible way to attack the grand jury, but the courts decided all technical questions in favor of its validity. However, few of the businessmen indicted for bribery ever stood trial. Attacks on the grand jury served to delay matters until District Attorney Langdon was out of office and his successor dismissed all graft charges.[46]

[44] *Ibid.*, May 4, 5, 16, 17, 18, 20, 21, 25, 26, 1907; Hichborn, *"The System,"* 201, 206; Bean, *Boss Ruef's San Francisco,* 211, 212–216.

[45] *San Francisco Chronicle,* May 23, 24, 29, 31, June 1, 4, 14, 15, 18, 19, July 17, 27, 1907.

[46] *People vs. Schmitz,* 7 *California Appellate* 330 (1908); Hichborn, *"The System"*, 328, 356, 387, 403.

The grand jury, which in the past had proved itself a bulwark against tyrannical monarchs, demonstrated repeatedly in the United States its effectiveness in rescuing cities and states from an equally despotic rule of fraud and corruption. Tyranny in the form of alliances between powerful corporations and avaricious politicians frequently threatened individual liberty. Time and again, when bribery riddled city councils or state legislatures, when public officials united to plunder, or when powerful industrial and political interests conspired to defeat justice, the grand jury stepped in. Under such conditions the grand inquest gained recognition as a powerful instrument of reform and correction, affording the citizen a secret body before which he could testify. Where corruption extended to the office of the district attorney, the grand jury's ability to act effectively depended upon its independence of the prosecutor. When necessary, juries demonstrated that they could take investigations into their own hands, ignoring the district attorney. New York City jurors found this the only way in which they could oust the Tweed Ring and subsequent juries followed their example. Frequently an energetic and enterprising foreman was the key to a jury's success. George H. Putnam in New York City, Hovey C. Clark in Minneapolis, and B. P. Oliver in San Francisco showed what a fearless foreman could accomplish in spearheading a municipal housecleaning. Under extraordinary circumstances grand juries proved that they could, if necessary, unseat an entire municipal administration and using their power of indictment, take over and run a city in the name of the people. In both Minneapolis and San Francisco, grand juries governed the city for long periods while they rooted out crime and corruption. City bosses, corrupt officials, and racketeering criminals learned to fear the grand inquest, but to citizens seeking to rid their city of corruption, it was often the only hope.

Chapter 12

Big Business

IN THE PERIOD FOLLOWING THE CIVIL WAR, corporations and gigantic business combinations mushroomed in the United States, partly because of business and legal advantages afforded by the corporate form of organization. As persons in the eyes of the law, they claimed all the prerogatives of an individual citizen but frequently accepted none of the responsibilities. As spokesmen for their communities, grand juries often found it necessary to speak out against corporations. The inquest proved an effective agency for investigating illegal business practices. Its broad inquisitorial powers were invaluable where corporate officials refused to co-operate. The authority to subpoena witnesses and documents, backed up by the contempt powers possessed by the court, made the grand inquest a powerful weapon in the struggle to control the corporate giants.

Banking failures were a fruitful area of grand jury inquiry. Citizen panels probed the causes, indicted those suspected of illegal activities, and suggested remedies. When several large New York City banks closed their doors in 1890, the local grand jury conducted a thorough investigation and issued a public report denouncing the "bold and reckless" financial dealings of bank officials. The jurors warned that state laws were hopelessly inadequate to meet the situation and provided no criminal remedy for many fraudulent banking operations. They disclosed that it had been perfectly legal for officers to transfer the entire capital stock of a bank without notifying stockholders or depositors. In Clark County, South Dakota, the grand jury investigated interest rates in its community and indicted the Security

209

Bank on charges of usury. The jurors protested that bankers demanded excessive returns on farm loans.[1]

The panic of 1893 increased the number of bank failures and the number of grand jury inquiries. In Milwaukee, a special grand jury, meeting in June, 1893, to investigate the cause of recent fires, launched an investigation of the defunct Plankinton Bank. After spending a month examining witnesses and checking bank records, the jurors created a sensation in the city by bringing criminal charges against officers and directors. They accused William Plankinton, well known Milwaukee industrialist, United States Judge James C. Jenkins, a bank director, and others of having accepted money for deposit when they knew that the bank was insolvent. Shortly after the jury adjourned, the South Side Savings Bank failed. Rumors spread through the city that fraud had hastened the bank's collapse and residents of Milwaukee's south side circulated a petition demanding another grand jury to investigate the situation. In response to the petition, Judge Emil Wallber issued an order for a second inquest and it began a probe of all bank failures. Its inquiry revealed criminal neglect in connection with the South Side Bank failure and the jurors returned thirteen indictments against officers and directors. In their final report, the jurymen sharply criticized many common banking practices and suggested legislation to make them illegal. In October, 1893, members of a St. Paul grand jury reported that they had uncovered procedures "almost criminal in their nature" in connection with bank failures. They called for state laws to rescue banking from "its deplorable condition." In the same month, a grand inquest at Fargo, North Dakota, denounced local bankers for engaging in improper practices.[2] A New York jury investigating the failure of the Madison Square Bank demanded that the legislature institute "radical changes" in the system of bank examinations.

[1] *New York Times*, March 1, 1890; *State vs. Security Bank of Clark*, 2 *South Dakota* 538 (1892).

[2] Milwaukee, *Evening Wisconsin*, June 5, July 3, 12, 19, 22, 25, August 3, September 4, 5, November 1, 1893; St. Paul, *Pioneer Press*, October 21, 1893.

The jurors called the work of most state examiners "insufficient and misleading."[3] A federal grand jury in Denver charged executives of the Commercial National Bank with fraud and neglect of duty. Jurors in Atlanta employed an expert accountant to check the books of the Georgia Loan, Savings and Banking Company. The bank was hopelessly insolvent so the grand jury closed it and indicted the officers for neglect of duty.[4]

In April, 1897, the Globe Savings Bank of Chicago failed and took with it the life savings of many residents. Public opinion demanded action, and the local grand jury began an inquiry. After several days the jurors reported that bank officials had "deliberately wrecked" the institution for private gain while state officers looked on in "criminal apathy." Further investigation revealed that bank executives had shifted assets indiscriminately to benefit themselves and borrowed large sums through "dummy" persons. They had dissipated over $130,000 of University of Illinois endowment funds. Examination by a state bank examiner three months before its failure had disclosed that the institution was insolvent, yet it had remained open for business. The grand jurors indicted officers and directors of the bank on eighty-nine counts of fraud, embezzlement, and negligence. Their own regret was that the statute of limitations saved many "of that coterie of insiders who sapped the life of the bank." In their final report, the jurors demanded more frequent bank examinations and immediate publication of all findings, and they asked for a special grand jury to continue their investigation. Special grand jurors took up the inquiry and indicted State Bank Examiner George W. Hayden for misconduct in public office. They looked into other Chicago banking firms and uncovered "many queer financial manipulations" in the dealings of the E. S. Dreyer and Company banking and investment house. A complete

---

[3] *New York Times,* November 23, 24, 30, 1893.
[4] *Phoenix Weekly Herald,* May 21, 1896; *Atlanta Constitution,* April 30, May 1, 7, 1897.

investigation of Dreyer and Company revealed a systematic scheme to plunder the unsuspecting public of over $1,300,000. The firm had been insolvent for three years, but Dreyer had used funds of the Park Board, which he headed, to hide the insolvency. The grand jurors issued a scathing denunciation of banking practices. They warned financiers "if there is no moral sense in banking . . . then some legislation shoud be had which will produce an observation of honesty." But the jurors observed that legislation was not enough and called upon the people of Chicago to arouse themselves against "bank wreckers" and embezzlers, regardless of their supposed respectability and standing in the community.[5]

Grand jury probes revealed similar practices in other cities. A New York City jury exposed fraud in the failure of the Seventh National Bank. In Lexington, Kentucky, the grand inquest conducted an investigation of investment companies and indicted several persons for fraudulent activities. It advised all future grand juries to make periodic inspections of bank and financial houses. A Baltimore jury uncovered illegal practices among local brokerage firms.[6]

Insurance companies also came under grand jury scrutiny when their activities threatened the public interest. New York City jurors launched an insurance investigation in April, 1877. They subpoenaed officers and records and discovered that many reports made to the commissioner of insurance had been fraudulent. The jury indicted officers of the Security Life Insurance Company and the American Popular Life Insurance Company for perjury and put the latter firm into the hands of receivers. Before concluding their work, they issued a strong protest against Wall Street speculators who circulated false reports in order to drive stock prices down.[7] In the same year, a grand jury at Newark indicted five directors of the New Jersey Mutual Life

[5] *Chicago Tribune,* May 2, 9, 11, 15, 16, 1897.
[6] *New York Times,* July 25, 1901; *Louisville Courier-Journal,* March 30, 1902; *New York Tribune,* April 30, 1904.
[7] *Ibid.,* April 30, May 1, 3, 4, 1877.

Insurance Company for gross negligence. The five men had divided a bribe of $30,000 and had allowed the assets of their company to be transferred to the National Capitol Insurance Company.[8]

Large campaign contributions by insurance companies drew protest from New York City jurors in March, 1906, and later in the same year a grand inquest began a thorough probe of the New York Life Insurance Company. It found that executives had falsified records and entered "dummy transactions" to improve the company's annual report. The jurors indicted George W. Perkins of the House of Morgan, former Secretary of the Treasury Charles S. Fairchild, and other New York Life officers on charges of forgery. Inquiries into other insurance companies were undertaken. Investigation of the Metropolitan Life Insurance Company in May, 1907, disclosed a series of security manipulations designed to mislead the public as to the company's true financial condition. A double set of books enabled officials to hide loans made to Metropolitan executives at very low rates. On the basis of this evidence, the grand jury indicted President John R. Hegeman and other officers for forgery and perjury. Next, the jurors turned their attention to the Equitable Insurance Company, where they found that executives had manipulated securities and books in order to distort reports made to the State Insurance Department. They reported that it had been common practice for officers to conceal loans they did not wish to appear in the records.[9]

When the policies of large companies or the activities of racketeering labor leaders led to strikes and violence, grand juries intervened to investigate and denounce the practice of both companies and unions. In the summer of 1877, the Pennsylvania Railroad and other lines announced a ten per cent cut in pay. A strike followed rapidly on the heels of the declaration and the workers took possession

[8] *New York Times,* May 2, 9, 1877; *New York Tribune,* May 8, 1877.
[9] *Ibid.,* March 7, 24, 30, 1906; *New York Times,* December 28, 29, 1906, May 22, 23, June 4, 12, 14, 1907.

of railroad property. At Pittsburgh, the arrival of the state militia on July twenty-first led to a pitched battle. The troops opened fire and killed twenty-eight persons. That evening a mob of four thousand infuriated strikers, aided by miners and factory workers, besieged the militia in a roundhouse and set fire to the building. The troops finally fought their way out of the city, abandoning all railroad property to the strikers. A night of pillaging and destruction followed, and the mob destroyed locomotives, freight cars, and buildings. In October, Judge John M. Kirkpatrick asked that the Allegheny County inquest investigate the strike and riots. The court issued subpoenas for Governor John F. Hartranft, the secretary of state, and the adjutant general of Pennsylvania, but they refused to testify and the State Supreme Court upheld them. The jurors proceeded with their inquiry, however, and after a month of examining witnesses and listening to testimony, made a special report to the people of Pittsburgh. The grand jury announced that officials of the Pennsylvania Road and state officers were the real culprits. They had provoked the strike and "the riots followed inevitably the conduct of the military, too largely controlled by railway officials." The report denounced the role of the militia in the affair as a "blunder from first to last," culminating in the "wanton murder" of twenty-eight persons. The strikers did not escape censure for their part in the riots. The grand jury condemned their lack of respect for lawful authority. In conclusion, the jurymen rebuked state officials for hampering their inquiry and advised the city and county not to pay for damages that had been caused by "unlawful acts of the military."[10]

Grand jurors reflected the opinions and interests of the communities in which they served and many regarded union activities as dangerous to freedom. Employers occasionally tried to take advantage of this prejudice and press for in-

[10] John R. Commons, *History of Labor in the United States* (New York, 1918–1935), 2:187–191; *Appeal of John F. Hartranft, Governor of the Commonwealth, et al.*, 85 *Pennsylvania State Reports* 433 (1877); *New York Times*, November 20, 22, 1877.

dictments against their striking workers. In Chicago, in May, 1886, talk of anarchist activity in connection with the International Harvester strike frightened many citizens. On the evening of May fourth, a mass meeting of three thousand workers met on Haymarket Square to protest against police interference in the strike. When the police moved to break up the meeting, a bomb fell among them and the patrolmen opened fire on the crowd. The Cook County grand jury began an immediate investigation amid public cries for punishment of the alleged anarchists. The jurors indicted ten persons for murder in connection with the bombing, but announced that many of the arrests had been due solely to panic and were unjustified. They condemned the hysterical reactions of public officials, reactions which had led to mass arrests, and declared that officials had greatly magnified the number of enemies of law and order.[11]

During the week of the Haymarket bombing over seventeen thousand union workers in Milwaukee went on strike for an eight hour day. Strikers tried to shut down factories that used non-union labor to continue operations and this led to riots and street battles with police and the militia. When the violence had ended, Judge James A. Mallory summoned a grand jury, the second such body to meet in Milwaukee since the abolition of grand juries in 1871, to investigate the riots. The judge urged the jurymen to expose the "anarchists and demagogues" responsible for the violence and bloodshed, and public opinion supported him. The grand jury questioned witnesses and heard testimony for two weeks. It then delivered a crushing blow to Milwaukee labor unions by charging seventy of their members with conspiracy. Many of those indicted were important leaders in the eight-hour movement.[12]

In June, 1892, members of the Amalgamated Association of Iron and Steel Workers went on strike against the Car-

[11] Commons, *History of Labor*, 2:392–394; *Chicago Tribune*, May 5, 26, 27, 28, June 6, 1886.
[12] *Milwaukee Sentinel*, May 14, 20, 23, 24, June 2, 6, 1886; Bayrd Still, *Milwaukee: The History of a City* (Madison, 1948), 292–294.

negie Steel Company at Homestead, Pennsylvania. A pitched battle took place on July sixth when three hundred well armed Pinkerton detectives tried to enter the steel works and striking workers repulsed them. Twelve persons died in the clash. In October, 1892, Chief Justice Edward H. Paxson told the Allegheny County grand jury to investigate the cause of the disorder. He demanded treason indictments against the workers and urged the jurors to have no sympathy for men "receiving exceptionally high wages" who resorted to violence and bloodshed. The grand jurors followed the chief justice's advice and indicted thirty-one strikers for treason, conspiracy, and murder. However, they also examined the role of the Carnegie Company in the struggle. They charged H. C. Frick and other Homestead officials with conspiring to lower the wages of employees. They also charged the company officers with attempting to intimidate workers by hiring and arming three hundred detectives as strike breakers.[13]

Frequently, grand juries reflected public fear of violence and radical activity and indicted union leaders. In the spring of 1894, workers at the Pullman plant in Illinois went on strike. As a gesture of sympathy, members of the American Railway Union refused to handle trains with Pullman cars. The strike spread over most of the nation and resulted in violence and rioting in many places. Federal authorities in Chicago summoned a special inquest to investigate strikers stopping the mails. Judge Peter S. Grosscup denounced the strike and called upon the grand jurors to vindicate the law. In obedience to public opinion, the jurors returned conspiracy indictments against Eugene V. Debs, three other officers of the American Railway Union, and forty-three striking workers. Federal grand juries throughout the country followed the lead of the Chicagoans. In St. Paul sixty strikers faced charges of interfering with the

[13] "Investigation of Labor Troubles," *Senate Report No. 1280,* 52nd Congress, 2nd session (1893), xv–xix; Commons, *History of Labor,* 2:495–497; Arthur G. Burgoyne, *Homestead* (Pittsburgh, 1893), 197–203; *New York Times,* October 11, 12, 1892; *Cleveland Citizen,* October 15, 1892.

mails, while in San Francisco jurors indicted a hundred and thirty-four strikers on the same charge.[14]

During the course of the miners' strike at Cripple Creek, Colorado, in 1894, the local grand jury sitting at Colorado Springs reflected the antagonism that many of the residents felt for the miners and the Populist administration of Governor Davis H. Waite. The jurors indicted thirty-seven of the strikers on charges of riot and protested vigorously that Governor Waite and the adjutant general had interfered with the sheriff's efforts to restore order.[15] However, grand jurors attending court at Hazelton, Pennsylvania, made little effort to hide their sympathies for striking coal miners. In September, 1897, three thousand strikers clashed with a sheriff's posse near Latimer, Pennsylvania. The well armed deputies killed nineteen and wounded forty miners, and the whole community was up in arms over the incident. The grand inquest investigating the affair laid full blame on the sheriff and indicted him and his men for murder.[16]

Grand jurors in Chicago, in June, 1905, inquired into charges of collusion between employers' associations and corrupt labor leaders. They found that officers of the Teamsters' Union had accepted bribes from the National Wholesale Tailors' Association to prevent a strike. The streetcar company had also paid the union officials to forestall threatened labor troubles. An investigation of the Illinois Brick Company revealed that it had a "labor fund" of $25,000 to foment strikes against independent brick manufacturers. By conspiring with unscrupulous labor leaders, the trust had forced independents out of business through a system of prearranged walkouts. The jurors voted conspiracy indict-

[14] "Report on the Chicago Strike of 1893," *Senate Executive Document* No. 7, 53rd Congress, 3rd session (1895), xviii–xix; Commons, *History of Labor*, 2:502–503; *Chicago Tribune*, July 10, 11, 19, 20, 1894; *New York Times*, July 20, 1894; *United States vs. Cassidy*, 67 *Federal Cases* 698 (1895).

[15] *New York Times*, August 9, 19, 1894; Portland, *Morning Oregonian*, August 8, 1894; "Labor Disturbances in Colorado," *Senate Document No. 122*, 58th Congress, 3rd session (1905), 84–85.

[16] *New York Times*, September 11, 12, October 29, 1897; *Commonwealth vs. Martin et al.*, 9 *Lazerne Legal Register Reports* 69 (Pennsylvania, 1898).

ments against executives of both the Illinois Brick Company and the International Teamsters' Union. The jury's final report scored the "greedy vampires" among union leaders and condemned business men for conspiring with them against others. It demanded heavier punishments for persons who practiced such extortion.[17]

The development of trusts, pools, and other monopolistic business combinations led both federal and state governments to take action to curb them. In 1889 an amendment to the Interstate Commerce Act empowered federal grand juries to indict railroad companies and shippers who engaged in illegal practices. State grand juries could indict monopolies for the common law crime of conspiracy, but in a few states anti-trust laws broadened the scope of their action. By 1890 Populists and farm groups in six states had secured anti-trust laws that provided criminal penalties for attempts to restrain trade.[18] In July, 1890, Congress passed the Sherman Anti-Trust Act, making illegal all combinations in restraint of trade. With this, federal grand juries became free to indict for monopolistic practices.[19]

In November, 1891, a federal grand jury in Chicago indicted meat packers for receiving rebates. They had begun their probe after scores of small meat packers had complained that they could not compete with Swift and Company in eastern markets because it received more favorable shipping rates. The jurors had subpoenaed Swift's traffic clerks and the freight agents of all principal railroads and compelled them to bring their books into court. After a searching examination, they had discovered that Swift had received rebates totalling $25,000 over a six month period. The jurors returned indictments against two Swift brothers

[17] *Chicago Tribune*, June 12, 13, 15, 16, 18, 22, 23, 24, 29, 30, July 2, 1905.
[18] *United States Statutes at Large*, 25:857 (1889); Joseph E. Davies, *Trust Laws and Unfair Competition: Report of the Commerce Department* (Washington, D.C., 1916), 9. Maine, Michigan, Tennessee, and Texas passed anti-trust acts in 1889. Iowa and Kentucky did so in 1890. Arkansas and Georgia had constitutional provisions declaring monopolies unlawful.
[19] *United States Statutes at Large*, 26:209 (1890).

and the agents of the guilty railroads. A few of the "hot-headed farmers" on the panel favored wholesale indict-ments covering all persons involved in the scheme, but they were in a minority. Following their probe of beef shipments, the grand jurors investigated an alleged glue monopoly held by the Fermenich Manufacturing Company of Iowa. They found that the Iowa firm enjoyed special rebates to the ex-tent of $80,000 a year from one railroad.[20] In 1892, a United States grand jury in Boston began an inquiry into the dis-tilling industry and returned the first indictments under the Sherman Act. The jurors charged officers of the Distilling and Cattle Feeding Company of Peoria, Illinois, with at-tempting to monopolize the sale of liquor. In the same year, federal grand jurors in Minneapolis investigated price fix-ing agreements among retail lumber dealers and indicted all members of a pool formed to standardize prices.[21] In October, 1894, a grand jury in the District of Columbia in-dicted agents of the sugar trust for refusing to testify before a Congressional committee. In their report, the jury-men condemned the trust's political campaign contributions as a bribe given to obtain favorable tariff schedules. In the same month, a federal inquest at Chicago charged the Santa Fe Railroad, members of the beef trust, and cattle shippers with conspiring to give rebates.[22]

When decisions of the United States Supreme Court weakened the Sherman Act, state grand juries gave in-creased attention to the problem of trusts. Judge James P. Tarvin reminded jurors at Covington, Kentucky, to look into monopolistic activities, since there was "little likelihood that the McKinley administration will destroy the trusts." Governor Levi P. Morton of New York signed an anti-trust law in 1896, and almost immediately a grand jury indicated officials of the American Tobacco Company. In Frankfort,

[20] *Chicago Tribune,* November 20, 1891.
[21] *United States vs. Greenhut,* 50 *Federal Cases* 469 (1892); *United States vs. Nelson,* 52 *Federal Cases* 646 (1892).
[22] *Washington Post,* October 2, 3, 1894; *New York Times,* October 2, 3, 1894; *Chicago Tribune,* October 20, 1894.

Kentucky, a jury broke up a pool formed by fire insurance companies. Jurors of Kenton County, Kentucky, inquired into trade agreements designed to raise coal prices and indicted the participants for violating the state law.[23]

Coal shortages caused by the prolonged anthracite strike in 1902 set off a series of local grand jury investigations. In Delaware County, Ohio, the grand inquest forced retail dealers to disband their coal exchange. In Chicago the city council referred the problem of an acute coal shortage to the local grand jury, and it discovered a dealer's plot to set minimum prices and destroy all competition. Retailers had thousands of tons of coal at a time when families could not get enough fuel to heat their homes. The jurors indicted officers of twenty-seven corporations for conspiring to create an artificial coal shortage. In Toledo, Ohio, a grand jury charged coal dealers with criminal conspiracy, while Cleveland retailers dissolved their association in preference to facing a grand jury probe.[24]

Federal juries, despite the weakness of federal law on the subject, also regularly sought to expose and eliminate monopolistic practices. In June, 1902, federal jurors at Atlanta examined shipping rates for cotton and named five railroads on charges of conducting a freight pool. In the same year, a United States grand jury at Minneapolis summoned representatives of large milling companies and the principal railroads to testify and exposed widespread discrimination in freight rates. At San Francisco a federal inquest charged the salt trust with eliminating competition and forcing the price of salt from $3.00 to $30.00 a ton in less than three years. A federal grand jury in Chicago spent over three months untangling the complicated agreements between railroads and the large meat packers. The panel,

[23] *New York Times,* November 18, 1896, June 15, 1899; *Aetna Insurance Company vs. Commonwealth,* 106 *Kentucky* 864 (1899); *Pittsburgh Gazette,* October 8, 1902.
[24] *Gage vs. Ohio,* 1 *Ohio Circuit Court* (new series) 221 (1903); *Chicago Tribune,* January 6, 8, 12, 15, 20, 22, 1903; *Chicago, Wilmington and Vermilion Coal Co. vs. People,* 214 *Illinois* 421 (1905).

made up of farmers and small businessmen, examined a hundred and eighty-five witnesses and subpoenaed the records of all suspected companies. During the course of their probe, they indicted the superintendent of Armour and Company for trying to influence witnesses and preferred charges against executives of the Schwarzchild and Sulzberger Company for trying to prevent their employees from testifying. On July 1, 1905, the jurors ended their inquiry by indicting J. Ogden Armour, Louis F. Swift, E. W. Cudahy, and other important meat packers located in Chicago for attempting to destroy competition.[25]

In the years between 1905 and 1907, grand juries in counties throughout the state of Kentucky attacked the stranglehold that the International Harvester Company had on the farm machinery business. Inquests in Spencer, Trimble, and Oldham counties indicted the corporation, in 1905, for attempting to fix the price of harvesting machines. In 1906 and 1907 grand juries in four more Kentucky counties hailed the gigantic trust into court for violating the state anti-trust law.[26] Jurors in Hancock County, Ohio, cited an equally formidable corporate giant when they returned nine hundred and thirty-nine separate indictments against the Standard Oil Company for attempting to force competitors out of business. The jurymen of Lyons County, Iowa, discovered that the Standard Oil Company used the same tactics in their state, cutting prices in some communities in order to destroy competition and making the losses up elsewhere. Throughout the country in those counties where they continued to stand guard over the public welfare, grand juries spoke out forcefully against monopolies that sought to plunder the people. Lumber pools, milk trusts, oil

---

[25] *Atlanta Constitution*, June 21, 1902; *Minneapolis Journal*, September 4, 10, 19, 1902; *San Francisco Chronicle*, March 1, 1903; *Chicago Tribune*, March 29, April 13, May 3, 4, June 22, 29, 30, July 2, 1905; *United States vs. Armour and Co.*, 142 *Federal Cases* 809 (1906); *United States vs. Swift et al.*, 186 *Federal Cases* 1002 (1908).

[26] *Commonwealth vs. International Harvester Co.*, 124 *Kentucky* 543 (1909); 131:151 (1909); 131:768 (1909); 137:668 (1910); 147:557 (1912); 147:573 (1912).

monopolies, all brought their records into court when grand juries summoned them.[27]

The success of grand juries in probing corporate activities was not lost upon business leaders. In 1905, the American Tobacco Company challenged the authority of grand juries to subpoena witnesses and compel corporations to produce their records. However, the United States Supreme Court rejected all attempts to curb them. The court held that grand juries possessed the broadest kind of investigating powers and could probe any and all instances of suspected illegal activities.[28] Although the Sherman Act gave United States attorneys power to institute criminal proceedings by information rather than on the indictment of a grand jury, no prosecutions originated in this manner.[29] Federal prosecutors found that they could not supplant the grand jury in investigating corporate activities. Their lack of subpoena powers made it impossible for them to secure records and compel the testimony of company officials, and grand juries demonstrated, in practice, that they were not mere relics of the past. In 1908, a federal inquest at Phoenix, Arizona Territory, exposed a conspiracy to monopolize meat sales in the city. Pennsylvania jurors charged the American Sugar Refining Company with maneuvering to force independent manufacturers out of business. In 1910, a special grand jury in New York City, by indicting members of the cotton pool on conspiracy charges, broke up attempts on the part of brokers to corner the cotton market. In August, 1910, federal jurors in New York undertook a thorough inquiry

[27] Salt Lake City, *Salt Lake Tribune*, January 18, 1907; *State vs. Standard Oil Co.*, 150 *Iowa* 46 (1911); *Arnsman vs. State*, 11 *Ohio Circuit Court* (new series) 113 (1908); *State vs. Coyle*, 7 *Oklahoma Criminal Reports* 50 (1909); *State vs. Minneapolis Milk Co.*, 124 *Minnesota* 34 (1913).

[28] *Hale vs. Henkel*, 201 *United States Court Reports* 43 (1905); *United States vs. American Tobacco Co.*, 146 *Federal Cases* 557 (1906).

[29] John H. Lewin, "The Conduct of Grand Jury Proceedings in Anti-Trust Cases," in *Law and Contemporary Problems*, 7:112–113 (Winter, 1940); "Information and Indictment Under the Sherman Act," in *Yale Law Journal*, 54: 707 (June, 1945). Violation of the Sherman Act is not a capital or infamous crime and prosecution on an information does not violate the fifth amendment of the United States Constitution.

into activities of the United Wireless Telegraph Company. Officers of the firm refused to produce their books, protesting that the inquest had no right to examine corporate records. However, in May, 1911, the United States Supreme Court reaffirmed the broad inquisitorial powers of grand juries, and the Telegraph Company brought its books into court.[30] With their power still intact, grand juries remained important in investigating business activities. By 1916, federal inquests had indicted eighty-four corporations for violations of the Sherman Act.[31]

In a period when crimes of corporate mismanagement and the threat of monopolies constituted serious menaces to society, the grand inquest proved indispensable in securing evidence and protecting the public interest. However, many of the areas of the West which felt most keenly the arbitrary power of railroads and other monopolies had already abandoned the grand jury system. The people discovered then that district attorneys could be tools of the large corporations or even if they did want to curb them, they lacked subpoena powers and found it difficult to secure the witnesses and records necessary for a thorough investigation of a business organization. In such cases legal training, efficiency, and singleness of purpose were not enough.

[30] *Tribolet vs. United States,* 95 *Pacific Reporter* 85 (1908); *United States vs. Kissel,* 173 *Federal Cases* 823 (1909); *New York Times,* June 18, 1910; *Wilson vs. United States,* 221 *United States Court Reports* 361 (1910).

[31] Davies, *Trust Laws and Unfair Competition,* 121; *United States vs. Philadelphia and Reading Railway Co.,* 225 *United States Court Reports* 301 (1915).

Chapter 13

Tradition and Reform, 1917–1941

IN THE PERIOD BETWEEN the two world wars a cen-
tury-old trend was checked, then reversed.[1] The grand jury
gained prestige in the eyes of many Americans. Examples
of juries at work, improving government and protecting
the public interest, led many citizens to take up the cause
of preserving the inquest. Associations of ex-jurors dedi-
cated themselves to breathing new life into the ancient institution. They helped give jurors a sense of strength and
responsibility and fought efforts of judges and prosecutors
to dominate panels. The grand jury system died in England,
but in America it lived on, revitalized.

Early in 1917 grand juries ceased to exist in England.
Pressure of the life and death struggle with Germany led
Parliament to suspend them for the duration of the war.
Although the noise of battle hushed all but a few critics of
the move, there were Englishmen who saw the paradox in
fighting for democracy abroad while restricting it at home.
They suggested that even a democratic government such as
Britain's might need the strong check that grand juries
provided against arbitrary rule. However, such protests
were dwarfed by cries of a manpower shortage. The issue
of a war emergency enabled English legal reformers to accomplish what they had been unable to do in the name of
efficiency and economy: kill the grand jury.[2]

---

[1] The bulk of the material in this chapter originally appeared in the author's
"The Grand Jury Under Attack, Part Three," in *Journal of Criminal Law,
Criminology and Police Science,* 46:214–225 (July-August, 1955), and is used
with permission.
[2] *Hansard's Debates,* fifth series, 95:380, 736, 1086–1097 (1917); London *Times,*
January 3, 8, 29, 30, February 13, 14, 15, 17, March 29, 1917.

American legal reformers hailed the British action as a step in the right direction. They attributed the move to parliamentary fear that the power of indictment would become an instrument of oppression in the "hands of an inflamed populace." Opponents of the jury in United States observed that suspension of English juries had come just in time to avoid "a flood of indictments" against pacifists and persons of German extraction. In England, however, officials had expressed the fear that inquests would refuse to indict individuals arrested by the government.[3]

Wartime suspension of grand juries in England ended in December, 1921, but solicitors and magistrates throughout the island requested that the Parliament make the order permanent. The London *Times* supported the move, characterizing grand inquests as expensive and inefficient, but it drew a host of replies defending the system. Judges as well as laymen objected to eliminating the panels of citizen accusers. Judge L. A. Atherley-Jones praised their wholesome influence and warned that justice was already too tightly controlled by "an official and professional class." Sir Alexander Wentworth Macdonald, a layman, declared that a group of non-professional men should stand above judges and courts. However, Lord Justice J. Eldon Bankes agreed with most jurists that grand juries were of little value in reviewing the work of experienced magistrates. In spite of charges of inefficiency Parliament refused to extend the suspension order and citizen investigators resumed their traditional place at English courts.[4]

But the experts finally had their way in England. As the war had in 1917, the depression of the 1930's came to their aid. In January, 1930, the Lord Chief Justice observed that grand inquests no longer served any useful function. Other jurists followed suit and called for an end to expensive juries in view of "the grave national emergency." Gradually, anti-

[3] *New York Times,* January 22, February 20, 1917; Minor Bronough, "Shall the Grand Jury Be Abolished?" in *Law Notes,* 25:187 (January, 1922).

[4] London *Times,* October 24, 28, 1921, January 3, 4, 9, 10, 11, 13, 1922; *Law Times,* 153:1–2, 17 (January 7, 14, 1922).

jury forces impressed upon the depression-pinched English people the certainty of great tax savings if they abandoned the system.[5] A commission of the House of Commons studied the matter and reported in favor of eliminating grand juries. The commissioners emphasized the burden of jury duty and the great expense of the system. Parliament accepted the recommendations of the special commission and abolished grand juries in England, effective September 1, 1933. Magistrates and others throughout the nation who disliked seeing an end to the system awoke only in time to deliver panegyrics over the corpse. During the spring and summer of 1933 they expressed their displeasure in grand jury charges and filled the columns of the *Times* with protests, but all to no avail. Professor W. S. Holdsworth castigated "the bureaucrats of Whitehall . . . and the lawyers who think with them" for establishing their own form of tyranny over the nation. It was only natural, Holdsworth observed, that they "should instinctively dislike anything which independently safeguards liberty." A national emergency finally accomplished what legal reformers had tried to do for over a century. The grand jury in England "succumbed to an acute onset of depression."[6]

Legal reformers in the United States were unable to turn the war to their advantage as had their counterparts in England. American entry into World War I in April, 1917, temporarily ended efforts to abolish grand juries. But, following the war, opponents resumed efforts to persuade additional states to abandon the institution. In January, 1920, Assemblyman Louis A. Cuvillier introduced a reso-

---

[5] "Lord Hewart on Grand Juries," in *Solicitor's Journal*, 74:47 (January 25, 1930); "Suspension of the Grand Jury System," in *Law Times*, 172:252 (October 3, 1931); "Grand Juries and Quarter Sessions," *ibid.*, 173:166 (March 5, 1932).

[6] "Report of the Business of the Courts Committee," *House of Commons Reports* (1932–1933), 10:14–19; London *Times*, March 9, 16, April 27, May 24, 27, June 14, 20, 28, July 5, 13, August 3, 1933; *Statutes at Large of England*, 23 and 24 *George V*, chapter 36 (1933), is the Administration of Justice Act; Albert Lieck, "Abolition of the Grand Jury in England," in *Journal of Criminal Law and Criminology*, 25:623–625 (November–December, 1934).

lution into the New York legislature to amend the state's constitution to eliminate the juries. The American Judicature Society advised delegates attending the Illinois constitutional convention in 1920 that grand juries were of little value and delayed the courts. The Society warned that time was the most important element in criminal justice. The State's Attorney's Association of Illinois agreed wholeheartedly and made a plea for abolition of the institution. However, delegates remained unmoved and refused to sacrifice the citizens' panel. In Massachusetts, Judge Robert Wolcott of Cambridge reiterated the appeal for judicial efficiency. In October, 1921, he told members of the state bar association that abolishing the grand jury was one means of ending congestion in criminal courts. His statement did not go unopposed, however. Former District Attorney Arthur D. Hill of Boston protested against a system of criminal law that eliminated "the popular element" and told prosecutors that they could learn a great deal from working with grand jurors.[7] In March, 1922, the New York County Association of the Criminal Bar announced that it planned a vigorous state-wide campaign to abolish the institution. Former District Attorney Robert Elder called upon prosecutors to take the initiative in replacing the "inefficiency, ignorance and traditional bias" of grand jurors. Judge Thomas Crain of New York gave the movement his support. Testifying before the Committee on Law Enforcement of the American Bar Association, he observed that "a judge or some other man learned in the law" should participate in grand jury hearings. In Minnesota, attorney Paul J. Thompson urged his state to adopt the Wisconsin system of prosecution on the order of a district attorney. In 1922, Judge Roscoe Pound and Felix Frankfurter conducted a survey of criminal justice in Cleveland and added the weight

[7] *New York Times,* January 24, 1920; "Grand Jury Reform," in *Journal of the American Judicature Society,* 4:77–80 (October, 1920); *Proceedings of the Illinois Constitutional Convention* (Springfield, 1921), 2:1929, 1941, 1944, 1948; "Report of the Annual Meeting of the Massachusetts Bar Association," in *Massachusetts Law Quarterly,* 7:27–29 (January, 1922).

of their expert testimony to those who sought to eliminate use of grand juries. Pound and Frankfurter reported that juries were inefficient and unnecessary, that trial courts could provide protection against executive tyranny.[8]

Professional oposition to the inquest of the people was faced with a serious challenge when, in 1924, the Grand Juror's Association of New York began publication of *The Panel*, a militantly pro-grand jury periodical. Through its pages, former grand jurors, judges, and prosecutors explained the importance of the institution to the average citizen. The Association urged inquests to exercise their full powers as representatives of the people and fought all attempts to make them mere agents of the court. As a result of its efforts grand juries took on a new importance for many citizens.[9] In 1927, a Grand Juror's Association crusade against judges who imposed upon jurors brought a sharp reply from Judge Otto A. Rosalsky of the New York Court of General Session. He denounced an article in *The Panel* that charged judges with maintaining a "judicial dictatorship." In January, 1929, when former District Attorney William Jerome likened the grand jury to the appendix on the body and called for its abolition, *The Panel* took up the challenge and replied, "Impatient prosecutors may denounce the system as archaic, but the alternative is a surrender to bureaucracy."[10]

Meanwhile, a series of crime surveys conducted by criminologists and sociologists sought to impress upon the Ameri-

---

[8] *New York Times,* March 15, 19, 1922; *Journal of the American Bar Association,* 8:326 (June, 1922); Paul J. Thompson, "Shall the Grand Jury In Ordinary Criminal Cases Be Dispensed With In Minnesota?" in *Minnesota Law Review,* 6:616 (June, 1922); Roscoe Pound and Felix Frankfurter, *Criminal Justice in Cleveland* (Cleveland, 1922), 176, 211–212, 248.

[9] Robert Appleton, "What Is An Association," in *The Panel,* 6: no. 1, p. 1 (January, 1928); "Grand Jury Association Notes Its Twenty-Fifth Anniversary," *ibid.,* 15: no. 3, p. 15 (May-June, 1937).

[10] *New York Times,* February 5, 1927; Charles H. Tuttle, "Grand Jury Criticism Answered," in *The Panel,* 7: no. 1, pp. 7–8 (January-February 1929); Charles H. Tuttle, "The Grand Jury System," *ibid.,* no. 3, p. 3 (April-May 1929); Charles J. Dodd, "The Grand Jury," in *St. John's Law Review,* 3:225 (May, 1929).

can people the futility of the entrance of a panel of laymen into a field about which they knew nothing. Crime commissions in both Minnesota and New York recommended broader powers for district attorneys to institute prosecutions. After careful study, experts surveying conditions in Illinois reported that grand juries handicapped prosecutors and delayed justice. In 1928, drafters of the American Law Institute's model code of criminal procedure suggested that all prosecutions be begun by information and that only one grand jury a year meet in each county. They based their recommendation on advantages of speed, economy, and efficiency.[11] In 1929, Professor Raymond Moley of Columbia University approved increased power for prosecutors and characterized grand jury investigations as "cumbersome and ineffective." Judge Roscoe Pound went even further and warned that inquests of the people constituted "a power needing check."[12]

In 1928, the Social Science Research Council had commissioned Professor Moley to make a survey to obtain accurate information on the relative efficiency of grand juries and public prosecutors. He and his staff compared criminal justice in three states in which the information was used with three in which the indictment was required. At the same time Dean Wayne L. Morse of the University of Oregon conducted a poll of judicial opinion. Early in 1931 Moley and Morse released summaries of their findings. They concluded that the evidence showed public prosecutors to be "more efficient, economical and expeditious" than panels of citizen accusers. Moley contended that most grand juries were content to "rubber-stamp" the opinions of prosecutors and thus served to relieve district attorneys of

[11] "Report of the Minnesota Crime Commission," in *Minnesota Law Review,* 11 supplement: 30 (January, 1927); "Report of the Crime Commission," in *New York Legislative Document No. 23* (1928), 6:167; *The Illinois Crime Survey* (Chicago, 1929), 218, 298–299; *American Law Institute Code of Criminal Procedure* (St. Paul, 1928), sections 113–114.

[12] Raymond Moley, *Politics and Criminal Prosecution* (New York, 1929), 127–128; Roscoe Pound, *Criminal Justice in America* (New York, 1930), 109, 186–187.

the idea of reform is not a new one!

their rightful responsibility. The Moley survey focused public attention on the weakness of the grand jury system, but in doing so it took into account only the tangible factors in criminal proceedings: speed, economy of operation, and the percentage of convictions.[13]

Defenders of the grand jury system refused to agree that efficiency was an adequate basis for determining the best method of criminal procedure under a democratic government. Many hastened to point out that criminal justice deals with people and that the number and speed of convictions does not necessarily indicate a superior system. Others emphasized the broad investigating powers of grand juries. John D. Lindsay, former New York district attorney, observed that "the grand jury is the public and they have a right to investigate any evil condition of a criminal nature." United States District Attorney George Z. Medalie warned that the inquest "breathes the spirit of the community" as no prosecutor could ever do.[14] Other critics charged Moley with bias in interpreting his statistics and drew vastly different conclusions from the survey data. They maintained that grand juries were far from being "rubber-stamps" and that they caused little delay in criminal proceedings.[15]

But, shortly after Professor Moley made his findings public, the reformers received another vote of confidence when a presidential commission headed by George W. Wickersham submitted its recommendations on law enforcement to President Hoover. It advised abolishing grand juries because they served no useful purpose and impeded criminal

[13] Raymond Moley, "The Initiation of Criminal Prosecutions by Indictment or Information," in *Michigan Law Review*, 29:403–431 (February, 1931); Wayne L. Morse, "A Survey of the Grand Jury System," in *Oregon Law Review*, 10:101–160, 217–257, 295–365 (February, April, June, 1931).

[14] "Analysis of the Moley Survey," in *The Panel*, 9:no. 2, p. 14 (March-April, 1931); John D. Lindsay, "Grand Juries As the People—A Reply to Professor Moley," *ibid.*, p. 1; George Z. Medalie, "Grand Juries Value," *ibid.*, p. 16.

[15] Criticisms of Professor Moley's conclusions may be found in Jerome Hall, "Analysis of Criticism of the Grand Jury," in *Journal of Criminal Law and Criminology*, 22:692–704 (January, 1932), and in George H. Dession, "Indictment to Information," in *Yale Law Journal*, 42:163–193 (December, 1932).

courts. Thinking only in terms of efficiency, the commission viewed the grand jury as a "mitigating device and opportunity for escape" for criminals.[16]

Associations of grand jurors hoped to counter the efficiency experts by increasing the importance and scope of grand jury activity. Exposures of corruption led Chicagoans to organize the Grand Juror's Federation of America in 1931. The group sought to encourage public interest and prevent domination of juries by courts and prosecutors. Also in 1931, Lloyd N. Scott, a New York attorney writing in *The Panel*, suggested that each county summon "auditing grand juries" at regular intervals, to check all departments of government in an effort to prevent corruption rather than merely to correct it. The New York County Grand Juror's Association threw its support behind the proposal and conducted a vigorous campaign to secure newspaper backing. *The Panel* urged citizens to make inquests a vital force in their communities and not be misled by "college professors and others roaming the country with loud cries that the grand jury is an archaic institution." It scored the efforts of "reformers and well meaning progressives" who would take away the last stronghold of the layman in the law.[17]

Though a few prominent jurists and prosecutors came to the defense of the institution, in the final analysis, its best spokesmen were fearless grand jury panels in action. Successful jury probes attracted attention throughout the na-

[16] *Report on Prosecution of the National Commission on Law Observance and Enforcement* (1931), 34, 124.

[17] Lloyd N. Scott, "An Auditing Grand Jury Is Suggested," in *The Panel*, 9:no. 3, p. 32 (May-June, 1931); Bryan Cumming, "Georgia Grand Juries Check on Public Officials and Funds," *ibid.*, 11:no. 1, p. 1 (January-February, 1933); "Auditing Grand Juries," *ibid.*, p. 2; Robert Appleton, "Letter to Editor Explains Need for Grand Juries," *ibid.*, p. 10; Martin W. Littleton, "Official Conduct Grand Juries," *ibid.*, no. 3, p. 21 (November-December, 1933); Thurston Greens, "Auditing Grand Jury Bill Before the Legislature," *ibid.*, 12:no. 1, p. 1 (January-February, 1934); *Chicago Daily News*, September 17, 1930, January 14, 1931; Thomas S. Rice, "Chicago Planning an Association of Grand Jurors," in *The Panel*, 9:no. 1, p. 5 (January-February, 1931); E. J. Davis, "Grand Jurors Federation of America Organized in Chicago," *ibid.*, 10:no. 3, p. 30 (May-June, 1932).

tion and awakened interest in their work. In states where grand juries no longer existed, many citizens learned of them for the first time. In other areas, residents organized to revitalize and protect their system of inquests. Grand juror's associations became more numerous and worked to give a dynamic quality to the old institution.

In the 1920's numerous spectacular probes in widely scattered areas, and often in the face of judicial and official opposition, effectively demonstrated the versatility of the grand jury. In Okmulgee, Oklahoma, an inquest probing state corruption was about to indict twenty-one officials when the judge dismissed the jury. Aroused citizens of Okmulgee County exercised their authority under the state constitution and petitioned for another panel to complete the investigation. In 1923, a Philadelphia jury visited the Eastern State Penitentiary and after it discovered that guards had beaten several of the inmates, conducted a thorough investigation. In Kansas City, Kansas, the chief of police, a judge, and two county commissioners resigned when the local grand jury launched an inquiry into rumored corruption. In September, 1928, a special jury in Chicago accused thirteen local officials of protecting vice and crime and condemned "the vicious spoils system" under which municipal employees had to make donations to political parties. After a five week investigation, a Pittsburgh grand jury reported in October, 1928, that police and underworld had co-operated in racketeering, bootlegging, and gambling ventures. It indicted over two hundred and fifty persons, including aldermen and police officials. In the following year another Pittsburgh jury recommended legislation to end fraudulent assessment of taxes and illegal registration of voters. A survey of the work of the county board convinced the panel members that "drawing their salaries" seemed to be the only concern of many commissioners. Also in 1929, jurors in Philadelphia discovered a similar situation in their city. Their four month probe led to a complete reorganization of the police department. In May, 1929, another Chicago

inquest indicted police officials for working with hoodlums
and accused fifteen officials of embezzlement in connection
with the construction of a sanitary canal. Failure of the City
Trust Company of New York in 1929 saw juries in Brooklyn
and Manhattan begin investigations. Indictments were returned against State Superintendent of Banks Frank H.
Warner for accepting over $100,000 in bribes to approve
bank mergers and waive periodic examinations of the City
Trust Company. In a three month probe, the juries found
that officers and directors had forced the company into in-
solvency through fraud and deception. Judge Francis X.
Mancuso, Chairman of the Board, resigned his seat on the
Court of General Sessions.[18]

Grand juries thrived on publicity and official opposition.
Their spectacular exploits captured the public imagination
and led citizens of city after city to use them as a weapon
against government by corruption. In April, 1933, a panel of
citizens in Atlanta, Georgia, threatened to indict the county
commissioners if they did not institute reforms. Judge John
D. Humphries, speaking for the five judges on the Atlanta
bench, rebuked the jurors for departing from their duties.
He reminded them that they were mere agents of the court
and would be "as helpless as a body of citizens meeting on a
street corner" without the power of the court behind them.
The jurors demanded a new prosecutor and judge to work
with, but the court denied their request. Before they adjourned, the jurymen indicted the county commissioners and
appointed five citizens to conduct a thorough probe of the
municipal and superior courts and report to the next grand
jury. The attack of the Atlanta judges on the powers of the

---

[18] Albert H. Ellis, *A History of the Oklahoma Constitutional Convention*
(Muskogee, Oklahoma, 1923), 165; *Commonwealth ex rel James Fraley vs.
Rotan*, 82 *Pennsylvania Superior Court* 172 (1923); Nat Spencer, "Charges of
Lawlessness and Bribery Bring Municipal Turmoil in Kansas City, Kansas," in
National Municipal Review, 15:674 (November, 1926); *Chicago Tribune*, Sep-
tember 30, 1928, May 1, 4, 1929; *Pittsburgh Post Gazette*, October 31, Novem-
ber 3, 1928, October 5, 7, 1929; *New York Times*, September 1, 8, October 30,
December 26, 30, 1928, July 23, August 26, 27, 29, September 7, October 11, 12,
17, 1929.

local grand jury led residents to organize a grand juror's association to encourage future panels to uphold their inquisitorial rights.[19]

In October, 1933, a Cleveland grand jury began a probe of the city police department. Led by its energetic and fearless foreman, William Feather, the panel spent three months investigating and issued a report that shocked the people of Cleveland. The jurymen announced that the entire city had been intimidated by union racketeers who received protection from city officials. They denounced law enforcement officers and declared that the local criminal court "neither merits nor receives the respect or confidence of the people." The jurors noted that the talent of the prosecutor's office was well "below par" and chided the Cleveland Bar Association for its lack of concern in the matter. Before concluding its report, the jury reminded inquests throughout the state of Ohio that they too could initiate independent investigations. The succeeding Cleveland grand jury began a thorough inquiry into the defunct Guardian and Union trust companies, and returned indictments for fraud against officers of both companies. In October, 1934, citizens of Cleveland followed the example of those in Chicago and Atlanta and organized a grand juror's association to preserve the rights of their investigating body.[20]

In New York it took a fighting body of grand jurors to combat the hampering tactics of city officials and mobilize public opinion for a thorough investigation of rackets. The March, 1935, grand jury took up a probe of policy rackets begun by a predecessor. It soon broke with District Attorney

---

[19] *Atlanta Constitution,* April 15, 19, 20, 21, 25, 28, 1933; Charles H. Tuttle, "Grand Juries by Exercising Their Initiative Can Put Fear Into Criminals and Unfaithful Public Servants," in *The Panel,* 11:no. 3, p. 13 (March-April, 1933); Phil C. McDuffie, "Fulton County Georgia Grand Jurors Assert Independence," *ibid.,* no. 6, p. 31 (November-December, 1933).

[20] *Cleveland Plain Dealer,* October 10, 14, 24, November 3, December 22, 1933, February 2, April 3, 14, October 23, 1934; "Ohio Grand Jury Report Startles County," in *The Panel,* 12:no. 1, p. 11 (January-February, 1934); William Feather, "Foreman Tells Why Criminals Fear Action by Grand Jury," *ibid.,* no. 2, p. 17 (March-April, 1934).

William C. Dodge and began summoning its own witnesses. Foreman Lee Thompson Smith took charge of the inquiry and demanded that the district attorney appoint a special prosecutor. Racketeers threatened jurors and their investigators, but they continued their work. When Dodge and the panel could not agree, the jurors asked the court to discharge them and appealed to Governor Herbert Lehman to summon an extraordinary grand jury and appoint a prosecutor to assist it.[21] Governor Lehman named Thomas E. Dewey as special racket prosecutor and summoned a new panel to convene September 5, 1935. During the following four months the special jury examined over five hundred witnesses. It investigated loan sharks and racketeering in labor unions and trade and protective associations. In December, 1935, the panel returned twenty-nine indictments and reported that control over racketeering in New York City centered in the hands of a dozen or so major criminals who extorted millions from the city each year. A second extraordinary grand jury took up the racket probe in January, 1936. It uncovered a $12,000,000 prostitution racket and put vice lord Charles "Lucky" Luciano and his lieutenants on the road to prison. When the court discharged the panel in August, 1936, after seven months of service, it had broken the back of organized racketeering in New York City.[22]

People all over the United States followed the exploits of Prosecutor Dewey and his "racket busting" grand juries. In October, 1937, the *Reader's Digest* publicized their work and told citizens in communities throughout the country that they could attack corruption in the same manner. As a result, the New York County Grand Juror's Association received inquiries from all over the United States and from

[21] *New York Times*, March 12, June 4, 5, 7, 9, 11, 1935; Robert B. Wilkes, "A History-Making Grand Jury," in *The Panel*, 13:no. 5, p. 1 (September-October, 1935).

[22] *New York Times*, December 27, 1935, July 1, August 11, 1936; L. Seton Lindsay, "Extraordinary Grand Juries," in *The Panel*, 14:no. 1, p. 3 (March, 1936); "Dewey Grand Jury Strikes at Rackets," *ibid.*, no. 2, p. 6 (May-June, 1936); "Grand Juries Active in Presentments to Court," *ibid.*, no. 3, p. 4 (November-December, 1936).

abroad, from individuals who had never before realized that such an institution as the grand jury existed.[23]

The example of New York gave a tremendous impetus to the work of laymen trying to revitalize the system. In January, 1936, a grand inquest in Minneapolis demanded the elimination of racketeer control of the city and it protested against use of the National Guard for strike breaking duty. A panel reported to the people of Boston that school commissioners were guilty of selling promotions and appointments. In San Francisco, the local grand jury found inefficiency and corruption when it investigated the city police commission.[24]

Beginning in September, 1937, a Philadelphia grand jury conducted a seventeen month crusade against vice and racketeering patterned after the Dewey investigations. In May, 1938, the jurors charged a hundred and seven persons with gambling and prostitution and accused police officials of accepting bribes to give immunity to criminals. The panel called for the immediate dismissal of forty-one police officers on grounds of inefficiency and dishonesty. The jurors reported to the people of Philadelphia again in August and charged city and county officials with a "criminal conspiracy" to protect crime and vice. In September, the grand jury indicted Mayor S. Davis Wilson on twenty-one counts of misbehavior in office and failure to suppress crime. But Mayor Wilson managed to have the indictments quashed on a technicality. In order to prevent further exposures by the grand jury, state officials withdrew financial support and the Philadelphia court discontinued the investigation. The grand jurors charged that the move was but "the culminating act of a long continued opposition which has crippled our work." They appealed directly to the State Supreme Court, which allowed them to continue their inquiry. Free to go

[23] J. C. Furnas, "The People's Big Stick," in *Reader's Digest*, 31:5–9 (October, 1937); "Reader's Digest Article on Grand Juries," in *The Panel*, 17:no. 1, p. 4 (January, 1939).

[24] *New York Times*, January 6, 1936; "Boston Grand Jury for School Reform," in *The Panel*, 14:no. 1, p. 3 (March, 1936).

ahead once more, the panel lashed out at the district attorney, accusing him of using the vice investigation for political purposes. The jurymen demanded a complete reorganization of the police department, including dismissal of incompetent officers and reapportionment of police districts to end the influence of politicians. They concluded their work in March, 1939, by re-indicting Mayor Wilson, accusing him of permitting vice and crime to flourish, while "he issued blasts of meaningless words."[25]

Investigations in other communities also advertised effectively the capabilities of an alert grand jury. In Buffalo, New York, a special panel exposed bribery and fraud in the municipal government. Seventeen city officials faced trial for perjury and bribery. A Miami, Florida, inquest found that bribery had played an important part in establishing electric rates for the city, and indicted Mayor Robert R. Williams, several councilmen, and other municipal officials. After a two month investigation of city affairs, the jurors condemned the police department for protecting criminals and criticized a newly instituted program to refinance the city debt. Members of the jury did not cease to be concerned after they completed their work but as private citizens inaugurated a recall movement that eventually removed Mayor Williams from office. At Greensboro, North Carolina, a grand jury initiated an inquiry into a primary election, and in spite of determined opposition from the court, it discovered and reported many irregularities to the people.[26]

Opposition to investigations frequently developed when grand juries threatened to expose prominent officials and upset the balance of political power. In April, 1938, Pennsylvania politicians were engaged in a heated primary elec-

[25] *New York Times*, February 6, May 5, 15, August 18, November 20, 24, December 2, 28, 1938; March 2, 3, April 7, 1939; *Shenker vs. Harr*, 332 *Pennsylvania State Reports* 382 (1938); *Commonwealth vs. Hubbs*, 137 *Pennsylvania Superior Court* 229 (1939).

[26] *New York Times*, January 9, 11, 18, 25, February 2, April 15, 1938, March 2, 1939; Frank C. Miller Jr., "Grand Juries—Independent Investigations," in *North Carolina Law Review*, 17:43 (June, 1938).

tion struggle. Dissident elements within the Democratic Party leveled charges of corruption and fraud against the Democratic administration of Governor George H. Earle. The district attorney at Harrisburg petitioned for a special grand jury investigation and the Court of Quarter Sessions summoned a panel. Governor Earle took to the radio and in an address to the people of Pennsylvania charged that the proposed probe was "a politically inspired inquisition, to be conducted by henchmen of the Republican State Committee." Two days before the inquiry was to begin, the attorney general asked the State Supreme Court to restrain the grand jury from beginning an investigation, but the court declared that it had no such power. The panel prepared to convene early in August. On July 22, 1938, when it appeared that the administration had exhausted all efforts to block the inquiry, Governor Earle summoned an extraordinary session of the state legislature "to repel an unprecedented judicial invasion of the executive and legislative branches of our government." Three days later he stood before the lawmakers and warned them that "the Inquisition and the Bloody Assizes . . . stand as grim reminders of judicial tyranny." He charged the judges and the district attorney with abusing their authority and asked the legislature to look into their conduct. He then requested legislation to block the threatened grand jury probe. The Democratic legislators rushed through a retroactive law suspending all investigations of public officials once the House of Representatives had taken jurisdiction and begun an inquiry. They also empowered the attorney general to supersede any district attorney. A House committee launched an immediate investigation, but the court impounded all evidence awaiting the grand jury. Again the matter went to the State Supreme Court. In October, 1938, that court declared the law restricting investigations unconstitutional and reminded the legislators that they could not abolish the grand jury.[27]

[27] *New York Times*, July 26, August 8, 11, 1938; *Dauphin County Grand Jury Investigation*, 332 *Pennsylvania State Reports* 290, 342 (1938); *Laws of*

The example of public officials going to any length to prevent a panel of citizens from investigating led New Yorkers to strengthen their grand jury system. Rallying behind the slogan, "What happened in Pennsylvania can happen here," the constitutional convention meeting at Albany in 1938 made certain that the grand jury would remain the people's shield against official corruption. A new clause added to the state constitution provided that inquiries into official misconduct could never be suspended by law. In addition, all public officers summoned before grand juries had to testify without immunity or be removed from office.[28]

Pennsylvania's lesson did not go unheeded in other states. In June, 1941, citizen's groups in Washington succeeded in getting the state legislature to approve a constitutional amendment making one grand jury a year in each county mandatory. In addition, the amendment barred prosecuting attorneys from advising grand juries. Special prosecutors would serve in that capacity. However, the State Association of Prosecutors conducted a vigorous campaign against the proposals and managed to defeat them in a referendum held in November, 1941. Citizens of Missouri were more successful. The convention that met in 1943 to revise the state constitution inserted a specific provision that the power of grand juries to investigate misconduct in public office could never be suspended.[29]

The growth of dictatorship abroad and the entry of the United States into World War II seemed to convince many Americans that institutions that protected the people's rights were not outmoded. Fear of executive tyranny and

---

the *General Assembly of Pennsylvania, Extraordinary Session, 1938,* 18–19; "Legislative Interference With the Grand Jury," in *Harvard Law Review,* 52:151–153 (December, 1938); "Power of the Legislature to Suspend Grand Jury Investigations," in *Columbia Law Review,* 38:1493–1501 (December, 1938).

[28] *New York Times,* August 8, 11, 1938; *Journal of the Constitutional Convention of the State of New York* (Albany, 1938), p. 248, article 1, section 6, of the New York Constitution as revised in 1938.

[29] *Session Laws of the State of Washington,* 1941, pp. 436–437; Ewen C. Dingwall, "Independent Grand Juries Opposed in Washington State," in *National Municipal Review,* 30:374 (June, 1941); *Journals of the Constitutional Convention of Missouri* (Jefferson City, 1944), 3:13.

infringement of individual liberty gave a new importance to the grand inquest. Those who had previously called for its abolition for reasons of economy and efficiency remained silent when Prosecutor, now Governor, Thomas Dewey denounced "the bright young theorists, the fuzzy minded crackpots and others of less idealistic purpose who would like to see the grand jury abolished" or when Judge Francis Martin of New York dismissed charges that juries were rubber stamps, as "the rantings of inexperienced and highly theoretical professors." With war and other threats to freedom close at hand, mere efficiency had less appeal. It became apparent to many that the grand jury was more than a means of bringing individuals to trial. It was an integral part of American democratic government.[30]

[30] Thomas E. Dewey, "Grand Jury, the Bulwark of Justice," in *The Panel,* 19:no. 1, p. 3 (May, 1941); Francis Martin, "Grand Jury Must Be Just, Free and Fearless," *ibid.,* p. 8; Lamar Hardy, "Grand Juries," *ibid.,* no. 2, p. 5; H. L. McClintock, "Indictment By a Grand Jury," in *Minnesota Law Review,* 26:153–176 (January, 1942); Martin H. Weyrauch, "Grand Jury, a Bulwark Against Tyranny of Dictatorship," in *The Panel,* 20:no. 2, p. 5 (December, 1942); Frank S. Hogan, "Advice to Grand Jurors in the Present World Crisis," *ibid.,* no. 1, p. 3 (March, 1942).

Chapter 14

Whither?

ALTHOUGH GRAND JURIES have repeatedly demonstrated their value in speaking out in the public interest, there remain threats to the continued existence of the institution. In 1946, opponents of the grand jury in New York put a bill through the state legislature prohibiting inquests from making presentments or otherwise censuring persons for misconduct that did not constitute a crime. The Grand Jury Association of New York, metropolitan newspapers, and civic and business groups conducted a vigorous campaign to get Governor Dewey to veto the measure. They pointed out that the grand jury was the only local body that could effectively reprimand lax and indifferent public officials. Pleas that the bill be vetoed poured into Albany. In his message vetoing it, Governor Dewey warned legislators that the power of grand juries should not be impaired and that they should remain "the bulwark of protection for the innocent and the sword of the community against wrongdoers."[1]

Threats to the continued existence of grand juries come from another quarter as well. Recently there has been a tendency for other investigators to take over the inquisitorial role. Legislative investigating committees in particular have intruded upon the work of the grand inquest. Frequently this has constituted a serious threat to individual

[1] *New York Times,* March 3, 14, 15, 19, 27, April 4, 1946; Richard H. Kuh, "The Grand Jury 'Presentment': Foul Blow or Fair Play?" in *Columbia Law Review,* 55:1136 (December, 1955); J. Hadley Edgar Jr., "The Propriety of the Grand Jury Report," in *Texas Law Review,* 34:755 (May, 1956). Both writers agree that grand juries should be able to report on matters from which no indictment is framed, although the function must not be abused.

liberty. The rules of evidence and other traditional safeguards which control the deliberations and conclusions of a grand jury do not protect witnesses before legislative committees. Hearings often take place in a carnival-like atmosphere and investigations become little more than publicity devices for participating congressmen. In 1947, Federal Judge Simon H. Rifkind emphasized this problem when he reminded grand jurors in New York that legislative investigations constitute "a dangerous tendency" which juries can combat only by increased attention to their responsibilities. In 1950, the grand jury of Merrimack County, New Hampshire, faced a threat of legislative interference. The inquest investigated a large public utility company and at the conclusion of the probe a committee of the state legislature sought to question the jurors on their deliberations. Members of the panel refused to testify and the State Supreme Court upheld them. The court warned the lawmakers that they had no power to interrogate grand jurors regarding their investigations.[2]

In addition to legislative investigators there are others encroaching on the work of grand juries. In some states experts have already supplanted citizen panels for inquiries into official misconduct. This has been accomplished by establishing substitute officers to take over the tasks normally performed by inquests. Three states, Michigan, New Hampshire, and Connecticut, have created "one man grand juries" in the person of a magistrate empowered to launch investigations, summon witnesses, and return indictments. This innovation has followed as a logical step in the process of excluding laymen from law enforcement activities. In other states, legislatures have given judges powers similar to those of a grand jury, enabling them to conduct "John Doe" hearings to determine whether crimes have taken place. But no matter how efficiently magistrates may exercise their newly acquired authority, it is not entirely in keeping with

[2] *New York Times,* October 8, 1947; "Opinion of the Justices," in 96 *New Hampshire* 530 (1950); Kuh, "The Grand Jury Presentment," 1118–1119.

democratic procedure to destroy an investigating body composed of representative citizens and to delegate its broad inquisitorial powers to public officials.[3]

As an instrument of discovery against organized and far-reaching crime, the grand jury has no counterpart. But, in spite of its broad investigating powers, legislation is needed in most states to strengthen the people's weapon by giving grand juries greater freedom to act. They frequently find themselves in the embarrassing position of dependence on the police department for evidence and the public prosecutor for legal advice. Inquests should have the authority to employ investigators, expert accountants, and separate counsel if they see fit.[4] In large cities regular grand juries are often kept too busy with routine criminal matters to supervise the conduct of public officials. Where this is true, it would be an important advance in the fight against racketeering and corruption to have special panels meeting at stated intervals to guard against abuses in government.

Inquests have always been particularly vulnerable to charges of inefficiency. They are seldom able to act as swiftly or as decisively as a public prosecutor and their inquiries often try the patience of both judge and district attorney. Few opponents of the institution recognize, however, that efficiency is not a normal product of democratic government. A careful concern for the rights of those who have been arrested and the ability of citizens to participate in their government and to initiate investigations of abuses may be more important. Condemning the grand jury system strictly on a utilitarian basis has the effect of narrowing debate to one of democracy versus efficiency and popular government versus government by expert.

[3] Pliny W. Marsh, "Michigan's One Man Grand Jury," in *Journal of the American Judicature Society*, 8:21–123 (December, 1924); William P. Lovett, "One Man Grand Jury in Action," in *National Municipal Review*, 33:292–294 (June, 1944).

[4] "Grand Jury Contracts," in *Minnesota Law Review*, 7:59 (December, 1922); Harold W. Kennedy and James W. Briggs, "Historical and Legal Aspects of the California Grand Jury System," in *California Law Review*, 43:262–264 (May, 1955).

Grand juries are occasionally vulnerable to other charges. Opponents have found instances where inquests have abused their authority. American juries have not been infallible and they have not always dispensed perfect justice or conducted their investigations impartially. Panels have represented a cross section of their communities and have been as full of faults and prejudices as the people who served upon them. However, the solution to this problem is not to destroy the institution, but to make it more effective. The work of inquests may be improved by selecting competent individuals to serve. It is important that political factions within a community do not dominate the selection of grand jurors and use them for partisan purposes. In a few states jury commissioners have replaced sheriffs and other officials in choosing grand juries and have done much to remove the procedure from politics. In New York City, county jury boards maintain a list of persons qualified to serve. Any citizen may ask to be included on the list, but the board attempts to obtain a cross section of the community.[5]

It is not enough to secure capable individuals to serve on grand juries. They must also be persons who understand their great responsibility and realize their tremendous powers for good. Jurors who perform their work in a routine and superficial manner betray the public interest and reflect upon the institution as a whole. They must take the initiative and remain independent of both court and prosecutor. They must not wait for the district attorney to lay cases before them. Judges have been partly to blame for the failure of some grand jurors to understand the full extent of their powers. Many jurists have intimated to juries that they were limited to considering matters suggested to them by the court or the prosecuting attorney and have failed to inform jurors of their power to launch investigations on their own initiative. This has made many panels unwitting rubber stamps. Unless grand juries know and exercise their powers

---

[5] *Manual for Grand Jurors in the City of New York* (New York, 1948), 4–6.

in the public interest and thereby refute those who seek to abolish them, they sacrifice the confidence of the people.

If Americans are to take full advantage of the opportunity offered them by their grand juries to make government more responsible, every citizen must know what grand inquests are and what they can do. Toward this end, associations of grand jurors have conducted vigorous educational campaigns and alert juries have shown their value. But to counteract the preachings of those who would restrict or abolish it, there is need for more widespread publicizing of the importance of the institution to democratic government. In states that have abandoned the people's panel, few persons realize the full extent of their loss.[6]

In the three hundred and more years since grand inquests first convened on American soil, panels of representative citizens have spoken out against all manner of threats to individual liberty. Agents of the British Crown, territorial political appointees, meddling abolitionists, corrupt machine politicians, corporate monopolies, racketeering criminals, and many others have had occasion to know the wrath of an aroused grand jury. Although the object of their investigations has shifted from place to place through the years, grand juries have remained guardians and spokesmen of their communities. Grand juries have the effect of placing criminal justice in the hands of members of the community. They possess broad inquisitorial powers derived from the government, yet they are of the people, not of the state. Their constantly changing personnel prevents small groups from gaining a vested interest in law enforcement and gives all persons an opportunity to participate in their government. The grand jury enables the American people to act for themselves rather than have an official act for them. It is the one institution that combines the necessary

[6] *The Panel*, 24:no. 1, p. 5 (February, 1950), sets forth the educational program of the Association of Grand Jurors of New York County. See also C. C. Mason, "Value and Importance of Grand Juries," in *Alabama Lawyer,* 11:473–477 (October, 1950).

measure of disinterestedness with sufficient authority to investigate effectively malfeasance and corruption in public office. Today, as in the past, it is the one body that can effectively handle the complaints of individual citizens, whether the grievances be against their fellow citizens or against their government.

The most significant aspects of the grand jury are its democratic control and its local character. Governmental power has to a large extent replaced other threats to liberty in the United States. The increasing centralization of governmental authority and the growth of a huge bureaucracy in no way responsible to the people have made it vitally necessary to preserve the grand jury. In some instances it is the only possible means of checking on political appointees or preventing illegal compulsion at the hands of zealous law enforcement officials. At a time when centralization has narrowed the area of democratic control, grand juries give the people an opportunity to participate in their government and to make their wishes known.[7] In the past citizen panels proved an effective instrument of protest against centralized authority. They remain potentially the strongest weapon against big government and the threat of "statism."

[7] "Third Interim Report of the Special Committee to Investigate Organized Crime in Interstate Commerce," *Senate Report No. 307*, 82nd Congress, 1st session (1951), p. 3. The Kefauver Crime Investigating Committee warned Americans not to rely upon the central government to control organized crime, but to use their local grand juries to attack the problem in their own communities.

Chapter 15

Essay on the Sources

MATERIAL ON THE GRAND JURY in the United States
is widely scattered and often difficult to locate. This is particularly true of materials from the seventeenth and eighteenth centuries. Statutes and laws of the various colonies
and states set forth the legal basis of grand juries and some
of their duties. Published records of cities, colonies, and
states, setting forth their reports, presentments, and indictments, give a greater insight into their work. Among the
most useful records collections are A. D. Chandler, ed., *Colonial Records of the State of Georgia* (26 vols., Atlanta,
1904–1916), *Archives of Maryland* (65 vols., Baltimore,
1883–1952), *Records of the Court of Assistants of the Colony of Massachusetts Bay, 1630–1692* (3 vols., Boston, 1901–
1928), *Records of the Governor and Company of the Massachusetts Bay in New England* (5 vols., Boston, 1853–1854),
Documents Relating to the Colonial History of New York
(15 vols., Albany, 1856–1887). Contemporary newspapers
are valuable for accounts of grand jury proceedings. Particularly useful for the Revolutionary period are the *Boston
Gazette, Boston Evening Post,* Boston, *Essex Gazette,* Philadelphia, *Pennsylvania Gazette,* Philadelphia, *Pennsylvania
Journal,* Charleston, *South Carolina Gazette,* and the Williamsburg, *Virginia Gazette.* The published works and mem-
oirs of prominent individuals—John Adams, Thomas Jefferson, James Iredell, Francis Hopkinson, and others—con-
tain references to the work of grand juries, as do histories
of cities, colonies, and states. An excellent discussion of the
grand jury system in New York is in Julius Goebel and T.
Raymond Naughton, *Law Enforcement in Colonial New*

York (New York, 1944). Oliver P. Chitwood's *Justice in Colonial Virginia* (Baltimore, 1905) and Arthur P. Scott's *Criminal Law in Colonial Virginia* (Chicago, 1930) give some information about the grand jury system in Virginia. The movement to abolish the grand jury in the United States may be traced partially through the debates and proceedings of the many state constitutional conventions and partially through legislative journals and newspaper reports of legislative action. Beginning in the 1830's, American law reviews and legal periodicals present the attitude of lawyers toward the grand jury system. Most valuable of these are *The American Jurist, The Western Law Journal, The Law Reporter, The United States Monthly Law Magazine*, and *The North American Review*. For the period after the Civil War the proceedings of state bar associations are very useful. Court decisions are also important for tracing judicial efforts to limit grand jury powers. Treatises on the law, including Bird Wilson, ed., *The Works of James Wilson* (3 vols., Philadelphia, 1804), Francis Wharton, *A Treatise on the Criminal Law of the United States* (Philadelphia, 1857), and John N. Pomeroy, *An Introduction to Criminal Law* (New York, 1864) reveal the attitudes of legal scholars. The campaign to eliminate the grand jury in England is traceable in articles in such English journals as *The Jurist, The Legal Observer, The Solicitor's Journal and Reporter*, and the *Juridical Society Papers*. Articles in and letters to the editor of the London *Times* are very informative. Debates in the House of Commons and Reports of Royal Commissions are also valuable.

Reported decisions of courts in the several states give important data on the role of grand juries in the slavery controversy. Helen T. Catterall's *Judicial Cases Concerning American Slavery and the Negro* (5 vols., Washington, D.C., 1926–1936), is indispensable in this regard. Charges to federal grand juries contained in the reported decisions of federal district and circuit courts are important in connection with the Fugitive Slave Act. Information is also found in accounts of specific incidents in the abolition campaign. Two of these are W. U. Hensel's "The Christiana Riots and the Treason Trials of 1851," in the *Lancaster Historical Society Papers,* 15:18–59 (1911), and Hazel Wolfe's *On Freedom's Altar* (Madison, 1952). For the South, decisions of courts as well as histories of slavery and the ante-bellum South are useful. Of special value are Howell M. Henry's *The Police Control of the Slave in South Carolina* (Emory, Virginia, 1914), Russell B. Nye's *Fettered Freedom* (East Lansing, Michigan, 1949), James B. Sellers' *Slavery in Alabama* (University, Alabama, 1950), and Clement Eaton's *Freedom of Thought in the Old South* (Durham, 1940).

Newspaper accounts and reports of state and federal courts provide the best information on the work of grand juries during the Civil War. The *New York Times, New York Tribune, Baltimore Sun,* and *St. Louis Democrat* are particularly useful. James G. Randall's *Constitutional Problems Under Lincoln* (New York, 1926) covers arbitrary arrests and military usurpation of the functions of the grand jury. William M. Robinson's *Justice in Grey* (Cambridge, 1941) treats the work of local grand juries in the Confederacy. For the Reconstruction period, histories of Reconstruction in each of the southern states show how southerners used their grand juries to advantage. Most important among these are Francis B. Simkins and Robert H. Woody, *South Carolina During Reconstruction* (Chapel Hill, 1932), Ella Lonn, *Reconstruction in Louisiana after 1868* (New York, 1918), C. Mildred Thompson, *Reconstruction in Georgia* (New York, 1915), and Charles W. Ramsdell, *Reconstruction in Texas* (New York, 1910). Reports of the many Congressional committees investigating conditions in the South and reports of the attorney general of the United States are also valuable.

Newspaper accounts of grand jury deliberations and reports of grand jury activities contained in county histories are important records of the role of the people's panel on the American frontier. State and territorial court reports and Clarence E. Carter, ed., *The Territorial Papers of the United States* (26 vols., Washington, D.C., 1934–1962), are also useful. The work of many vigilance committees is set forth in Nathaniel P. Langford's *Vigilante Days and Ways* (Boston, 1890) and James A. B. Sherer's *"The Lion of the Vigilantes": William T. Coleman and the Life of Old San Francisco* (Indianapolis, 1939).

The labors of grand juries in combatting municipal corruption are best traced through newspaper accounts. Court reports also give important information. Individual grand jury probes have been treated in detail in Franklin Hichborn's *"The System." As Uncovered by the San Francisco Graft Prosecution* (San Francisco, 1915), Gustavus Myers' *The History of Tammany Hall* (New York, 1917), *The Autobiography of Lincoln Steffens* (2 vols., New York, 1931), and Lincoln Steffens, *The Shame of the Cities* (New York, 1948). Newspapers and court reports also provide the most complete information on the grand jury and big business. Also valuable are reports of Congressional investigations into strikes and labor disturbances.

For the period between the two world wars, only newspaper sources provide sufficient material on the investigative activities of grand juries. *The Panel,* published by the Grand Jury Association of New York County since 1924, provides important material from the campaign in defense of the inquests. Law review articles, crime survey reports, and proceedings of state bar associations present attacks on the grand jury system. Most important of these are Raymond Moley, "The Institution of Criminal Proceedings by Indictment or Information," in the *Michigan Law Review,* 29:403–431 (February, 1931), Wayne L. Morse, "A Survey of the Grand Jury System," in the *Oregon Law Review,* 10:101–160, 217–257, 295–365 (February, April, June, 1931), and Roscoe Pound and Felix Frankfurter, *Criminal Justice in Cleveland* (Cleveland, 1922).

Index

343.1Y78p
The people's panel

144 00086828 0